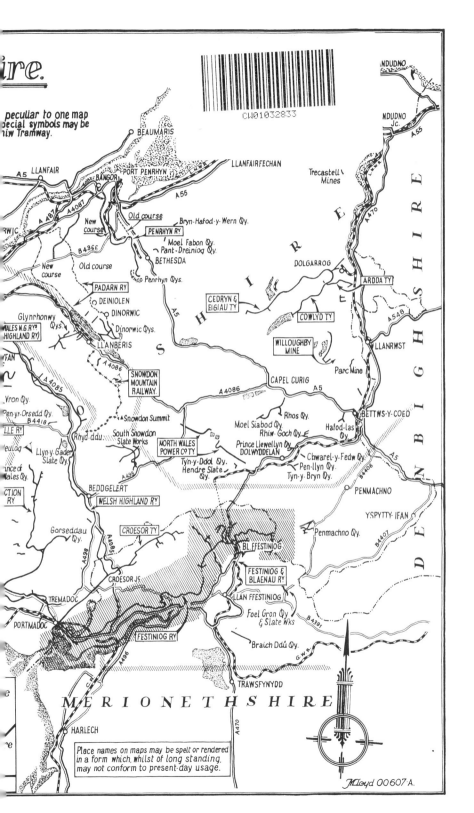

...ire.

...peculiar to one map
...pecial symbols may be
...niw Tramway.

NDUDNO

NDUDNO Jc.

A55

BEAUMARIS

LLANFAIRFECHAN

Trecastell Mines

A5   LLANFAIR

PORT PENRHYN

BANGOR

A55

A487 A4087

A470

New course

Old course

Bryn-Hafod-y-Wern Qy.

PENRHYN RY

Moel Fabon Qy.

Pant-Dreiniog Qy.

BETHESDA

B4366

Old course

New course

Penrhyn Qys.

DOLGARROG

ARDDA TY

PADARN RY

DEINIOLEN

DINORWIC

CEDRYN & EIGIAU TY

Glynrhonwy Qys.

WALES N.G RY's HIGHLAND RY)

Dinorwic Qys.

COWLYD TY

LLANBERIS

WILLOUGHBY MINE

LLANRWST

A4085

A4086

Pen-yr-Orsedd Qy.

B4418

Vron Qy.

Parc Mine

A548

SNOWDON MOUNTAIN RAILWAY.

CAPEL CURIG

A5

BETTWS-Y-COED

Rhos Qy.

LLE RY

Llyn-y-Gader Slate Qy.

Rhyd-ddu

Snowdon Summit

South Snowdon Slate Works

Moel Siabod Qy.

Rhiw-Goch Qy.

Hafod-las Qy.

A5

A4086

NORTH WALES POWER Cº TY

Prince Llewellyn Qy

DOLWYDDELAN

Chwarel-y-Fedw Qy.

ince of ales Qy.

Tyn-y-Ddol Qy.

Hendre Slate Qy.

Pen-llyn Qy.

Tyn-y-Bryn Qy.

B4406

CTION RY

BEDDGELERT

A498

WELSH HIGHLAND RY

PENMACHNO

YSPYTTY-IFAN

Gorseddau Qy.

CROESOR TY

A498 A4085

Penmachno Qy.

B4407

CROESOR JC.

BL. FFESTINIOG

FESTINIOG & BLAENAU RY

TREMADOC

LLAN FFESTINIOG

PORTMADOC

Foel Gron Qy & Slate Wks

B4391

FESTINIOG RY

A496

Braich Ddû Qy.

G.W.R.

TRAWSFYNYDD

M E R I O N E T H S H I R E

A470

HARLECH

Place names on maps may be spelt or rendered in a form which, whilst of long standing, may not conform to present-day usage.

JLloyd 00607·A.

H I R E

S

O

N

D E N B I G H S H I R E

CW01032833

NARROW GAUGE
RAILWAYS IN
NORTH
CAERNARVONSHIRE

Volume 2
THE
PENRHYN QUARRY
RAILWAYS

The near-vision of phantasy – the Quarry as it appeared to the Victorians.

NARROW GAUGE RAILWAYS IN NORTH CAERNARVONSHIRE

Volume 2

THE PENRHYN QUARRY RAILWAYS

by

JAMES I. C. BOYD

THE OAKWOOD PRESS
1985

© Oakwood Press & J. I. C. Boyd 2001

British Library Cataloguing in Publication Data
A Record for this book is available from the British Library
ISBN 0 85361 312 5

First Edition 1985
Reprinted 2001

Printed by Inkon Printers Ltd., Yateley, Hants.

DEDICATION

This volume is dedicated to the many friends both within and without the Quarry and Railway who throughout my lifetime have increased my vision of life and industry.

Published by The Oakwood Press, P.O. Box 13, Usk, Mon., NP15 1YS.
E-mail: oakwood-press@dial.pipex.com
Website: http://ds.dial.pipex.com/oakwood-press

CONTENTS

Page

The work of pick, shovel and black powder was to become one of the Wonders of Wales to our forebears.

FOREWORD

By E. H. Douglas Pennant

The last time that a member of the Penrhyn family wrote a foreword, at the author's invitation, for a book about local railways was when the Rt. Hon. Hugh Napier, 4th Baron Penrhyn of Llandegai, my great-uncle, wrote the foreword to Charles E. Lee's book, which also included a section on the Penrhyn Railway. It is therefore an honour, for me, to be invited to write the foreword to this book.

It is a fact that Caernarvonshire had large mineral deposits, including slate, which attracted speculators and landowners to tap the source. Some were successful and as a result of their success, railways such as the Penrhyn were built to transport the product to the coast, from where it would be exported.

From the year 1768, in the days of Hugh Warburton and John Pennant, when they leased to tenants the right to quarry slate from what became Penrhyn Quarry, Bethesda, until 1973 when Lady Janet Douglas Pennant sold the remaining 51% of shares she held in the quarry to Marchwiel Holdings Ltd., my family has been involved in the slate industry for just over two hundred years.

The section on Penrhyn not only deals with the railway and the locomotives that worked on it and in the port and quarry, but also with the ships associated with it, which carried the slate to other parts of the country and Europe. Other sections of the book deal with the Dinorwic Quarry Railway, the tramroads in the mines of the Trefriw and Llanrwst areas, the reservoir construction lines west of Dolgarrog and also the Great Orme Tram.

At home, I have the other books in the series of which this book is the latest, so the author is not unknown to me. When I first met him in early 1984 at the archives at the University College of North Wales, it was a pleasure and an honour to be invited to write this foreword.

I have enjoyed the other books he has written and I hope that all who read this book will enjoy doing so. I wish Mr. Boyd every success with his latest volume.

Penrhyn, 1985   E. H. Douglas Pennant

AUTHOR'S NOTE

So to the penultimate and most formidable volume of a series begun about forty years ago in youthful enthusiasm, and the desire to expose what I then thought was – and do still – a most neglected subject. In those times I was endured by others as a non-conformist, for in my native Cheshire the standard-gauge railway strode from border to border and upon it rode the products of Crewe, Gorton, Derby and Horwich . . . more than sufficient for others to dote upon. When at 13 years my headmaster exposed us (literally) to a week climbing in Snowdonia and I experienced the Welsh Highland and Festiniog, my mind was made up: before World War II had started my notebooks were full of all that might be learned of that district, and it was preciously small! It was to be the opportunities offered by His Majesty in the next few years which would enrich my field notes, and base the foundations for this series.

The canvas of these last two books is widespread; if I had a personal choice it would be for the area so rich in colourful subjects even though at that time my limited opportunities had found the Welsh Highland almost dead, the Festiniog geriatric, the Glyn Valley defunct, the Corris and Talyllyn each running an uncertain service but yet – and what important exceptions these were! – both Penrhyn and Dinorwic railways were operating daily and their quarries were oases of railway wonderment.

Now almost everything has gone. Well-meant but mostly iconoclast are the tourist railway substitutes, and it is beyond the brief of Marchwiel Holdings at Penrhyn or the Central Electricity Board at Dinorwic (to name the two most important places around which Volumes 2 and 3 are written) to preserve any semblance of the two centuries of Welsh industrial history which was made there. Something of the feeling of a crusader who comes to the end of his mission with a mixture of relief and regret is almost unavoidable for one who has watched this pattern of a bygone age of transport disappear, and knows how limited is his skill to re-create it!

Colwall, Herefordshire.   James I.C. Boyd.
November, 1985.

PREFACE

This is the second of a three volume work in a series to cover a part of North Wales where lay some of the earliest railways in the Principality, if not in the world. They were certainly the first built to carry slate, that intractable roofing material which is most economically carried by water. Herein lies the competition between the great 19th century quarry/landowners who used the railways to achieve the most efficient transport between quarry and sea, a critical factor in not only their own survival but for whole communities both on land and water. The most efficient railway system could ensure domination of a market and as that market grew less, so more effective did the railway system have to become.

Over the period of almost forty years since the first in this series was published, an explosion of Further Education, and the spread of radical beliefs has given enormous emphasis to the social impact of commerce and industry, with the result in the subject under consideration here that publications on the slate industry (for instance) have completely lost sight of the technology of the industry itself, in exchange for social impact. One cannot overlook the change from agricultural to industrial communities which took place in certain parts of North Wales, but the manner and means of this revolution, the detail of the pockets of industrial expertise almost always in isolation from the remainder of the country, the initiative and individuality of the end-products . . . these have become the neglected basic issues and in this final publication an effort has been made to correct this ill-balance.

The railways herein were of infinite individuality, reflecting the character of the owner. Unlike railways in other parts of the Kingdom, they were not territorially ambitious, governed by remote Boards of Directors in far-away London or subject to scrutiny by Board of Trade inspection. They operated under an umbrella of semi-feudal relationship between landlord and employee (sometimes landlord/tenant and employee/tenant – a far more demanding situation) in a pattern of employment which few other railwaymen would have accepted and yet clearly was largely accepted and appreciated by those involved! Changes were slow until the business was threatened; when changes came they did so with consuming rapidity. From horse-power to steam-power within a matter of months, or from ancient tramway to modern railway in as short a time; no Directors of a share-holding company could develop at such pace, let alone the ponderous undertakings in public ownership!

In short, we may look back on an age where imagination, ambition, drive, confidence and success in a few men could ensure the employment of hundreds. And the lynch-pin of that complex was none other than the railway!

ACKNOWLEDGEMENTS

This work has involved over one hundred persons in the three decades of preparation, and besides the fact that many are no longer living, it would be impossible to mention each by name; among those deceased are the Engineers of the Penrhyn and Dinorwic undertakings, and many of their colleagues also. Survivors amongst the employees may still be found in The Welsh Slate Museum and at the National Trust's Museum in Penrhyn Castle; their reminiscences together with those who have come forward from retirement to help, have given life to the script. Sources less closely-connected include Eric Foulkes who made his extensive researches into Penrhyn archives available to me, loaned his unpublished notes and checked my first rough draft. Next, Douglas Carrington, who has been especially interested in Dinorwic and published a small book on the subject, has shared his knowledge with me and supervised my rough draft. The unselfish collaboration of these two good friends has saved me hours of tedious research and added beyond measure to my personal experiences of these two sites.

Visits to archival depositories in Wales have become opportunities of real pleasure, no less because of the helpful and friendly welcome which always awaits! These include Gwynedd Archives at Caernarfon, The Library Archives at University College of North Wales, Bangor, The Welsh Industrial & Maritime Museum at Cardiff with its branch, The Welsh Slate Museum, Llanberis; here Gareth Williams, Tomos Roberts, Stuart Owen-Jones, Dafydd Roberts and their supporting staff have tended to make me linger in their company for longer than was really necessary for my objectives!

Roy Fenton has ensured that with his close knowledge of coastal shipping, I was fully informed on the maritime links of these Welsh quarries; Dr. C. V. Waine gave me details of individual ships. Bernard Roberts, Philip Hindley and Victor Bradley with their keen curiosity in railways on industrial sites, have helped me over many points of locomotive and rolling stock details; Ivor E. Davies, full of years and experience, assisted with many aspects concerning local history and the granite industry, as did Eric Jones with Dolgarrog notes. W. H. Roberts (Port Dinorwic) recalled his life as a guard on the Padarn Railway, Iowerth Jones and J. K. Jones of Bangor their personal reminiscences of Penrhyn.

Edmond Douglas Pennant has spent much time retrieving archive material from his ancestors' collections, and has contributed a Foreword. Much of the material from his patient work has been used herein.

No writer can afford to be without the fullest collection of photographic material; C. C. Green, Ifor Higgon, Eric Hannon, Hunslet Holdings PLC, E. D. Chambers and David Chatfield have been especially generous in this regard.

As to drawings, several capable persons have contributed either from their own collections or made a special assignment to my requirements. In this respect Chris. G. Down, Philip Hindley, Alan Holmes, Alan Kidner, G. R. Page, W. A. D. Strickland and Don Townsley should be mentioned, not omitting Tony F. Rushworth who made available the work he did for Mr. Carrington's book.

Finally, to the small team whose contribution is without measure: John M. Lloyd who is responsible for the greater part of the drawings, maps and diagrams – to meet his exacting standards some have been re-draughted up to half a dozen times. Jeremy Wilkinson has supplied a stream of supporting information ranging from statutory statistics, through commercial information to the valuable availability of technical services at manuscript stage . . . and that is not all! Then in the ultimate my wife must address herself to the assemblage I have made from so many sources and proceed to construct an acceptable typescript: on the way I expect her to know every subject as well as I do, to be on personal terms with my associates, assist me with research, entertain my collaborators, insert missing facts from the formidable array of material in this study and keep callers at bay. The finished work must be well typed, grammatically correct, and impeccably spelled. The story must be crystal clear – these are her standards! She more than anyone else involved will dispel an enquirer's illusion that writing railway history is a casual, speedy, free-time relaxation . . . and equally that it is either financially rewarding or undemanding.

A simple list of appreciation must follow:

J. L. H. Bate and D. E. Bick	Mining information
Rev. E. A. Boston	Access to preserved rolling stock
M. Cowley	Use of drawings
Emlyn Evans (Gee & Sons, Denbigh)	Background publications
Mrs. Catherine Hughes	Translations
Peter Hughes	Quarry information
L. Humphries	Quarry information
Dr. K. A. Jaggers	History
Gwynfor P. Jones	Quarry histories
Hugh R. Jones	Engineer, Dinorwic
H. A. Lewis	Translations
Dr. Jean Lindsay	Quarry histories
W. J. Milner	Archival material
A. S. R. Parsons	Loan of unpublished essay
Douglas Rendell	Photographic work
Ernie Roberts	Quarry information
Dr. E. A. Shearing	Genealogical and architectural notes
Einion Thomas	Penrhyn Estate information
Rev. H. Thomas	Reminiscences

SOURCES

A NOTE ON SOURCES TO VOLUMES 2 AND 3

Two main sources of information have been used herein; firstly, the close personal familiarity of the author with all systems which survived to 1940 and, secondly, such records of these systems which have come available during and since their demise.

Private railways which formed the greatest mileage herein are especially difficult to research as owners naturally treat their records as not for public scrutiny. In the case of the Padarn Railway instructions went out to burn all paper-work when the railway closed and little recent paper-work has survived . . . if indeed there ever was the close written account such as fortunately has been made available concerning the Penrhyn Railway – and which is still coming to light. So it is these two historic lines, whose ancestry goes back to the earliest days of rail transport, cannot enjoy equal status.

The Dam Disaster at Dolgarrog in 1925 carried away many of the records of the North Wales Power & Traction Co. Ltd and its associated interests. Ironically, the circumstances surrounding the many small tramways can often be pieced together from company records whilst the unique Great Orme Tramway – so relatively modern – is embarrassingly rich in material !

Some variation in the presentation of place names will be noted; for examples there is documentary evidence for the vernacular at Penrhyn of Felin-Fawr Slab Mill (not Felin-Fawr slab mill) or Spoon Points (not spoon points) and this characteristic has been followed. Elsewhere documentation is scarce and does not support this presentation e.g. galleries with the same name at Penrhyn and Dinorwic would be Twlldyndwr Level and Twlldyndwr level respectively.

General National Library of Wales: Manchester Central Reference Library: The Science Museum: The Bodleian Library: The J. S. Wilkinson Collection: Clwyd Record Office: The National Museum of Wales: The House of Lords Record Office: The Public Record Office: Festiniog Railway Archives: Institution of Civil Engineers: Gwent Record Office.

Periodicals The Quarry Manager's Journal: The London Gazette: The Stock Exchange
and Annuals Official Intelligence: Bradshaw's Railway Manual: The Engineer: Engineering: The Railway Magazine: The Railway Times: The Railway News:
Stone Trades Journal: The Quarry: Industrial Railway Record: The Stock
Exchange Year Book: The Mining Yearbook: Skinner's Mining Manual:
Skinner's Register of Defunct Companies.

Other sources are listed under ACKNOWLEDGEMENTS, and to avoid a long list of book titles
and newspapers, appropriate footnotes have been given to specific sources in the text. A
detailed list of directories, registers and maps is given on p.274 of Volume I, and is
applicable also herein.

With special reference to the content of Volumes 2 and 3, Accident Reports published by
H.M.S.O. are relevant to the Great Orme Tramway, The Museum of English Rural Life
to the use of oxen, and the extensive records held at the City of Birmingham Reference
Library have wide-ranging application.

Note on Maps and Diagrams

Those drawn herein may not always be to scale and care must be exercised where, in
order to show detail, some exaggeration has been necessary.

Care must also be taken with Ordnance Survey maps; those of similar date but differing
scales do not always agree, especially in the detail of such places as quarries. The plans of
quarries and port arrangements have been prepared in the knowledge that in these areas
railways were being subject to continuous alteration. Where documentary evidence has
been available, this has been used in preference to Ordnance Survey maps.

Note on Place Names

No attempt has been made to bring Welsh place names into the modern form, but the
spelling of the period has been retained. Many records were kept for years without the
correction of place name mis-spelling and something of a compromise has been attempted
throughout.

Note on abbreviations of Titles

B.R.	British Railways
C.C.R.O.	Caernarvonshire County Record Office (more recently – Gwynedd Archives)
C.E.G.B.	Central Electricity Generating Board
C.&H.R.	Chester & Holyhead Railway (Company)
F.R.	Festiniog Railway (Company)
G.W.R.	Great Western Railway (Company)
L.N.W.R.	London & North Western Railway (Company)
N.W.P.&T.C.L.	North Wales Power & Traction Co. Ltd (ex North Wales Power Co.)
P.&W.G.C.L.	Penmaenmawr & Welsh Granite Co. Ltd
P.B.S.S.R.	Portmadoc Beddgelert & South Snowdon Railway (Company)
P.R.O.	Public Record Office, Kew
U.C.N.W.	University College of North Wales, Bangor
W.H.R.	Welsh Highland Railway (Company) – a Light Railway

Note on motive power in certain more obscure locations

The Birmingham Locomotive Club Pocket book 'F' of 1968 INDUSTRIAL & INDEPENDENT
LOCOMOTIVES & RAILWAYS OF NORTH WALES – almost the only publication available – is
used wherever necessary. In 1982 the compilers stated that certain lists 'dogmatically
published in the past . . . may contain errors of fact'. Wherever possible the authors of
the Pocket Book have collaborated to bring information herein up to date.

Note on changes effected by statute since 1962

The content of this volume largely ceased to exist during the 1960s. It ignores therefore:

Changes of place names etc. brought about by Local Government re-organisation in April 1974. In consequence the titles of the period are retained (e.g. Carnarvon or Caernarvon and not Caernarfon) and present-day titles do not appear e.g. Gwynedd.

The change to decimal money – almost all transactions herein were made before this was introduced.

The change to metric measurement, which was seldom used in the period concerned, save for an occasional exception.

PART 5
THE PENRHYN QUARRIES AND RAILWAYS

(Quarries open by 1719 and still at work)

PENRHYN QUARRIES LTD. Registered November 1951

OWNERS   *Acquired*

(1)   General Warburton & John Pennant   1768
      (1695–1771)   (?–1781)
(2)   John Pennant & Richard Pennant   1771
      (?–1781)   (1739–1808)
(3)   Richard Pennant (later Rt Hon. Richard,   1781
      Baron Penrhyn of Penrhyn, Co. Louth
      1783)   (1739–1808)
(4)   George Hay Dawkins[1]   (1763–1840)   1816
(5)   Col. The Hon. Edward Gordon Douglas[2]   1840
      (later, Rt Hon. Edward Gordon, 1st Baron
      Penrhyn of Llandegai 1866)   (1800–1886)
(6)   Rt Hon. George Sholto Douglas-Pennant,   1886
      2nd Baron Penrhyn of Llandegai
      (1836–1907)
(7)   Rt Hon. Edward Sholto Douglas-Pennant,   1907
      3rd Baron Penrhyn of Llandegai
      (1864–1927)
(8)   Rt Hon. Hugh Napier Douglas-Pennant, 4th   1927
      Baron Penrhyn of Llandegai (1894–1949)
(9)   Lady Janet Marcia Rose Harper[3] (1923–)   1949
(10) Lady Janet Marcia Rose Douglas Pennant   1965
      (formerly Harper) (1923–) & Marchwiel
      Holdings Ltd.
(11) Marchwiel Holdings Ltd.[4]   1973

NOTES

1. Assumed name of Dawkins-Pennant on succeeding to Estate in 1816 on death of Richard Pennant's widow. His daughter married (5). He was a grandson of Lady Pennant's sister. (Name of Hay also given as Henry elsewhere).
2. Assumed name of Douglas-Pennant in 1841 – new Barony created 1866. Succeeded to Estate on death of his father-in-law. In May 1885 handed responsibility for the Quarry to his son, George Sholto Douglas (6), 17th Earl of Merton.
3. Assumed name of Douglas Pennant in lieu of Harper in 1951 (she is a niece of the 4th Baron). Sold 51% shareholding to Marchwiel Holdings Ltd. in 1965.
4. From November 1951 had operated as Penrhyn Quarries Ltd; from 1973 remainder of shares acquired from (9); Quarry now a wholly-owned subsidiary of Marchwiel Holdings Ltd.

LLANDEGAI TRAMWAY

24½ ? ins. gauge	Open	(see text) c. 1798
(over rail centres)	Closed	greater portion used as part
		of Penrhyn Railroad:
		remainder 1831

PENRHYN RAILROAD (mainly the conception of Benjamin Wyatt)

24½ ins. gauge	Begun		September 1800
(over rail centres)	Open	(part)	February 1801
		(remainder)	25th June, 1801
	Closed	(last train)	2nd October, 1879
	Lifted		1882

(Route amended near Llandegai to accommodate improved Holyhead road: Autumn 1819)

PENRHYN RAILWAY (basically the conception of Charles E. Spooner)

1 ft 11 ins. gauge (inside rails)

Tyn-y-Clwt Deviation	Begun 9th March, 1876
	Opened 15th October, 1876
Dinas Top to Port Penrhyn	Begun 18th March, 1878
	Opened 6th October, 1879
Last steam working on main line	28th June, 1962
Official date of closure main line	24th July, 1962
(Workmen's Train	Started 16th January, 1880
	Ceased 9th February, 1951)

QUARRY TRAMWAYS

First noticed	29th August, 1801
Steam haulage ceased	January 1965
Last workings	May 1965

Standard Gauge Port Penrhyn Branch

| Open | January 1852 |
| Last working | 2nd March, 1963 |

THE PENRHYN RAILWAY – THE PENNANT INHERITANCE

As with the lands owned by the Assheton-Smith family – an account of which follows in the next section – a part of the inheritance included one of the most prolific slate-bearing regions in North Wales. The excavations created by the enterprise of these two families living almost side by side in that district were to become (whatever else they may have been) two of the largest man-made holes in the world at the time, created solely by explosive, pick and shovel, and only the merest assistance from modern earth-digging machinery.

Commercial rivalry between the two families was constant, but they had the foresight to see that by working together they could command the whole of the North Wales slate industry . . . and this they did. The finished products of these quarries were conveyed to the waterside and then transferred to the most cost-efficient transport of all, the sea. The intermediate journey was for the greater part of time by rail, and although claims are legitimately made for other Welsh rail carriers of slates, there is no doubt that in the field of industrial archaeology the Penrhyn and Padarn Railway systems were second to none; but such is the fascination of the North Wales narrow gauge railway picture that individuality makes comparisons a worthless exercise.

Whilst the history of North Wales slate quarrying, of commercial rivalries and social problems have been favourite subjects for Welsh students for years, the contributions of transport have received relatively scant attention; yet, as any slate producer could market his goods at competitive rates at the edge of his quarry, his ability to deliver them *on board ship* at a cost which undercut his rivals, was essential to his survival. So it was the railway which became the prop of the business, the lessee, the landowner and its employees – a point which the sociologist generally overlooks.

Tenants on what was to become the Penrhyn Estate are recorded as early as 1413 to be working for slates on sites which they rented; some were for personal use and the remainder for sale. The exploitation was very simple, as the rock was dug from shallow pits, so that it was not until the second part of the nineteenth century that roofing slate manufacture on a large scale began, entirely due to the take-over of the workings by the English owners of these two estates in particular. However, even then on the Penrhyn Estate the right to win slate, build dwellings and the very boundaries themselves were confused and in dispute. Nonetheless, the growing importance of the slate business had been emphasised by the appointment in 1719 (during the ownership of the Yonges) of a Slate-Reeve when royalties to the Estate were fixed at one eighth, 'fetched at the waterside'.

Richard Pennant (1739 – 21 January, 1808) son of immensely rich John Pennant, a merchant of Liverpool and Hanover Square, London, had begun his public career in 1761 when he became M.P. for Petersfield, Hampshire. He married Sarah Anna Susannah, the only child of Lt Gen. Hugh Warburton (1695–1771) of Winnington Hall, Cheshire on 13th November, 1765, he being then 26. Through her grandmother she was heiress to half of the Penrhyn Estate.[1] Back in 1757 Sir George Yonge and Lt Gen. Hugh Warburton were joint owners of the Estate, having acquired the title nearly a century previously through Sir Griffith Williams. Whilst prosecuting his family's Jamaican interests, Richard was to apply the large fortune coming from the work of several generations of forebears' connections in the Jamaica sugar estates, to his North Wales manor and create the basis of the North Wales slate industry. His wife also had Liverpool links and in 1767 he became one of the two Members for Liverpool, holding the seat again in 1768, 1774 and 1784.[2] His experience in running the sugar estates, the employment of slaves and the shipment of cargoes made him a most suitable Parliamentary representative for Liverpool, then one of the chief centres of the slave trade and with strong ties in shipping, merchanting and overseas estates.

On the death of his father-in-law (1771) he inherited through his wife the Warburton portion of the Penrhyn Estate and on the death of his father (22nd October, 1781) took up residence at Penrhyn House in 1782; this latter event enabled him to succeed to the leasehold of the Yonge moiety and in 1785 he purchased the moiety from Sir George Yonge (5th Baronet) of Escott, Devon, negotiations to this end having been started by his late father in 1737.[3] In 1783 he was made Baron of Louth in the peerage of Ireland. "Richard inherited his father's business sense, along with a belief in the 'progress of mankind'. They had no misgivings about the state of slavery as an acceptable form of labour. Provided the slaves were cherished and humanely treated, their consciences were not troubled" writes Dr. Lindsay.

By September 1768 his father's share of the Estate had been clarified (he leased the Yonge moiety from 1768 until his death in 1781), thus from 1781 enabling Richard and General Warburton to commence the issue of 21-year leases to win slate on the Estate. He prepared a large map of the Estate showing all features including roads and field-names. Ultimately about three thousand leases would be granted to local men, but their working was so casual that by 25th October, 1782 he decided to work the ground himself, and commenced an active policy of buying out the leases. He was keenly aware of competition from Cilgwyn Quarry at the head of the Nantlle Valley, a historic working where lighter and good quality slate was won. From the same tonnage of rock extracted, Cilgwyn could produce more slates and was well placed to dispose of rubbish. As a quarry however, it was not well-organised.

The next stage developed from the purchase of the Yonge lands; at the time there were two sites in use, the first on the common at Chwarel Goch (enclosed by 1800) and east of the present Quarry and the second on the high ground above the present working, Y Ffrith, another common. The Quarry proper was developed on pasture then called Cae Braich-y-Cafn, a name at first adopted by the Quarry. It had been a condition of the former leases that lessees cart the slates to the nearest sea-board and place them ready for shipment; at that time Aber-Ogwen (and later, Aber-Cegin) was the coastal venue. Growth of the Quarry under Pennant may be judged by employee strength: 80 in 1782, 120 in 1800 due to men serving in the Militia, and 600 in 1808.

The dates on which slate quarrying in Caernarvonshire ceased to be a casual operation on the three major sites where quarrying was done in the open (as opposed to underground) were important milestones in the history of the industry:

Bethesda – becoming the Penrhyn Quarry under 1782 takeover by Richard Pennant

Llanberis – becoming the Dinorwic Quarry under 1787 takeover by partnership

Nantlle – the Cilgwyn Quarry under 1800 partnership with lease from The Crown

This much-simplified summary[4] demonstrates how competitors were lined up during the French Wars (begun February 1793). Ffestiniog area underground workings first opened about the same decade; later output here was to be of prodigious tonnages. In each of these situations primitive rail transport developed early among the workings and when more sophisticated railroads linked them with the sea, their technical independence gave each a very personal character. Pennant and Assheton-Smith had the edge over every competitor – they owned the quarry, the land, the sea-board and later, the ships. They were nearer Merseyside and Deeside, centres for industry and terminals of railways, waterways and canals. Their own tenants were closely involved and their rail links did not have to stand commercially as independent businesses as did the Nantlle, Festiniog or North Wales Narrow Gauge Railways, systems whose fortunes waxed and waned with the slate trade itself, and being statutory undertakings, were unable to manipulate their operations to suit a single proprietor. At all times the Penrhyn party was well to the fore; by 1793 they were shipping 11,000 tons a year (also quoted as 15,000 tons) and Dinorwic, the next in total was then only 2,652 tons; nonetheless, by then they had created together 57% of the North Wales output.

George Hay Dawkins inherited the Pennant Estates in Great Britain and Jamaica in 1808, and the Quarry rights after the death of Lady Penrhyn in 1816.

(In those times and since, any person employed on the Estate was deemed to be the employee of the estate's owner. At his death, every employee lost his job; if his work was of importance he would be re-employed by the new owner that same day; otherwise within a week. Outside a week it could be accepted the new owner had not given re-employment.)

RAILWAYS ON THE PENRHYN ESTATE – A HISTORICAL SUMMARY

Much of the credit for the enthusiastic development of the Penrhyn Estate under Pennant must go to William Williams of Llandegai (1738–1817), his Manager[5] and Slate-Reeve, who between 1761 and

1802 controlled production, sale and transport at the Cae Braich-y-Cafn Quarry; it was he who suggested the expansion of the quarry and supervised it.[6] In the person of Williams (a former Anglesey weaver, later becoming a surveyor), among the first of a list of faithful retainers, Pennant could well afford to turn his personal attentions elsewhere and he made himself responsible for agricultural development which was generations overdue.

In former times the slate was carted from the district to primitive quays on the shore by the east mouth of the Ogwen; only drainage tunnels and certain stoneworks may now be discerned here. At that time the only easterly coastal route lay along this shoreline; it was impassable at high tides. There was a second quay at the highest tidal point of the River Cegin at the Pool, and in Bangor there was the Hirael Quay. Pennant's aim was to improve the Cegin inlet and a lease of the foreshore from John Warren of Pen-y-Bryn (Bishop of Bangor) on 25th December, 1786 enabled him to build the first quay.[7] By 1790 it was a 'commodious harbour, capable of admitting vessels of 300 tons burden' and eight years later there were to be found there ships bound for London, Bristol and Liverpool, though Liverpool and Runcorn came to be the most important destinations; however, during this period the overall trade was with Ireland.

The creation of what came to be called Port Penrhyn in the mid-1790s was planned by another of His Lordship's gifted servants, Benjamin Wyatt (a member of the celebrated family). That Wyatt had had the advantage of earlier work done here is revealed by an Estate map of 1768 showing an existing Ballast Bank at the mouth of the Cegin (not to mention 'Muscle Beds' at that of the Ogwen!) The tonnages handled by the new port speak for themselves: 1,800 in 1780 and 12,000 in 1792 the latter being about half the North Wales seaborne slate output for the year. This new port on the east side of the muddy Cegin creek cost in the region of £15,000; at low water it dried out, so a lockgate was installed to allow boats to pass from the Port into the Pool above when the tide level was suitable, thus water remained in the Pool whilst the gate was closed; to clear the Pool of mud it was flushed by opening the gates at low water. Further improvements in 1800 allowed 50 vessels to use it at the same time, but even so, the Port area remained for many years incapable of doing the trade offered to it, and expansion was only possible by tipping slate waste into the Straits and enlarging the apron.

The effects of the Napoleonic War were immediate, and shipments fell as mariners feared the French pirates round our coasts. So began the long see-saw of slump and boom in the industry, whilst Pennant tried to find other work for his employees to keep them out of trouble when the Quarry was slack; in this wise his immediate attention was to put the men to building roads, a weak feature of the Estate. By 1790–1 a good road was built from the Port right up Nant Ffrancon; this grassy track passed up the western side of the Ogwen Valley south of the Quarry and is still walkable. By 1797 it was extended to Capel Curig where Pennant built the Inn which is now the Plas-y-Brenin Outdoor Pursuit Centre. In 1802 the Capel Curig Turnpike Trust built another road; this kept to the western side of the Ogwen initially and then formed the basis for the present road as it went southward over Nant Ffrancon on the east side of the valley.[8]

Roads will have further mention but it should be emphasised that The Old Road (as it became known) was essentially a Quarry link (though extended beyond it) designed by Benjamin Wyatt shortly after his appointment as Agent in 1785 to accommodate horsedrawn wagons in place of pack animals.[9] Seasonal weather conditions were a perpetual enemy to the roads but were only one factor in a larger problem. The French Wars had brought taxation which hit Pennant twice; firstly, in the form of a Slate Tax (June 1797) and secondly, on farm horses. ('A HISTORY OF TAXES & TAXATION IN ENGLAND FROM EARLIEST TIMES TO THE PRESENT DAY' (Stephen Dowell) Section V. Longmans Green & Co. 1884). The former was among other taxes placed by William Pitt on building materials from 1794; a 20% tax on slate was also intended to alleviate distress in the tile industry whose complaints were conveniently ventilated in the nearby London Parliament. A tax whose principal victim was North Wales, was of little consequence in the Capital.

The tax on horses began as an attempt to pay for the rise in Navy wages following the Spithead mutiny in 1797: until then carriage and race horses only had been affected, but this was extended to farm horses, thus hitting the transport of slate to the coast; the rate was '£2 5s. 0d. per quarter', but in the following year full credit might be given to an owner if he passed over the animal for use by the Military. The price of horses thus rose, and the cost of horse fodder rose with it and anyone in the transport business began to seek ways of mitigation. A well-tried method was to run wagons on either edge rails or plateways, by which a horse might draw three times more its load than on a cart road. Some (including Pennant) tried oxen for a time. (The Museum of English Rural Life, Reading, displays material concerning the use of oxen until the First World War. Also, 'AGRICULTURAL TRANSPORT IN WALES' (J.G. Jenkins) Nat. Mus. of Wales, Cardiff, 1962. Chap. IV discusses the relative merits of oxen and horses.) Horse Tax survived for ninety years. Fortunately The Old Road was under construction two years before Horse Tax took effect; it reached Pont-Coetmor from the Quarry in 1784, Llandegai Bridge in 1786 and Aber-Cegin in 1788 and in one move the horse, ass or donkey with its pannier of 64 slates was relegated in favour of about 100 two-wheeled carts requiring 400 horses (all animals and vehicles being hired from estate farms, the property of tenants) in the exercise of moving slates. A contemporary account writes of 'apple-cheeked boys and girls singing merrily' and leading these caravans.

Countrywide, inventive minds were directed to reducing the need for horses on such a scale and Pennant set about investigating the economies of either a canal or a railway, for he was now facing competition from quarries already connected by canal (e.g. in Leicestershire). Slate Tax – finally repealed in 1831 – was levied on each ton of slate carried coastwise at a rate of 10/- . . . the tax on tiles was already 4/10d. per thousand and bricks also carried tax. Due to their reliance on seaborne transport, Penrhyn and Dinorwic were severely hit by Slate Tax; quarries in the Lake District and Leicestershire were not affected by it, and as the new Lancaster and Leicester Canals were more efficient, less horses were in use per ton of slate. Some customers were switching orders to these sources.[10]

But taxation was not to be the final arbiter leading to the establishment of a rail system; Pennant had an interest in a writing slate factory in Westmoreland Street, Liverpool, and also in the opening on 15th December, 1796 (on the site of Roe's Copper Works at Toxteth Park, Liverpool) of the Herculaneum Pottery. The latter was an enterprise directed by a Quaker, Samuel Worthington, a Liverpool corn merchant, where at first earthenware was made, but Worthington's aim was to manufacture porcelain but, having no waterpower available at Toxteth to grind flint, Pennant and Worthington teamed-up.[11]

There was adequate waterpower above Port Penrhyn (from the Afon Ogwen) where a grinding mill could be built, and the product shipped to Toxteth Dock. The flint could be shipped in from Sussex; the same ships would continue to Liverpool with the loading. As to the writing slates, there was no tax on these. By 1797 Port Penrhyn had taken the form of what today would be called an industrial estate, for the writing slate factory had been established, a flint mill had been built in Nant-Gwreiddiog, (a slate mill would be built at the Port in 1801) and Worthington moved house from Liverpool to Llwyn-On, a stone's throw from the mill, then known as Llwyn-On and later as the Upper Mill – there was a Lower Mill adjacent and both acquired the collective 'Penrhyn Mills'. A leat brought the water to the east side of the mill where were housed two overshot wheels 16 ft diam. × 6 ft wide. Until then the Swiss had enjoyed world monopoly of the writing slate trade but the new factory turned out 136,000 slates requiring 3,000 ft of wooden framing in 1804 and employed 25–30 men and boys. The Swiss firm went bankrupt. Of the new mill, Dodd writes[12] (It) 'must have helped to relieve local distress when the market for slates fell off . . . a Mill was erected to grind cherts and quartz from the neighbouring hills . . .'.

In this now much-changed situation, the transport of stone between port and mill was effected by the building of a tramway . . . at whose instance is not clear but each of those involved was already shown to be a man of great concept.[13]

The Llandegai Tramway (1798–1831)

This historic step is worth a moment's reflection. Much unthinking opinion has credited it with being the first railway in North Wales, but this is not the case as in the Wrexham area there had been feeder tramways to connect collieries and ironstone workings since the 1750s. Also, somewhat earlier and nearer than this, certain coal measures were linked to the south bank of the River Dee: for instance, the primitive wooden-railed Mancot Railway near Hawarden had had iron plates substituted in 1793.[14] There were other smaller tramroads between Point of Ayr and Chester and travellers from North Wales would be aware of them as they took ship from Bagillt or Connah's Quay . . . in short, the Llandegai Tramway could only claim to be the first over-ground system in northwest Wales.[15] It was about a mile in length and included a balanced incline from the Cegin valley to the higher ground which marks the hinterland of Bangor, there being a second incline from thence whereby the tramway fell to the Mill: both had vertical drums for the cable, fixed on the side of the line, and the short journey would involve much wagon handling in consequence.

The tramway was positive evidence of the first collective industrial enterprise in Caernarvonshire and sprung from Worthington Senior's wide range of interests which did not confine themselves to Herculaneum. Together with other Liverpool entrepreneurs who included Samuel Holland,[16] Michael Humble and Nicholas Hurry, he was involved with other North Wales quarrying and mining enterprises, but the conception of the grinding mill was to make it possible to use clay bodies and flints from the chert of local limestone. This source, together with flint from Ireland (such Irish shipping as survived was not at risk in the Irish Sea) could be brought back as ships' ballast and for a brief period the Llandegai line was a critical link in the trading chain.

A copy of the first lease dated 21st March, 1800 between Lord Penrhyn and 'Michael Humble & Co.' still survives[17] being a 'Lease of several Corn, Flint & Ochre Mills and a Quay and a Farm . . . for 21 years determinable on the 7th or 14th years by either party . . .'

Worthington and Hurry were to make four separate Agreements with Lord Penrhyn in 1803, and the pattern for these was an Agreement with Lord Sefton to lease the Liverpool Toxteth site for the Pottery from 31st October, 1800 for 50 years. The Agreements at Penrhyn were to usher in a second phase of railway building, for they enabled Worthington and Hurry 'to exploit the mineral and agricultural assets on the Penrhyn . . . Estates'. Thus Worthington became the focal point of reformation.

His influence was to last many years, much longer than the work of the flint mill for by 1817 Toxteth was complaining about inconsistency in supplies and irregularity in documentation and sought independence from outside grinding. By 1818 they had installed a beam-type steam engine to drive their own mills but long before then the original Llandegai Tramway had found other uses (though the small length of line between Llandegai village down the incline to the mill was closed in 1831; by that date the main portion of the Tramway had been a part of the Penrhyn Railroad for three decades!)

The Penrhyn Railroad (1801–1879)

The experience gained with the tramway was sufficient to encourage all concerned that a similar system could convey slate from Cae Braich-y-Cafn to Aber-Cegin, and reduce the number of horses involved in transport. This reduction was to prove considerable and A. H. Dodd maintains that 'Agriculture gained in the long run by the release of horses for farm work, but farmers long missed the subsidiary source of income'.

Lord Penrhyn had been relieved of the difficulties of selling slates during the long depression by appointing Worthington to do this for him, an arrangement which lasted the whole of Worthington's lifetime. James Greenfield became the Quarry Engineer in 1802 (after two years as Chief Overseer) and equally convinced that rail transport was required, he and Lord Penrhyn approached a mutual friend, Thomas Dadford, who was well acquainted with canal construction and the various forms of rail tramway feeder lines thereto.

Dadford produced a survey for a canal in 1799, for though he had been given a wide brief his personal inclination was likely to adopt the mode of transport with which he was most familiar. Though the canal was not taken up, he reported again on 5th June, 1800 for a fee of £51 for his survey for a railway instead. The plans for the canal are very crudely done and reflect the limited schooling of the engineers of those times; fortunately they have been recently traced.[18] (The Railway Survey was kept in the Engineer's Office at Coed-y-Parc in the 1940s, but the original document is missing – reference to it is taken from a copy made by J. H. Battersby and given to the Author).

The canal would have begun in the quarry below 650 ft and followed the contour northwards; it would begin 'where an oblong bason should be formed to hold 10 boats on each side to take in their loading . . .'. Dadford gave no precise route but rather general instructions to the effect that the route should continue along levels to geographical points where inclines could make the greatest descents. His generalised instructions (the mis-spellings in place names are as given) would have created:

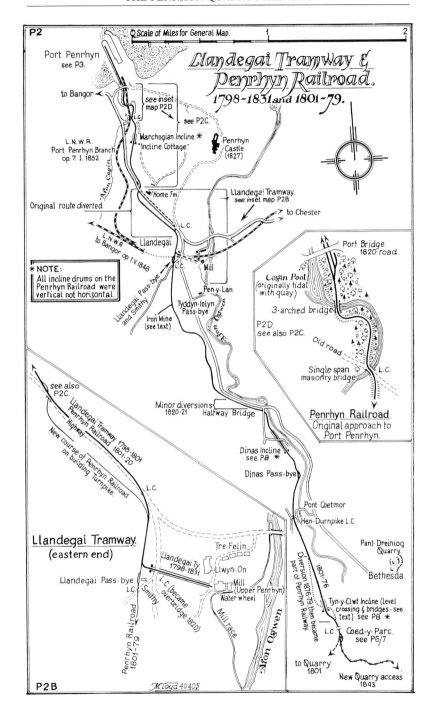

First Canal: Quarry – Coach House – Gorse –
  Pen-y-Bonk – Gwern Arfe – Ty Hen –
  Kilgeraint – Nant-y-Gryan – Pen-y-Dob   = 191 chains
  (There followed two consecutive inclines   = 213 ch. total)
Second Canal: Tyn-y-Loan – Tyddyn-Sarn   = 253 ch. total
  (There followed two more consecutive inclines = 275 ch. total)
Third Canal: Ty Gwyn – Coed Hywel-Ucha –
  Coed Hywel-Isa – Ffraeth   = 352 ch. total
  (There followed three consecutive inclines   = 381 ch. total)
Fourth Canal: (no distinguishing names in Survey) = 485 ch. total
  (There followed one incline to Pont
  Marchogian at its foot   = 495 ch. total)
Fifth or 'Lower Canal': Tan-y-Bryn – Port Penrhyn = 517 ch. total
  (The chain distances quoted are measured along the horizontal
  throughout).

The heading given is 'Leveling for Canal 1799 & Estimate'
followed by an 'Explanation'.

The waterway was to be 12 ft wide at surface, 6 ft wide at
bottom, 4 ft deep (but only 4 ft wide 'in rock cuttings and similar').
'Boats 20 ft long × 3 ft wide × 3 ft deep to carry 3 Tons & a Horse
supposed to draw 8 to 10 of them'. The total distance was 6.45
miles. It is not possible to plot a route accurately; a possible course
would take it to a point above Tregarth at Pen-y-Dob where
inclines would carry the boats on trolleys down to Tyn-y-Lon (near
the west end of the Penrhyn Quarry Railway passing loop). Thence
further north-westerly-directed inclines would fall to near Felin-
Hen whence a level continued to a point north and near Coed-
Hywel Isaf, falling then by inclines to near the White Bridge on the
east bank of the Cegin. A single plane would then lower the boats
on the final stage to where the old road crossed the Cegin at Pont
Marchogian (and where the third Railroad Incline found its base).
Thence by the fifth and last level into the Port. Whatever else the
problems of working such a waterway, a plentiful supply of water
in this part of Wales would not be one of them!

The Estimate accompanying is worth a partial quote, as several
Railroad features are linked to it; it appears to have been prepared
by Chrles Jones (sic) but the caligraphy is not clear. The items
include:

Bridge over Canal to go to Upper Slate Quarry	£ 30 0s. 0d.
Bridge to the Yellow Ochre Mill	40 0s. 0d.
Aqueduct at Glyddford average height 6 yds. × 110 yds.	357 10s. 0d.
5 Bridges	230 0s. 0d.
To the above must be added Machinery for 4 inclined planes 546 feet fall	546 0s. 0d.
NB. 4 of the Bridges may be saved, as Fords will do (less)	205 3s. 9d.

The total gross amount was £3,605 3s. 9d.

The Dadford Railway survey starts from the cart-loading wharf at the south edge of the Quarry and gains the banks of the Afon Cegin by a somewhat circuitous route via Llandegai (where he may have been instructed to link up with the existing tramway, accepting the fact that it is not known if this line was operational by this date). The most remarkable feature of the Report is the recommendation for a plateway of 5 ft 2 in. gauge: Dadford, who had been associated with certain 3 ft 4 in. gauge edge rail railways of South Wales, in this instance seems to have been completely influenced by Benjamin Outram's Report in favour of plateways to replace edge railways: the former method used a flange on the rail – allegedly to make the rail stronger – whilst the latter had the flange on the wheel.[19] Many edge railways in South Wales and Monmouthshire were converted into plateways about this time . . . a backward step as time was soon to show. As to the proposed gauge, it may be Dadford was providing to carry two small wagons from the Quarry, side by side on the back of a transporter, such as was done at Dinorwic Quarry in later times. His route involved three double-acting balanced inclines linked by a single line falling regularly from Quarry to Port at 1 in 96 . . . the figure of the eventual construction.

There were two Thomas Dadfords, father and son. It is suggested that Pennant met the elder when he was Engineer to and working on a section of the Trent & Mersey Canal close to his home at Winnington. He (Dadford) was familiar too with the 1777 tramroad off the Caldon Branch of that canal which linked Froghall Basin with the Caldon Low limestone quarries in Staffordshire by Act of 13th May, 1776 (said in 1797 to have had wooden rails faced with 1½ inch cast-iron strips). In his later life – he died in 1809 – and assisted by his sons as both contractors and engineers, they worked together in South Wales, Monmouthshire, Herefordshire and Worcestershire. Hadfield[20] has called them 'the mid wives of the new age', and rightly.

With Pennant being a Member of Parliament he may have been influenced by a Report of 1787 which Richard L. Edgeworth (Lord Edgeworth) of Edgeworthstown, Co. Longford had shown to his friends in the Commons; it was titled 'For improving the bogs of Ireland' and published in 1810, when it included the following '. . . it had been adopted in various places and in particular, at the Penrhyn Quarries, North Wales' though this sentence is more likely to apply to the portable tracks used at the quarry working faces. Sufficient to mention that Samuel Worthington and Edgeworth were on visiting terms.

If there was any hesitancy, then the low state of trade in the late 1790s brought matters to a head; by 1797 75% of Pennant's men were unemployed. There was an urgency to utilise this labour which, suffering privation, was in riotous mood. The standard of living in North Wales was much lower than in England, as were wages. Worse, there was a considerable migrant population among the quarrymen; these moved from place to place as work offered. Starvation was never far away and Williams confirms that workmen's wages were always quickly spent, as no one considered that a little careful budgetting might make difficult times a trifle easier. When there were Corn Riots in Caernarvon in 1800, quarrymen were prominent; on 2nd September in that year Lord Penrhyn had 'taken the plunge', deciding to super-cede the Llandegai Tramway by absorbing it into a larger system, and work on the 'Penrhyn Rail Road' as a contemporary report put it, began. He had put his faith in the future, and many of his unemployed tenants to work. Of Dadford's Report, some but not all was adopted.

REPORT ON A CONVEYANCE OF SLATE FROM THE QUARRIES TO PENRHYN PORT

We have surveyed and examined the country for both a Canal and a Railway, and find it greatly unfavourable to the former, owing to the great and irregular falls of ground; and it would require a Mile of Locks and Incline plane to pass the Boats from one Canal to the other. The expense of making and keeping it in repair would be very considerable, and the carriage would not be done on it for less money that by Rail Roads. The Country is not so forbidding to a Railway and will admit of one as convenient as most places which be recommended to be as follows beginning from the present Quarry and going Northwards Two Mile and 5 Furlongs with a fall of 8 inches in a Chain (Twenty two yards). Then to descend by an Incline Plane 142 yards long and fall 63 feet (5.3/10 ft in a yard). From thence the Road to continue three quarters of a Mile with a like fall of 8 inches in a Chain and descend an Incline Plane of 220 yds in length, 58 feet fall (3.1/10 in a yard). From thence continues the Road seven Furlongs [error in Report – should be 1 mile 7 Furlongs] falling 8 inches in a chain and then descend by a third Incline 330 yds long falling 102 ft (3.7/10 in a yard), and from thence to go to Penrhyn Port and Shipping Place, making in the whole a length of Six Miles, Six Furlongs, and a fall of 558 feet. For the line refer to the Plan.

The Road to be formed as follows, six yards wide and covered with gravel or broken stones three yards wide, nine inches thick, on which place blocks of stone nearly one hundred weight, with a circular hole drilled in the middle 6 inches deep and 1½ inch diameter into which drive a wood pin to receive a nail for fastening the Rails, after which the Road to be raised with gravel and c. well rammed round the stone blocks. See Section. [Here is shown an end-elevation of a tram-road wagon on a plateway – Battersby's copy retains this item.] It is headed "TRAMWAY, QUARRIES TO PORT PENRHYN."

The Rails to be made one yard in length to the Tram-rail plan with flanches and to weigh 40 lbs. each, which will be 80 lbs. to the yard, and 63 tons to the Mile. On this Road, waggons with iron wheels properly constructed carrying from 30 cwt. to 2 tons each and a tolerable Horse will take six or more of them with ease, and return with the empty ones carrying 2 to 3 tons.

The Incline Planes to be on the Rotative principle or endless chains working by a wheel at top and bottom and a double rail road for the loaded waggons coming down and the empty ones going up, by this means, slate and c. will be taken down at about 7d. a ton and from one to two hundred tons per day.

– ESTIMATE –

		£ s. d.
To	forming stoning and c. the Road 11066 yds. in length at 2/6	1383 3. 0.
"	forming and stoning the Incline Planes 692 yds. in length at 4/-	138 2. 0.
"	24902 stone blocks, nails and c. at 8d.	830 0. 0.
"	457 Tons of cast iron Rails and c. for the Road and Incline Planes in length at £11	5027 0. 0.
"	laying down rails and c.	150 0. 0.
"	Bridges, water ways and c.	150 0. 0.
"	Wheels, chains and c. to Incline Planes	300 0. 0.
		7978 5. 0.
	Contingencies and c.	350 0. 0.
		£8328 5. 0.

T. Dadford & Son. June 5th 1800

So 2nd September, 1800 marked the start of a Railroad, when Benjamin Wyatt, adopting certain Dadford recommendations, began civil engineering work with the help of about twenty-five workmen. Recasting the Tramway where necessary, he is likely to have completed the length between Port and the foot of the Dinas Incline by the following February, the work being fairly straightforward – this date is suggested by the fall in cartage rates. Up to this point, Dadford's route was followed, but southwards Wyatt increased the length of Dinas Incline (to which he would have road access about its middle point), so allowing the length of the ensuing Tyn-y-Clwt Incline to be shortened – but unfortunately steepened in consequence! Wyatt incorporated a difficult crossing with the 1803 Turnpike at Hen-Durnpike.

The basic facts about the Llandegai Tramway have not materialised, but if it is assumed the Railroad adopted similar standards and a junction was made at the top of the Llwyn-On Incline, the new edge railway (for such it was) was laid to a gauge of 24½ inches measured over the rail centres; the wagons were probably those used in the flint traffic and had double-flanged wheels so that the surface of the edge rail made contact between the flanges – a weakness as this was to prove. Some enlargement of the Port was essential and a first train of four wagons with two horses ran the whole length (not the final operating procedure, be it added) on 25th June, 1801; an official opening by Lord Penrhyn took place on 1st July, 1801, with the usual junketing at a cost of £25 5s. 0d.!

Almost at once the physical problems of the system, and the lack of experience of its operatives, led to chaotic conditions, and it was not for several months that teething troubles were largely overcome and an actual rail connection to the Quarry by incline was begun on 29th August. The Railroad was soon to become a 'must' for the excursionist-diarists of the day – Paterson's 'ROADS' (16th Edition of 1822) has this to say about the London–Holyhead route: '. . . and the wonderful power of machinery will also be viewed with considerable pleasure as exemplified in the iron tram road constructed for the more easy and expeditious conveyance of the waggons to and from the quarry at the expense of £170,000. The net profit of these quarries at a moderate calculation amounts to £15,000 per annum as no less than 100 tons per diem are conveyed to Port Penrhyn and from 500 to 600 tons are shipped every week'. (This cost given is widely quoted elsewhere and probably for the first time by Nicholson in 1808).

So the first of a long line of Welsh narrow gauge slate railways came into being and some new characters took the stage alongside; foremost was Benjamin Wyatt, who claimed to be the inventor of this form of railway and who eschewed Dadford's scheme for plates in favour of an edge railway. In 'A PRACTICAL TREATISE ON RAILROADS' published in 1837, Luke Hebert writes: '. . . It was not, we believe, until the beginning of the present century that edge rails were much known; as it appears that Mr. Benjamin Wyatt of Lime Grove near Bangor imagined himself to have originated them'. This was not so, for cast-iron rails proper were in use at Whitehaven by 1738, replacing wooden ones. Be that as it may, Wyatt maintained the unusual design of the track was his, a proclamation he may later have regretted; of the system he wrote in 1803 'The wheel made use of on the rail has a concave rim, so contrived in its form, and the wheels are fixed on their axles, as to move with the greatest facility in the sharpest curves that can be required'. There were a number of other persons who contemporarily claimed the Penrhyn design was theirs, and certainly there were some unique features. Dendy Marshall[21] writes and quotes from 'An Account of the Penrhyn Railway' in the 'REPERTORY OF ARTS AND MANUFACTURES' Vol. III 2nd Series p.285 which Account states it was 'communicated by the Inventor, Mr. Benjamin Wyatt of Lime Grove, near Bangor.'

> The rail hitherto made use of in most railways is a flat one ['flat one' i.e. a plate-way], three feet in length, with a rib on one edge, to give it strength, and to prevent the wheels (which have a flat rim) from running off. Observing that these rails were frequently obstructed by stones and dirt lodging upon them; that they were obliged to be fastened to single stones or blocks on account of their not rising sufficiently high above the sills to admit of gravelling the horsepath; that the sharp rib standing up was dangerous for the horses; that the strength of the rail was applied the wrong way; and that less surface would create less friction; led me to consider if some better form of rail could not be applied; the oval presented itself as the best adapted to correct all the faults of the flat rail, and I have the satisfaction to say that it has completely answered the purpose in a railway lately executed for Lord Penrhyn, from his Lordship's slate-quarries in Caernarvonshire, to Port Penrhyn (the place of shipping).

Further details of the track are given by Thomas Tredgold[22] as follows:

> Of the Welsh railways, we shall only further notice the railway for conveying slates from the Penrhyn slate-quarries, because it differs from the ordinary railways. The

rest of the rail-ways in Wales have flat or tram-rails, almost without exception. Penrhyn rail-way, from the Penrhyn slate-quarries in Caernarvonshire to Port Penrhyn, extends a distance of 6¼ miles, and is divided into 5 stages; it has ⅜ of an inch fall in 1 yard, that is 1 part in 96, and it has 3 inclined planes. This rail-way was begun in October, 1800, and finished in July, 1801. It has oval-formed edge-rails of cast iron, 4½ feet long, and 2 feet apart. Two horses draw 24 waggons one stage 6 times per day and carry 24 tons each journey, or 144 tons per day. The wheels of the waggons are of cast iron, 14 inches diameter, and weigh 35 lbs. According to Mr. Palmer's experiments, it requires 1 lb. to draw 87 lbs. on the Penrhyn rail-way, when the rails are level; while on the edge-rails of Newcastle, 1 lb. will draw 176 lbs.; this difference arises from the smallness of the wheels used on the Penrhyn rail-way. But, imperfect as it is, it has been of great value to the proprietors of the slate-quarries, by saving an immense expense in horse labour. The carriages are very low, and apparently convenient for conveying slates short distances; in fact, they are rather trams than waggons.

Tredgold supplies further particulars of the permanent way, and of changes made by 1825 in both rail and wheel form, thus:

> Some variety has occurred in the form of the edge-rail in Wales; for the rails of the Penrhyn rail-way were made at first of an oval figure, but it was found that the oval rail wore the concave rims of the wheels very fast into a hollow, fitting so close to the rail as to create much friction, and oblige them to change the wheels often. Hence they altered their rails to the form shown in the section of the rail-road, and the cross sills connecting them were at the same time made of cast iron, with dove-tailed sockets to receive the ends of the rails. The rails are 4 feet 6 inches long, and 2 feet apart. Each rail weighs 36 lbs., each sill 14 lbs., and each waggon carries 1 ton.
>
> The form of these rails is considerably inferior to that of the Newcastle edge-rails; the swell in the middle of the depth of the Penrhyn rail, collects the greatest quantity of iron to that part of the depth where it offers the least resistance.
>
> The mode of connecting the two lines of rails by cross bars or sills of cast iron, may perhaps be used with advantage in other cases, but we think the connexion of the rails to the sills not so good as by means similar to the metal chair used for the other edge-rails.

In the Second Edition of Tredgold (1835) p.35 appears a heretofore unquoted paragraph . . .

> On edge railways dust and dirt cannot so easily accumulate but when it does accumulate on rails where waggons with small wheels are used its retarding effect is so great as to induce the managers of railways to have water carried before each train of carriages to sprinkle and wash the rails. Mr. Palmer remarks that this is done on the railway of the Penrhyn slate quarries. In other edge railways where the wheels are larger and the rails further apart no such expedient is necessary.

It is notable that in publications dating from the 1830s far more attention is given to the problems of friction and Luke Hebert in the mid-30s remarks (p.12) . . .

> Tramroads are much esteemed in Wales . . . it is found desirable to divide the pressure upon the rails as much as possible; hence small carriages are used and these lead to small wheels so that effect of a given power is not above half what it ought to be
> . . .

The wheels of Penrhyn wagons 'only 14 inches in diameter' were certainly small in relation to existing standards and, having double flanges and running on an oval rail, these quickly ruined the profile of the concave flange; the effects of friction were soon apparent and a new rail section was tried in consequence – of this more later.

'THE PENNY CYCLOPAEDIA OF THE SOCIETY FOR THE DIFFUSION OF USEFUL KNOWLEDGE' Vol. XIX p.246 (London 1841) contains a few observations which differ from the several previous accounts of the Penrhyn Railroad. With the benefit of hindsight it sees the line as the first edge-way system to break from the then strong influence of Outram's plate-way dogma beginning . . .

> The serious disadvantages of the plateway led to the use of edgerails which have now almost entirely superceded the previous form. The first edgeway of any considerable extent was that completed in 1801 for the conveyance of slate from the quarries of Lord Penrhyn . . . rails of oval section the longest diameter being vertical . . . four feet six inches long and had a dovetail block cast beneath each end which fitted into an iron sill embedded in the road . . . the friction considerable yet the saving in power effected was such that two horses . . . pull twenty four waggons each containing about a ton . . .

We may ask why Wyatt, having publicised his invention, did not patent it?

It would seem that neither the original oval section nor the modified 1807 form was wholly efficient and to judge by the quantities of the flat topped type surviving in walls etc. to this day, its production was limited.

A return must now be made to the historical summary and the people involved. As regards Benjamin Wyatt's father, also Benjamin, he was the sixth son of John Wyatt of Weeford near Lichfield; he had stayed at home to manage the family farm and showing some enterprise in the timber business also, began building and then designing buildings. Of Benjamin (I) sons, Samuel and James became outstanding architects, the latter was a genious and owned the largest practice of any in the eighteenth century, becoming Surveyor General to H. M. Office of Works (1796–1813); he is buried in Westminster Abbey. In 1776 Richard Pennant commissioned him (James) to add to Winnington Hall, Cheshire (where he developed Salt Works), and on becoming owner of the Penrhyn Estate, engaged Samuel to rebuild its ruinous house 'Penrhyn House' of mediaeval origins (and rebuilt beyond the present period as Penrhyn Castle by Thomas Hopper in 1827–47, incorporating parts of Wyatt's work). (Samuel was eventually to build Lime Grove in the Penrhyn demesne, whilst Baron Hill at Beaumaris was carried out for Viscount Bulkeley by him.) In these tasks the potential of slate became fully appreciated by Samuel and this created new demands for the material; delighted by his work, Pennant asked Samuel if he could find him an energetic man to become his estate agent, and he commended his brother Benjamin (II) (1744–1818).[23]

The younger Benjamin secured the post at the age of 42; he was the fifth son of the family and with a wife and nine children he moved in from Staffordshire. He faced a daunting task as the whole estate was in a wretched condition, having passed through the female line which had accorded it little interest and even less expense.

In 'THE CAMBRIAN TRAVELLER'S GUIDE' by G. Nicholson (1st Edit. 1808 and 2nd Edit. 1813) there is a useful description of the works:

> The professional skill of Mr. Benjamin Wyatt, his Lordship's agent and brother to the celebrated architect . . . a Rail-way crosses the public road . . . here is exhibited the wonderful power of machinery. By means of an inclined plane, with an apparatus upon an eminence, about 20 small waggons are drawn up, and as many let down at the same time. They are drawn from the level by two horses with great ease to the adjoining quay on the Menai, called PORT PENRHYN. This Rail-way and its accompaniments cost about £170,000, . . . the wheels of the waggons are concave, which run upon a narrow convex bar. Six or 8 horses now perform the work which required about 80.
>
> Port Penrhyn (Aber-Cegid) is the grand depository of slates from the quarries . . . of Dolowen . . . it can hold vessels of 300 to 400 tons which take their loadings of extremely fine slates of a large size, and slabs of slate rock . . . there is also in the vicinity a slate factory for ciphering slates, inkstands etc. Also a building containing a set of hot and cold sea water baths with dressing rooms, a mill for grinding flints . . . owing to the disastrous war with France and to an impost of 20% laid by the government upon slate carried coast-ways which has checked the spirit of building . . .

A nice account is found in Edmund Hyde Hall's 'A DESCRIPTION OF CAERNARVONSHIRE' in 1809–11:

> The elevation of the quarry above the sea is . . . about 550 ft. and . . . a railway is constructed of cast-iron bars, oval and laid with their transverse axes vertically in parallel rows along which glide the wheels, grooved into a semi-circle. Of the small waggons which being 4 ft 4 ins. and 1½ ft, deep and wide, carry about 15 cwt. of slate each. Of these, 24 linked together form what is called a run, six of which on a fine day can be passed down to the port. But the short days narrow the time; windy or snowy weather suspend the work or prohibit the passage. Two horses can draw this enormous weight, but three are now more prudently employed. The descent to the sea is obtained by a fall of an inch in every 3 yds. . . . in the midway between the planes double ways are also laid down for the passage of each other of the waggons, and any confusions by these precautions prevented. The original expense of construction, the interest of the sum expended, the wear and tear of ironwork, carriages etc. have been amply repaid and recompensed by the diminution of breakage among the slates, the prodigious extension of their sale and above all (in a public point of view) by the reduced number of horses, an animal which like the sheep has become more oppressively consuming than the wolf. (This applies to the high cost of horse fodder due to war.) Heretofore the slates were carried first in panniers and subsequently in carts which, 140 in number, took an equal number of oxen and no less than 400 horses from the pursuits of agriculture. The business is now done upon its very extended scale by 16 horses and 12 men and boys . . . The quay at Port Penrhyn 'on which terminates the rail-way' extends 600 ft. into the sea and was completed in 1790.

Although some of Hall's figures are at variance with elsewhere, his was the first intelligent and broadly-based account of the transport business, and many of the facets including the use of oxen and the cost of keeping horses are delightfully expressed.

In 'CAMBRIA DEPICTA' (E. Pugh) published in 1816 the cost of building is given as £5,000 and the cost per ton of cartage as 5/- whereas the railroad was only 1/- and the usual figure of 100 tons per day carried is quoted. As to the Quarry, Pugh says "a man conducts a fourwheeled barrow loaded along these edges on a narrow rail-road. When a sufficient number are ready the slates are conveyed to Port Penrhyn in eight or a dozen of these little barrows or waggons and thus one horse will draw many tons. There are two inclined planes at this quarry . . ." Pugh was clearly impressed by the small size of the wagons and that the slates were already loaded into them before they were taken along the galleries to make up a train; the two inclined planes were probably the initial one at the base of the quarry, built 1801, and the second one of about 1811.

A last extract from Rev. W. Bingley's 'TOUR OF NORTH WALES' published 1804 (2nd Edit.) will show how the Railroad had become a major tourist mecca within a short time of its building, and gives figures at this early period. "Two horses are now able in fifteen waggons chained to each other to draw upwards of 12 tons of slate along the levels . . ." Of the inclines (he states there were four besides those in the quarry and must have included the initial plane from the wharf) he writes "At the top of each there is a windlass where by means of a lever pressed against the cylinder the velocity of the full waggons going down and drawing up the empty ones is regulated. Only three waggons when I saw them were suffered to go down at once and in the longest plane the whole fifteen occupied about twenty minutes in passing."

The success of the new Railroad compared with previous forms of transport did not require those early tourists to trumpet it, albeit that it required four or five times more rail wagons to carry the same load as a Bethesda road cart; the cartage rate of 5/3d. then applying was reduced to 1/- per ton/mile under the railroad system and put the Penrhyn Quarry well in advance of its competitors. The canal-using quarries of the East Midlands which could use the Grand Junction for ½d. per ton/mile whilst still able to halve Penrhyn costs, served a limited market, whilst once slates were on shipboard at Port Penrhyn there was a world market growing for them. Despite taxation, there came a big demand for slate for the better buildings in south-east England, for with the French war, timber had grown expensive and the clay tiles or stone slates used there heretofore were much heavier than the Welsh slates; the use of the latter enabled lighter roofing members to be used, so cutting costs. One large London tile manufacturer was hit so hard that he leased Crown land adjacent to Penrhyn to quarry slate for himself. From the 1820s all the best buildings were roofed in slate

Plate I Quarry galleries with three of the five initial 'Blondin' hoists installed from 1912, with rubbish wagons suspended.
Gwynedd Archives

Plate II Looking down from Sinc Bach to Red Lion Level, with Water Balance extreme left: 1962
D.L. Chatfield

Plate III   KATHLEEN hauls along Sinc Bach Level, pre 1913. Wagons, save for the rock probably bound for the Mill in the middle of the train, contain rubbish. *Gwynedd Archives*

Plate IV   Seen from alongside Felin-Fawr Incline, the upper yard and Coed-y-Parc complex extend below: 1962. *D.L. Chatfield*

Plate V CEGIN brings a train of 'Fullersite', empty slate and coal wagons along Red Lion Level to the Felin-Fawr Incline. *per J.I.C. Boyd*

Plate VI BLANCHE is prepared for the Down Workmen's Train run (July 1947) and an unwary D.C. Boyd (the only passenger so far) is due for a lively ride! *J.I.C. Boyd*

Plate VII   CHARLES is on main line duties, Coed-y-Parc: May 1951.

J.I.C. Boyd

Plate VIII   Workshop interior with GERTRUDE, OGWEN and LINDA. Engineer Mr. Stephenson explains progress to a visitor.

D.L. Chatfield

Plate IX Looking south from Foulkes' bridge, the Quarry tips tower above Coed-y-Parc Yard. Former Railroad stables are behind the wall (right); the main line is to the right hand: 1947. *J.I.C. Boyd*

Plate X Coed-y-Parc Yard from the south end; slab trains in attendance on the Mill and STANHOPE (derelict) outside the small engine shed. *J.I.C. Boyd*

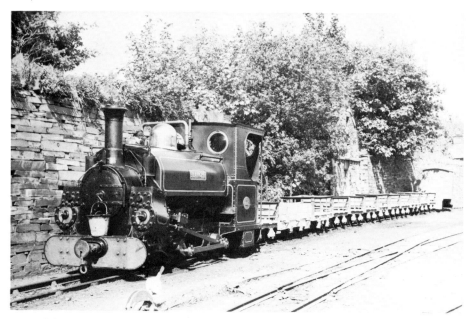

Plate XI   BLANCHE has arrived at Coed-y-Parc with the Up empties and takes water from the stand-pipe there. The water-tank brake van is in the rear of the train.   *Maid Marian Fund*

Plate XII   An evening Down Workmen's Train leaves Coed-y-Parc, fourteen coaches in the rear.   *J.H. Battersby*

Plate XIII A Down slate working cautiously passes Hen-Durnpike with
BLANCHE.   *Maid Marian Fund*

Plate XIV   Port Penrhyn about 1894 with cast-
and the shunting engines LILIAN and WINIFRED.

lge in foreground. The nearest ship is the ENTERPRISE
Gwynedd Archives

Plate XV Up 10.45 a.m. train passes Pandy (Tregarth) Loop with LINDA. 'Fullersite' wagons behind the engine, then loaded coal wagons and slate empties; the brakesman rides in the last wagon: May 1959. *Ifor Higgon*

Plate XVI BLANCHE approaches Felin-Hen with slate and sack-filled 'Fuller-site' wagons: July 1957. *Ifor Higgon*

Plate XVII LINDA halts awhile at Felin-Hen on a Down working; ex-L.N.W.R. branch overbridge in background. Note sanding gear fitted to these engines in later years: April 1962.   *D.L. Chatfield*

Plate XVIII Sunshine and shadows on the Port approach; standard gauge branch on the left: April 1962.   *D.L. Chatfield*

Plate XIX Entering the Port, BLANCHE trundles under the bridge with the last run of the day.

Maid Marian Fund

Plate XX The first empty run of the day prepares to leave the Port; the engine's blower is building up the steam pressure: June 1954.

J.I.C. Boyd

Plate XXI Port Penrhyn and vicinity. The Castle demesne covers the foreground, with the Menai Straits and Anglesey beyond.

Aerofilms

Plate XXII   The Port in the mid-1890s, seen from the upper floor of Port House, showing considerable stocks of slate on hand, the preponderance of which is due for rail loading rather than by sea.

National Museum of Wales

Plate XXIII   The handsome Port House of 1833, administrative centre of the
organisation and today a surviving feature of bygone times.   *J.I.C. Boyd*

Plate XXIV   WINIFRED takes over the loaded wagon run to shunt it around
the Port; main line engines were never used on this duty: July 1950.

J.I.C. Boyd

Plate XXV   SYBIL MARY berthed alongside the Coal Wharf in the late 1940s. At this period every slate produced was bound by legislation to reach the Home Market.   *R.E. Tustin*

Plate XXVI   Heyday of the Writing Slate Factory at the Port, which had rail access: about 1910.   *Gwynedd Archives*

whilst houses for the lower orders remained faithful to tiles or even thatch.

Benjamin Wyatt's brother Samuel, well-ensconced in the London building theatre, could not rely on a steady supply of Penrhyn slate for his needs; to this end Lord Penrhyn had long recognised the value of the Wyatt associations to widen his markets, and put buildings with slate (be it functional or decorative) before the public eye. In his Agreement with Worthington there was a clause specifically excluding slate supplied to Wyatts; Benjamin was a shareholder in the brig ALBION which worked to and from London carrying their slates. Despite Benjamin's wide experience he was happy to leave slate quarrying matters to William Williams (already noted) and afterwards to James Greenfield, though taking overall responsibility upon himself.

Ever anxious to keep his men employed and out of mischief, Wyatt designed the new cart road (now 'The Old Road'), and built the initial works at the Port in 1790. The mole there was extended about 1830, (a New Dock and second quay following in 1855) and his road up Nant Ffrancon (for which Lord Penrhyn took most of the acclaim) was primarily to obtain transport for the metal ores and stone from the head of the valley. Living at Lime Grove during his time at Penrhyn, he died aged 76 on 5th January, 1818 and is buried with his wife Sarah (1750–1815) under a prominent pyramid of slate slab in Llandegai Churchyard.

James Greenfield (1774–1825) became Chief Overseer at the Quarry in 1799, before William Williams's (Manager) retirement in 1802; he had married Wyatt's second child Charlotte (1774–1815) and his principal contribution was to be in improving the technique on the existing 'gallery' system of working the Quarry. The Greenfields lived at Bryn-Derwen, a villa built for them near Bethesda. (Bethesda, largest place in the locality, took its name from the Chapel built in 1820). On 19th January, 1825 during a period of considerable labour unrest at the Quarry, he was found drowned; his wife had pre-deceased him within days of her own mother's death. Greenfield was succeeded by James Wyatt (1795–1882), Benjamin's thirteenth child who had taken his father's position in 1819 but only as regards the Estate. During his employment, Quarry output rose from 46,000 tons in 1826 to 120,000 tons in 1859. James was the last Wyatt agent at Penrhyn, and Lime Grove was demolished after his retirement; his second daughter married her cousin Osmond Arthur Wyatt; their son Arthur became Quarry Manager in 1874 and he resigned after a disagreement with Lord Penrhyn in December 1885. (When his father James had retired he (James) lost a large fortune in trying to develop the Croesor Slate Quarry. James was replaced by Captain Pennant Athelwood Iremonger and henceforward the Port interests were divorced from those of the Estate.[24])

Turning back to the Railroad scene, near the Quarry was an area round the community known as Coed-y-Parc where the ground was suited to the building of a workshop to serve the whole Estate, where water power was available and there was a convenient road access. The site lay about quarter of a mile north of the Quarry boundary and in due course a group of workshops given over partly to slate and slab manufacture in connection with the Quarry was developed round a mill named Felin-Fawr (The Big Mill) and first begun in July 1803; further buildings followed, all on the east of the Railroad just south of the head of the Tyn-y-Clwt Incline and power was provided by water wheels. The complex began life with the building of a slate sawing mill conveniently placed alongside the storage sidings for the Incline; it was a Worthington project and from it fireplaces, window sills, man-tleshelves, monuments, slab tanks, and even inkwells emerged . . . in 1835 slate beds for billiard tables appeared, the first ever. Here the output of a small mine nearby whose mill supplied ground ochre, was loaded into wagons.

Apart from enlargements at the Port (which were never sufficient for Quarry needs!) the next improvement on the Railroad began in autumn 1820, mainly between Llandegai village and Ty-Newydd to the north-west. Here, John Provis's[25] newly-engineered Shrewsbury–Holyhead road created by Telford[26] took possession of the Railroad for that length and buried it five feet under the new road surface.

The Railroad was re-aligned and a tunnel made under the new road – built partly as a measure to relieve unemployment – being taken along a new course 35 yards to the south of the old one and creating a 'dip' in the section hereabouts.

From November 1823 extensive works were carried out to replace the wharf etc. at the east side of the Quarry. On the west side new inclines were taken up from the Railroad to new levels: at Railroad level a new weighing machine was of such capacity as to accommodate all output. These events coincided with the end of an era when the method of winning slate by digging deep holes in the quarry floor was ended.

Back on the main line, the wear and tear suffered by the vertical winding drums ('winches') on the inclines began to assert itself in early 1824, due mainly to the fact that the drums were so mounted (those in the Quarry were of the more common form and horizontal) and the bottom bearings were suffering. In 1825 Samuel Worthington, then aged 65, whilst still retaining ultimate control of his arrangements with Lord Penrhyn, allowed his sons Archibald and William to assume day-to-day responsibility for the business (his eldest son, Samuel seems to have gone back to his grandfather's business as a Corn & General Dealer in Liverpool). At the same period William Francis was to become Superintendent at the Quarry; his family were to exert some major influences over the next four decades, but not directly on the Railroad. The Worthington era came to a close; in July 1829 the family moved away to Llanfairfechan, where the evidence of their quarrying interests continue to the present day. Samuel died in 1847. With their departure Penrhyn Quarry annexed the Writing Slate Factory and enlarged it. The Flint Mill was converted into a Hone Mill, a business it was to follow until 1872. The associated kilns at the Port were readily converted into lime kilns, in which function they continued until 1863. Rail connection to the old Flint Mill (the incline down to the Mill had survived) was taken out – this move is suggested by an entry in the Daily Log in May 1831 – and in October 1839 the small ochre mine at Coed-y-Parc which had opened on 15th December, 1794 closed down.

Up at the Quarry end of the Railroad the years of depression in the 1820s had passed, and by 1830 1,400 were employed in the workings again. The Foundry at Coed-y-Parc came into use in 1832 and was extended in 1864 by the building of a Pattern Shop: a Brass Foundry was added later. At the Port the decorative iron bridge spanning the river was put up to replace a wooden one (which obviated a ford) in 1835 and whilst the Wyatt-designed Port House and a warehouse (to be the last) had been erected on 'The Import Quay' in 1833, back at Coed-y-Parc more alterations were made in 1835 when the Oil House (where wagon lubricants were stored) was given a new roof, the Saw Mill extended, a new Joiners' Shop built and the prominent high stone wall which thereafter concealed the stables, was put up. Five years later (1840) the weighing machine at the Quarry foot was replaced by a new one at Coed-y-Parc whereon the wagons were ingeniously assisted by water power; this was sited close by the later 'Baldwin (Loco) Shed'.

These matters apart, it may be noted that Lord Penrhyn had commissioned Thomas Hopper ('Judicious Hopper' as he was dubbed) to design and build a new Penrhyn Castle, complete with interior decor and furniture – all to be Hopper's responsibility – in 1827; over two decades were needed to complete the work and with foresight two special Document Chambers were incorporated. (The Castle is now administered by The National Trust).

All these developments were but outward signs of an industrial revolution on the Estate – in the early 1830s Thomas Roscoe wrote of Bethesda, the new town created beside the Quarry:

> On my way along the mail road . . . I was surprised by the rapid increase of population, houses and villages on the line of the mountain quarries, within the last thirty years, and by the marks of endless improvement . . . one serious drawback presented itself in the endless number of public houses. The extensive slate quarries in this neighbourhood are conducted on an admirable and enlarged scale, with the facilities afforded by railways and other improved methods of working . . . I was informed that upwards of two hundred tons of slates are conveyed daily by the railway from the quarries of Cae Braich y Cafn in Nant Ffrancon, to Port Penrhyn . . . and that nearly two thousand workmen have constant employment.

Though there were to be ups and downs in the slate business, the growth was constant and the removal of slate tax an important factor; markets abroad gave increased demand and there is much evidence that the Railroad frequently became choked with traffic which it could not carry; the wear and tear on primitive track and inferior incline equipment led to numerous failures. Only the technical ingenuity of the Workshops contrived to keep wagons moving along a rail-road system which had become outclassed. Over at Dinorwic a first railway system had also been built and like that at Penrhyn was proving incapable of carrying the traffic that offered, and there is a suggestion that in the late 1830s when Dinorwic was looking to ways of replacing their old line some thought was given to linking up the rail systems, though this would have meant Dinorwic products would have left the quarry at high level and Port Penrhyn would have to have coped with the shipment of both quarries! But nothing transpired: Dinorwic built its own railway and within a decade was operating it by steam power – suddenly Penrhyn was outdated too!

Evidence for official concern at the inadequacy of things is a Survey of May 1844 together with a Report of 7th November following submitted by a Mr. James Walker for a PENRHYN SLATE RAILWAY; Walker's work is based on the surviving Railroad Plan of 1829 and he proffers no less than three choices of route between Port and Quarry; summarized these were:

No. 1.   From Port, along the east bank of the Cegin to Felin-Esgob thence southeast past Coed-Hywel-Isaf, northeast of Llyn Cororian, north of Pen-y-Bronydd then alongside but west of the Dinas Incline and taking the west side round the hillock of Dinas knoll; then generally following the existing Railroad but to its west, to join it at Coed-y-Parc.

Nos. 2 and 3.   These were variations on No. 1 giving a total of three options between the Port and Hafod-Ty (two schemes) with a further option between Hafod-Ty and Coed-y-Parc. No. 2 follows fairly closely to the ultimate Penrhyn Quarry Railway route and is probably the key to later surveys by Spooner and Algeo.

Fortunately Sections of each scheme are given and on consideration of these one may conclude why no further steps were taken, for an incline of 1 in 18 takes No. 1 from 85 ft to 292 ft at Coed-y-Hywel, then after 3½ miles of 1 in 200 another incline takes the line from 330 ft to 516 ft whence – roughly about the head of the then Dinas Incline – a rise of 1 in 200 again would bring it to the Quarry (542½ ft) with a total length of 5 m. 42 ch. The route would naturally have been much higher up the hillside in order to achieve that altitude with only two inclines; an interesting note marks 'Viaduct for refuse from Quarry'. The foregoing was the least horrifically-inclined, the other options being hopeless. The Plan shows the proposed Chester & Holyhead Railway coming round from the northeast into Bangor to reduce tunnelling, and the existing course as 'Alternative'. No supporting documents have yet appeared.

Now, more of the impact which the Railroad made on visitors – probably the first that most had seen. Fenton writes (25th July, 1810): ". . . The scene on all sides was enlivened by the course of the Rail Road carriages laden with slates, a load that would be more perhaps than 20 horses could draw, drawn by two; neat cottages, mills for manufactures, cottages for the workmen employed in the mines . . ."

Fenton was back again in 1813 and said: ". . . We frequently saw the course of the Rail Road . . . where I saw Two Horses draw a vast number of Tumbrels with the greatest ease, each carrying a Ton-weight of slates. Two horses can often drag 30 of such Tumbrels, and can if occasion required, drag 40: and they can make three trips per day, a prodigious thing."

Fenton came to the Quarry but was unable to give it more than a cursory glance owing to a storm; he came to Coed-y-Parc: ". . . pass a little further on the manufactory for sawing slates, Chimney Pieces, occupied by Mr. Worthington, but did not see the process, the work being stopped owing to some reparation, for some days . . . Mr. Worthington . . . carries on Flint grinding work for the Potteries, on a grand Scale. The Flints he imports from Southampton, or other Ports nearest to the Downy Countries . . ." (which suggests the local flint stone was no longer the major source).

Of the processes which created the Llandegai Tramway, Fenton makes a later visit and wrote: ". . . he carries on here . . . a mill for reducing flint, first burnt with an impalpable powder, to make China, a very late discovery . . ." and of the Saw Mill: ". . . The Boards that were sawing then were for the frame of Cyphering slates, about 3 fourths of all that are used are made here, viz about 8,000 dozen. There is likewise a vast quantity of Pencils sold here which come from the North of England and are cut by Machine . . ."

There was an Admiralty Enquiry in 1844 which reported that 440 cargoes carrying 41,000 tons of slate were shipped westward from the Port and Parry's 'RAILWAY COMPANION FROM CHESTER TO HOLY-HEAD' of 1848 gives the quay as 1,000 ft long capable of holding 100 sail traders, whilst a later account of 1851 suggests a daily shipment of 250 tons which would require up to 300 wagons arriving at the Port (say 6 trips of 50 wagons each, per day).

The 'CAMBRIAN MIRROR' boasts that the quarries 'are alone worth a journey from London and back to see'. The amount of attention which the undertaking was receiving was due to the 'open house' afforded to visitors, the realisation that good publicity was good for trade and that in the initial years of the new century diarists who would normally be travelling the Continent were put off such excursions by the French Wars.

In the ultimate, the traffic on the Railroad depended not on the numbers of orders for slate but on the capacity of the Quarry to produce it. The high percentage of waste involved in the process made the careful disposal of rubbish around the Quarry a matter of prime concern, otherwise time and money would be lost in winning new rock buried by early rubbish disposal – this feature brought many a promising site to an early demise, especially where the tenure of land for quarrying did not allow sufficient area for rubbish dumping; the Penrhyn enterprise was fortunate, for land ownership created no problems. In March 1846 a new slab-cutting mill was opened at Coed-y-Parc; at the Quarry however extraction had gone deeper as well as being spread over the mountainside galleries, and methods of ridding the pits of water and lifting the quarried stone to the working level were devised which utilised water on a no-cost basis. Hydraulic balances of 5 ton capacity to lift wagons between the Levels first appeared in June 1852; on 4th January, 1842 the main line inclines' hemp ropes were exchanged for wrought iron chains, being renewed again in 1850: the wagon runs increased to 50 vehicles using three horses. Wire ropes did not find favour in North Wales until the late 1850s. ('A SHORT HISTORY OF BRITISH METAL MINING TECHNOLOGY IN THE 18th AND 19th CENTURIES' (Roger Burt) p.53.)

In the late 1840s the railway isolation of the Penrhyn system came to an end with the opening of the Chester – Bangor section of the Chester & Holyhead Railway on 1st May, 1848. The rights of the Penrhyn Estate were protected and there was to be no deviation in route, no station, shed or building permitted between the Ogwen and Bangor and all bridges, viaducts etc. were to be of ornamental character (which may explain the use of non-native sandstone to face interiors of slab, brick or iron). The line was to be tunnelled and the contractor or railway company servants were not to appear on the surface except during building or repairs, the land was to be restored within three months. Only 33 ft at rail level was to be allowed to be taken, the cuttings to be as steep as possible; the C.&H.R. was not permitted to obstruct any railway or tramroad to mines or quarries in existence or which in future might wish to cross it. The Act (7 & 8 Vic. Cap LXV)[27] appeared to protect Colonel The Hon. Edward Gordon Douglas-Pennant quite adequately for the very nature of the terrain required the new railway to pass through the Llandegai Tunnel and from the grounds of the Estate only the smokeshaft was visible from the gates of Grand Lodge! The Railroad was undisturbed but the visible remains of the Mill Incline disappeared in the cutting approach to the east tunnel mouth; even to this day the 1820 road overbridge (built by John Provis) survives over the remnants of the upper incline course – evidence of the rights of the Estate!

It should not be imagined however, that relations between Lord Penrhyn and the coming standard gauge railway were all milk and honey; the Estate Letter Book from early 1848 contains much bitter correspondence – 'I suppose you will be getting to work directly with your usual railway speed . . . as it is some months since promised . . .'

were among the contentious remarks exchanged. The diversion of the Cegin along whose bank the new Railway would run in after-years was a particularly sore point – 'the New Cut that was made for diversion of river Cegin is very imperfect . . . it will destroy not only the land . . . but will . . . injure the Viaduct . . . it ought to be paved with stones . . . do what is necessary to remove this evil'.

In October 1851 the first load of slate was taken to Bangor station by cart and despatched by rail to George Tavenor at Beswick, Staffordshire, but the cost of such cartage made the main line uncompetitive compared with sea freight, not to mention the extra handling and breakages. However, in January 1852 the 'L.N.W.R. Port Siding' came into existence and a standard gauge connection was brought right down on to the quays, necessitating some alterations to the narrow gauge layout there. That same month Mr E. I. Wood of Chirk became the first customer to receive his goods by main line. (The Port Branch as mentioned in C.&H.R. documents suggests it was worked by 'Lord Penrhyn's Loco', but there is no evidence that His Lordship owned such an engine – it may have been a small locomotive owned by the C.&H.R., and so dubbed.)

The branch was not actually a part of the Chester & Holyhead Railway promotion but was built under a number of Agreements by them on behalf of Colonel Douglas-Pennant under similar terms which were offered to Assheton-Smith to build the siding down to Port Dinorwic, also served by the C.&H.R. (Caernarvon Branch). A depot for slates was built at Saltney near Chester to receive both Penrhyn and Dinorwic stocks; Agreements made then and later were:

16th August, 1851	Installation & maintenance of structures and track (this item was similar to that agreed at Port Dinorwic)
14th August, 1870	Siding extensions
2nd February, 1881	Siding extensions
1st December, 1882	Siding extensions
17th July, 1888	Confirmation of original Agreement
18th July, 1923	Costs of Branch pass to new London Midland & Scottish Railway; rates adjusted to compensate

A series of letters exchanged in 1908 suggests that the 1851 Agreement was to be revised, but this was not carried out. The Euston Company continued to charge for maintenance, e.g.

9 May, 1912   Repairs to Culverts 1, 3, 5.   £8. 15s. 4d.

The Branch was designated 'Siding' in 1954.

In due course the standard gauge would be carrying away almost one-third of the Quarry output, but with increased tonnages along the Railroad, the number of ships using the Port, even allowing for their larger sizes, kept it near the limit of its abilities. Apart from local delivery, since 1819 the whole of the Quarry output had been funnelled down the Railroad, for in that year road haulage was suspended entirely; for the next 20 years its Railroad/shipping position remained pre-eminent in the North Wales slate trade; a look at competitors will underline the experience gained at Penrhyn:

Dinorwic Railway
  Port: Port Dinorwic .... Horse tramroad opened 1824
Nantlle Railway
  Port: Caernarvon .... Horse tramroad opened 1828
Festiniog Railway
  Port: Portmadoc .... Horse tramroad opened 1836

and the first real knocks were to come in the 1840s when the Dinorwic concern built a new railway which adopted steam power in 1848; after half a century the transport dominance of the Penrhyn Railroad was broken.

The coming of the main line railway changed the North Wales coast scene for ever: districts which had relied on the sea for supplies were now connected with any part of the Kingdom owning a railway; the warehouses at the Port (and elsewhere) became defunct. Only coal tonnages increased; much of this came from Flintshire collieries which were worked on the seaboard, and the Small Quay was modified to take bulk tonnages. Coal was taken up the Railroad for Estate purposes generally, but the Quarry needed much of it for steam engines' boilers (especially after 1860); also the area around Bethesda relied on it for domestic use[28] and ten new coal wagons appeared on the Railroad as a result. One of them was fitted with a roof to carry lime up the line from the kilns originally established at the Port by Worthington for burning flintstone: it still carried on sporadic duties when in 1863, the kilns were closed down and lime brought in by ship from Penmaenmawr.

In 1864 a rather sophisticated wagon-weighing machine was installed at the Port, powered by a stationary steam engine which hauled the wagons over the table; so for the first time an 'engine driver' appears on the wage sheets. (An earlier water-powered machine at Coed-y-Parc of 1840 has been mentioned previously.) In the early 1870s a significant addition to the Port came with the completion in May 1871 of the New Dock, and the extension of the L.N.W.R. siding towards the east side of the quays and this new work; it was nicknamed 'The Beaumaris Siding' pointing as it did, across the Straits to that town.

In the meanwhile Lord Penrhyn had received an unsolicited missive from Charles E. Spooner, the Manager, Engineer & Secretary of the narrow gauge Festiniog Railway which ran from Blaenau Ffestiniog down to Portmadoc and was also a slate carrier. That Company had within very recent years converted their system from a horse tramroad into a locomotive-hauled railway (albeit the down-grade trains ran by gravity) and had overturned earlier statutory legislation (Act 9 & 10

Vic. Cap. 87 of 1846) by acquiring the right to run passenger trains from 1866 on a gauge of less than 2 ft. Spooner, whose business interests were not entirely confined to the Festiniog, saw in the Penrhyn situation a close similarity to that which had recently pertained on the Festiniog (i.e. a horse tramroad which had potential as a locomotive railway), and on 5th June, 1868 wrote, with far-reaching effect:

Bron-y-Garth, Portmadoc.

I beg to bring under your Lordship's notice a matter that I presume will be of interest both individually and good to your Lordship's Quarry neighbourhood and workmen.

I have for some time considered that a small Railway to be of the same gauge as present tramway worked by Locomotive Steam Engine between Penrhyn Quarries and Bangor Slate Wharves would greatly facilitate transit . . .

He would retain the same gauge but build a new line from the Port to the head of the existing Dinas Incline, and from there to the Quarry would follow roughly the course of the Railway as would be built later on. At Ffridd, near Coed-Hywel-Isaf a branch would fork eastward and by a sweeping curve anti-clockwise and climbing, gain the Chester & Holyhead section east of the Llandegai viaduct and then run with that line into Bangor station; along the C.&H.R. section he suggested that the new line be brought in beside the existing Port branch of the L.N.W.R. either as a parallel track or run the narrow gauge inside the standard gauge (i.e. four-rail) inferring that the new narrow gauge Railway would usurp the existing Railroad site as it approached the Port . . . a state of affairs which was ultimately to come to pass. In fact, much of the whole conception thus far did come into existence – but not yet.

Spooner was doubtful if the C.&H.R. would accept his Bangor dream, for he writes:

. . . I do not know if the Chester & Holyhead Railway would approve of such a junction . . . This letter is based on the success of the Festiniog Railway passing from horses to Locomotives last Four Years [sic] . . . (otherwise) it would be very improbable that I should now take the liberty to trouble your Lordship with this letter . . .

He goes on to emphasise three facets which the Festiniog had just experienced:

    a) the successful introduction of Quarrymen's Trains
    b) the resultant reduction in the number of wagons required for traffic – ('abandoned slate trucks might be used for Quarry purposes')
    c) that all downhill traffic can be worked by gravity.

A detailed estimate follows showing 6¾ miles of new Railway @ £3,250 per mile (£21,937), with an additional £3,000 for the mixed gauge branch to Bangor; 3 locos and tenders – delivered (£2,860); altering 700 of the best present slate wagons and fitting tyred wheels, single flanges and fixed axles @ £5. 15s. each and 15–20 per time; 20 timber and coal trucks (£18 each); 20 quarrymen's carriages (£20 each) with, for public passenger traffic, six new carriages and a guard's van. In other words, a reflection of the Festiniog Railway. A total expenditure would be £37,737. Annual expenses would be £4,515 and income £8,200 giving an annual profit margin of £3,685. His costings were based on 120,000 tons of slate then passing plus 13,000 tons of materials, coal and goods for quarrymen and neighbourhood (a traffic which then was of limited extent). A significant suggestion is that the line might be worked by contract . . . (perhaps *he* hoped for such involvement?)

The approach was timely even if no more than food for thought; the historic costings are of value and the proposal was the first of three Spooner projects. Not insignificantly, within a short time steam power was to appear, together with the beginnings of the new Railway; in due course a new fleet of up-dated slate wagons would be introduced and a quarrymen's train would begin. Of the disappointments, Bangor station (not surprisingly) never played host to narrow gauge trains, and public passenger traffic was equally a non-starter on the Penrhyn line if for no other reason than it would have required a complete change of attitude by Lord Penrhyn towards the predominance of his slate traffic.

Arthur Wyatt had been the prime mover in demonstrating the problems of a decrepit Railroad; Penrhyn must face the effects of competitors who enjoyed a more modern railway. Another cloud on the horizon might be a standard gauge promotion between Bangor and Bethesda either by the L.N.W.R. or a railway running northwards from the Ffestiniog district and worked by the G.W.R.; within a few years local committees would pressurise Penrhyn to provide such a railway to serve his tenants and give outlying communities on the Estate a rail link . . . but it is probable that at this stage that cloud was too small to be noticed.

On 16th January, 1873 Spooner submitted 'Proposed Line of Railway from Port Penrhyn & Bangor to the Penrhyn Quarries, Bethesda';

> In compliance with your Lordship's instructions that I should ascertain the most practicable and best route to adopt for construction of a Narrow Gauge Locomotive Railway through your property . . . as a substitute for the present tramway . . . I understand from your Lordship that the Line should be arranged not only for quarry purposes, but also to be generally useful for the workmen and the district . . .

(Here Spooner acknowledges receipt of several plans sent by Pennant-Lloyd (the Quarry Manager).)

> . . . none of which were suitable for a Locomotive Line . . . and capable of being screened from view of the Demesne.

Spooner's object was to climb 490 ft in 6½ miles and lay out the line to the same gauge as the Railroad. It would embrace a section 'of the tramway with as light work in cuttings and fillings as possible'. Lord

Penrhyn had at last awoken to reality, with the reminder of competition from Ffestiniog-mined slate which now could enjoy steam/gravity haulage down to Minffordd exchange sidings on the Cambrian Railways' Coast Section, and give better service to the shipping potential of Portmadoc. Spooner's recommendations included plans of motive power, 'the most practicable and best route', and the transformation of the north end of the 1803 Slab Mill at Coed-y-Parc into a Locomotive and Carriage Repair Shop: he was at his most imaginative. There was to be a main passenger/goods station at the foot of Garth Road in Bangor, close beside the shore, and the narrow gauge line down to the Port for minerals would be but a branch off this. Along the standard gauge Port Siding the narrow gauge could be laid inside the wider, or on a parallel formation costing £1,300. There were to be passenger stations en route (e.g. such as at Tyddin-y-Felin, Tre-Garth and Hen-Durnpike) which took much the same course as his plan for the new length submitted in 1868. Beyond Coed-y-Parc the line would run into a Quarry station and make end-on junction with the mineral line which ran round the northeast corner of the workings i.e. the access route which existed 1843–1912. An inspiration was a branch from near Tyn-y-Clwt Incline foot which after using some of the Railroad course, crossed the Ogwen and forked to serve two termini in Bethesda, one beside the Gas Works on a site which would later be almost the same as that used for the L.N.W.R. branch terminal and the other further south on the east bank of the river.

Whilst the survey was to provide links between Bangor and Bethesda, the backbone of the Quarry – Port system would be retained for the slate traffic. Bangor, and its Menai-side wharves and slate stockyards would be served, intermediate stations would cater for the Estate and at the line's end, for Bethesda itself. The size of the tunnels and bridges – 11 ft x 10 ft – were dimensions which would be adopted for the Penrhyn Railway; a 'tunncl' would be cut through the huge embankment of the C.&H.R. main line. Felin-Hen cutting was necessarily deep in order to maintain a gradient of not more than 1 in 50. A nice touch at Coed-y-Parc was to extend the Slab Mill alongside the main Railroad line to the north and make this into an erecting shop for the Railway; nicer still was to cut through the west wall with a new siding and convert the stables into an engine shed! Of the branch line to Bethesda, an interesting feature would be a bridge over and near the mouth of the Quarry drainage adit, before the line took up a position along the bank of the Ogwen.

Spooner refers to 'a considerable number of rolling stock now made in the Erecting Shops on this principle' (i.e. wagons with single flanges, and fixed axles instead of double flanges and loose axles). He advocated that coal, lime and timber trucks be built on the same principle as the Festiniog and submitted drawings for a double Fairlie engine for the main line and a single Fairlie for passenger trains; for special light train and shunting a four-coupled engine would be needed. As on the Festiniog, Down trains would run by gravity with the proportion of 1 to 6 braked slate wagons; on mixed trains an engine and brake van would provide brake power. He estimated that the double engine, working exclusively on empty wagon trains, would haul 70 tons up and through the 2½ chain curves; the single engine would haul 32 tons. Farseeingly, he recommended 46 lbs. double-headed chaired track and estimated the cost ('less value of materials of old tramway @ £2,400') at £51,551 with a construction time of 12 months. Among the drawings submitted were (all dated 16th January, 1873):

Locomotives

1) Single Fairlie 0–4–4T JUPITER, inside driving bogie frame, disc wheels, outside cylinders, copper-capped chimney, Ramsbottom safety valves, curved front cab sheet (only), outside-framed rear bogie. No sanding gear. (Virtually a replica of the F.R. TALIESIN but pre-dating it by at least three years and possibly revealing the genesis of the Festiniog's engine?) Maker's oval plates on cab read 'Engineer's Office   Festiniog Railway'.

2) Four-coupled side tank VENUS, outside cylinders, inside frames, front cab sheet (only) and carrying oval plates as for JUPITER. (Virtually a replica of Spooner & Co.'s Class B industrial locomotive as first supplied to Braich Quarry in 1877 by Vulcan Foundry – again, possibly the genesis of this type?[29])

3) Double Fairlie 0–4–4–0T JAMES SPOONER. (Virtually a copy of the engine supplied for the F.R. by Avonside Engine Co. in 1872 at a time when the Penrhyn proposals were on the drawing board, and complete with bells and other F.R. features but having capped chimneys). Weather boards shown, and 'Avonside . . .' builder's plates.

(All the foregoing having taller boiler mountings than were possible on the Festiniog Railway, and the first two were perhaps conceived as Penrhyn engines without thought at the time of their subsequent construction for use elsewhere).

Carriages

4) Bogie passenger carriage 1st & 2nd composite (2+1+1+2) to seat 24. Three oil lamps in roof. Carries F.R. garter and 'No. 20', together with F.R. monograms. Length overall 24 ft 7 in.

5) Bogie passenger carriage. All 3rd, five compartment to seat 48 with two roof lamps. Carries F.R. garter etc. but number has not been added. Length overall 24 ft 7 in. Likely to have had open interior i.e. no partitions above seat-backs.

6) Bogie passenger carriage. 1st observation carriage with four doors, open above waist and exactly as isometric drawing in F.R. Archives (untitled).[30] To seat 24 and carrying F.R. 'No. 22'. Length overall 24 ft 7 in.

7) Bogie luggage van with dog compartment, and having balcony one end only. Length overall 20 ft 8 in. and height overall 7 ft 9 in. from rail. (Virtually from the same drawing as for F.R. No. 1 van of similar outline and dimensions and built in April 1873).

(All the foregoing carriages and van are approximately to F.R. loading gauge; only the van had a balcony, the carriages having conventional ends. F.R. No. 20 did not appear before November 1879 so Penrhyn drawings with their strange 'F.R. numbers' were six years earlier – they may have been given Festiniog identity to disguise the fact that work was being done for an outside enquiry in the F.R.'s Drawing Office!)

The last drawing shows a standard gauge plain track with Penrhyn rails laid inside it, and the necessary trackwork where the Penrhyn track broke out from the standard-gauge (as would have been necessary had the mixed-gauge line into Bangor station materialised).

The stage was now set for a metamorphosis. Between receipt of this 1873 scheme and a decision to re-vamp the whole undertaking from 9th March, 1876, some hard decisions were needed, in part forced on the situation by parties canvassing for support for a main line branch to Bethesda, to the irritation of Lord Penrhyn. Before the Tyn-y-Clwt Deviation was completed in October 1876 – the first step in replacing the Railroad – Spooner was asked to report again. By now he found a new "all-level" rail route emerged from the Quarry and continued to the head of the Railroad's Dinas Incline and his assignment was to replace the Railroad from here to the Port. In the meanwhile, he had been instructed to prepare plans to link his scheme to a Bangor and Bethesda railway which would counter branch proposals of 1876.

Spooner's conception of the task was again to convert Penrhyn thinking into Spooner thinking. The plans (31st January, 1877) had many features of his three 1876 suggestions, though the Bangor extension was shortened.

Despite all, Spooner failed to convince Penrhyn who chose to retain personal control over the Railway as had been over the Railroad; visions of public trains, liability to inspection by Government Department and other responsibilities at the risk of interruption to his own slate business were reasons enough, so when the old was replaced, the new retained the old image.

When Arthur Wyatt, Robert Algeo and Richard Parry were involved in final plans, survey and constructional work for the new Railway, it was sufficient but to cross the 'T's' and dot the 'I's' of Spooner's work.

The greatest changes resulted from the intended L.N.W.R. Bethesda branch which by 1878 had had its route and levels determined; it was imperative that the heights between the proposals be increased in the neighbourhood of Coed-Hywel; on the Penrhyn Algeo was obliged also to extend the embankment near Coed-Hywel-Uchaf by bringing it closer to the Cegin, so avoiding a line through the dairy farmyard! Spooner's 'Grand Design' with its extravagant limbs into Bangor and Bethesda survives . . . but only as a fine example of mid-Victorian brush work and penmanship!

A Sunday in July 1872 was to mark a far-reaching event when a vast tonnage of rock at the Quarry fell into the workings below . . . it was almost as if the Almighty Himself had ordained this should occur on a day when no one would be injured. 'The Great Fall' was caused by the discovery of commercially-desirable rock in 1852 which was worked to such extent that it undermined the galleries above. The resultant scar, involving the collapse of several galleries extending vertically 200 ft, is still a prominent feature today. (See 'THE TIMES' and 'LIVERPOOL MERCURY' 10 July 1872.) This fall had a direct effect on the Railroad and led to the introduction of steam locomotives working in the Quarry after an Enquiry and Report by John Hughes revealed the inefficiency of earlier working methods.[31] Two years later (August 1874) John Francis, the Quarry Manager, gave Messrs de Winton & Co. of Carnarvon an order for two vertically-boilered locomotives to cost £300 each; these were to be the first of a number of such units and of a wider use of mechanical power elsewhere. These engines were to work the Red Lion Level between the Cutting Sheds in the Quarry and a weighing machine at the head of a proposed new incline and give a direct outlet down to Coed-y-Parc; it was named the Felin-Fawr from the mills of that name near its foot. The main outlet thus formed was to remain the principal artery until the system closed down in 1962. Felin-Fawr passed its first train on 23rd November, 1874, its use having been delayed by two separate strikes among workmen from 31st July to 9th November. A feature of one strike was the resignation *en bloc* of all the Quarry management, including John Francis . . . in his case it led to embarrassment as, when in due course de Winton advised that the first locomotive was ready for delivery, no one on the new management had any knowledge of the order.[32]

Changes were pending and labour troubles hastened them; J. H. Battersby (Quarry Engineer from 1926) records that as early as 1874 a decision to build a new locomotive-worked Railway was made; with Spooner as Consultant a railway system based on the practices of seventy years before was unthinkable, and he put the forefront of narrow gauge trends before Penrhyn. The 'CARNARVON & DENBIGH HERALD' 17th July, 1875 writes: "We understand that Lord Penrhyn has decided upon running a locomotive engine on the tramway along which the slates are conveyed from the quarry to the port."

The second engine by Francis was still on the builder's hands, but in September 1875 a firm order was given for it, and for another to follow.

In March 1876 the two were named LORD PENRHYN and LADY PEN-
RHYN (whilst still at the Works, where until then they had been simply
No. 1 and No. 2). Delivery of the former had been set for 1st March.
The inauguration of steam on the main line was not to be to the credit of
de Winton & Co. however.

In late July 1875 a main line locomotive had been delivered to the
Dinorwic Quarry (perhaps named PERIS ?) accompanied by a Mr
Augustus Beatson of the firm, John Beatson & Co., of Irongate, Derby.
Augustus also obtained an appointment at Penrhyn and on such (by
then) fertile ground he received an order for a steam locomotive:
delivery was made as GEORGE SHOLTO NO. 3, by sea to Port Penrhyn
on 21st December following. It may have been transported up the
Railroad to Coed-y-Parc (if the Engineer's comments are to be taken
literally, without its chimney) and on 28th December a post-Christmas
crowd gathered to see the trials. These were confined to the short
section between Coed-y-Parc and the head of the Tyn-y-Clwt Incline
which, at the time was the steepest.

Even before Nos. 1 and 2 had been delivered, de Winton & Co. had
evolved a horizontally-boilered type and within a month received an
order for one; this was to be No. 4 EDWARD SHOLTO and its duty
would be to work the newly-constructed diversion of the Railroad
which substituted Tyn-y-Clwt Incline completely with a new Railway
using modern track materials and involved a gradient of 1 in 37 from
Coed-y-Parc to Hen-Durnpike. The foregoing foreshadowed the creation of the new Railway in five stages the first however being entirely
within the bounds of the Quarry:

1) 1870–74	Red Lion Level, including Felin-Fawr Incline, descending to Coed-y-Parc, opened November 1874
2) 1876	Tyn-y-Clwt Incline deviation (at Cilgeraint); begun 9th March, finished 15th October (Richard Parry, contractor) (These dates are to be found only in the Pay Bill records)
3) 1877	26th January, Robert Algeo accepts contract to build Railway from head of Dinas Incline to Port (sub-contracted to Richard Parry)
4) 1878–79	Head of Dinas Incline to Port Penrhyn; begun 18th March, 1878, finished and opened 6th October, 1879
5) From 1878	Alterations at Port Penrhyn; loco sheds etc., L.N.W.R. lines extended

No clear date completely divides the old Railroad era from the new
Railway as the work was staggered over a decade or more.

The Penrhyn Railway (1879–1962)

On 7th March, 1878 Richard Parry wrote to Arthur Wyatt: "I intend

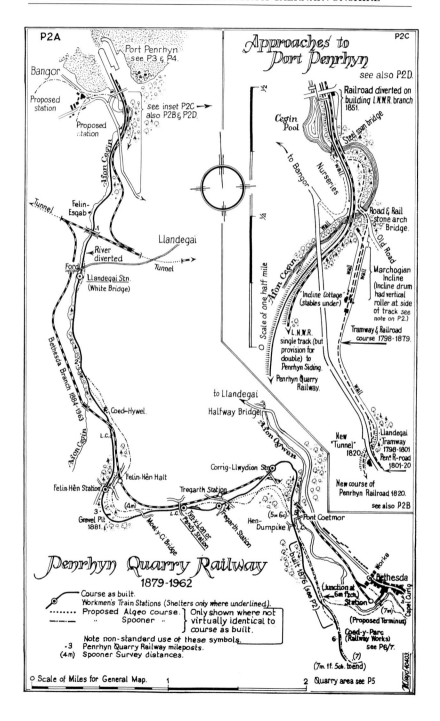

to put some few men at work on Monday next . . ." (i.e. 18th March) ". . . on the small cutting between the Shrewsbury Road and the L.N.W.R. viaduct . . . I mention this that you may have time to mark the trees that are to be cut down."

So a start was made. If evidence was needed that steam locomotives were envisaged even at this stage, the change in the design of bridges may be instanced; the old pattern involved a decked walkway for the horses; the new work carried the rails, one each on a longitudinal girder. The Tyn-y-Clwt Deviation was built with all speed; it opened on 15th October, 1876 and the disused incline was soon buried by rubbish; along it GEORGE SHOLTO could work between Felin-Fawr Incline foot and Dinas Incline head, and some traffic still came round to Felin-Fawr from the 'left hand side of the Quarry' via the old (1843) route. Upon delivery on 16th December, 1876 EDWARD SHOLTO took over this duty. Contemporarily, the 'main line' in the Quarry was in the hands of the vertically-boilered de Winton engines LORD PENRHYN and LADY PENRHYN, delivered in May and October 1876, respectively, the assignment for which they had been destined. Outwardly they were of differing appearance and, pleased with their performance, two more shunting engines were ordered from the same makers for the Port to become GEORGE HENRY and KATIE (later KATHLEEN) delivered in May and June 1877 respectively. In December 1876 another shunting engine (to be GEORGINA) for the Port, and yet a further '. . . the same as LADY PENRHYN . . .', were ordered. The last de Winton order for a vertically-boilered engine was placed early in 1878 – this was INA, which arrived the following October.

For a short time the rail system reflected 'something old and something new', the Railroad aspect remaining in force from Dinas head to the Port, but new development was envisaged when C. E. Spooner was engaged as Consultant, his plan being submitted on 31st January, 1877. In the February the L.N.W.R. was formally advised that a new Railway was to be built between the Quarry and Port, and that steam locomotives would be used. Spooner's arguments had carried the day.

Five days before Spooner's survey was received (26th January, 1877), Robert Algeo[33] of Menai Bridge, and Surveyor to Anglesey, was made Engineer to build a new railway from Dinas Top to the Port. He proceeded to make a personal survey – completed by 3rd May – but, apart from certain necessities to avoid the L.N.W.R. promotion, Spooner's ideas were retained. The final work involved Richard Parry (contractor), Arthur Wyatt (Penrhyn's agent), and Algeo. At Tregarth, near Felin-Hen and near Coed-Hywel bridge where the two intended railways were planned to cross each other, the Spooner route was amended.

Lord Penrhyn was now the target of advice from those who wanted a railway built to connect the growing town of Bethesda with its own satellite slate quarries – they having no rail links of their own – and

Bangor: it should also cater for as many communities on the Penrhyn lands as possible. The first murmurs are heard in the winter of 1875/6 perhaps born of the first steps at Tyn-y-Clwt and Red Lion Level. Committees, both of quarrymen and estate tenants, were formed in Bangor and Bethesda to solicit Lord Penrhyn's support, but when deputations met him they showed but scant diplomacy. On 28th March, 1876 Penrhyn had written to Wyatt:

> I do not like to withdraw what I said to the Deputation from Bethesda . . . got up with such evident determination to misrepresent and decry me. I think that your suggestion for a narrow line . . . is worthy of consideration and after these meetings are over I should like to consult Mr Spooner as to the cost. If I made it and *had* the *control*, we might then make it serve the *two* purposes of my own and public traffic, but it would never do to entrust my traffic to the management of a Radical Bangor Committee . . .

To represent him at local meetings, Penrhyn appointed H. Barber, a well-known Bangor solicitor; he wrote after one such gathering that the Bangor Committee was:

> disposed to do their utmost to clamour for a railway on their own terms entirely (broad gauge) and not to co-operate with any one who will not support them.

Again (6th April, 1876):

> . . . both Bangor and Bethesda Committees strongly in favour of a broad gauge railway and a vigorous effort to induce the Great Western to take it up with a through line as a check upon the L.N.W.R. Company . . . but that even the Bethesda Committee would be content with a narrow gauge line if they cannot get a broad one.

Even the Bangor and Bethesda Committees were divided, the former seeking the support of the L.N.W.R. and goodwill of Penrhyn, the latter of the G.W.R. and a break with Penrhyn!

Finding Lord Penrhyn unsupportive, a deputation from both places waited upon Richard Moon, General Manager of the L.N.W.R. at Euston, who diplomatically advised Lord Penrhyn of their visit and asked if he was aware what was going on?! Meanwhile Wyatt had approached Spooner who produced three plans on 1st May, 1876 for a 'Penrhyn Railway', (being the first ever actual use of that title) his brief being 'for a line similar to the Festiniog Railway'. The three proposals were:

No. 1 From L.N.W.R. station Bangor south-westerly then south-easterly through Waunwen and circling westward taking in Pentir to join by easterly section, the ultimate Penrhyn Rly. course (as built) at Tregarth. At Hen-Durnpike 'running over the same rails . . . as the present tramway . . . where the new quarry line [Tyn-y-Clwt Deviation then being built] diverges from the tramway in which case the work now being done will make this portion complete. If required by the Board of Trade the two ways can be kept distinct (which will probably be the case)'.[34] Thence across road at Tyn-y-Clwt, over Ogwen and into Bethesda (west side).

Maximum gradient 1 in 50; 'works of a heavy character' including viaduct 160 yd long × 40 ft high. ('A Branch to Port Penrhyn might be made near Tregarth and under the viaduct of the C.&H.R. to join the existing Port branch,' thence mixed gauge down to the Port. Gradient 1 in 45.)

Estimated cost: £55,675 (excluding Port Branch).

In the final footnote proposing a branch the seeds of the actual Penrhyn Railway can be seen; here is the moment of conception.

No. 2 Much as No. 1 but section preceding Waunwen provided with 814 yd tunnel with 2 smokeshafts in lieu of following contours; also includes 130 yd viaduct. Maximum gradient 1 in 50. The Port Branch again is shown as an additional option.

Estimated cost: £66,510 (excluding Port Branch).

No. 3 From Bangor Station Tunnel towards Chester with Up and Down lines in mixed gauge for 70 chains, thence southeast down into Cegin valley. Joins courses of Nos. 1 and 2 at Tregarth (follows much of course as built by L.N.W.R. initially out of Bangor with maximum gradient of 1 in 45). Included in the main scheme is a branch to Pentir 1¼ m. long running roughly parallel with the adjoining road. Maximum gradient 1 in 60. 'There would be considerable expense and awkwardness in working this short branch as it would entail the use of an engine and passenger carriages, specially for the purpose.' Again, the Port Branch is shown as an additional option.

Estimated cost: £52,834 (excluding Port Branch).

Included in these documents[35] is a fourth map without supporting text, showing a route almost exactly as the L.N.W.R. Bethesda branch out of Bethesda, but remaining on the east side of the Cegin to rise and join the main line on the east side of the C.&H.R. Cegin viaduct; about half a mile south of the viaduct a branch would have led along the courses of the other three schemes, to the Port. In short, almost every one of Spooner's schemes covering nine years from 1868, had part of their routes in common, and in course of time the new Penrhyn Railway and the L.N.W.R. Bethesda Branch would adopt much of his work. Summarised, the Spooner connection was:

5th June, 1868   Spooner's unsolicited approach to Lord Penrhyn proffering scheme to replace the Railroad

16th January, 1873 First survey commissioned by Lord Penrhyn for a steam railway to replace the Railroad

1st May, 1876   Three Schemes commissioned by Lord Penrhyn (plus another of the same period) to link Bangor and Bethesda and serve several villages on the Estate

31st January, 1877   Second Survey commissioned by Lord Penrhyn to replace the section of Railroad between Dinas Incline Top and the Port (the remainder having already been replaced)

It was to be 30th April 1879 before the closing correspondence about involvement in a Bangor–Bethesda promotion reveals that no further interest would be shown from The Castle. By then many persons and things had taken the stage and left it. For instance Mr. T. Lewis of Gwitherwen ('CARNARVON & DENBIGH HERALD' 7th December, 1878) wished that such a line might have a branch to the quay at Hirael (Bangor's rival place of shipment) but as in every suggestion, Lord Penrhyn found something to his disadvantage. The L.N.W.R., anxious to acquire more of the Quarry traffic, tried to interest Penrhyn in a narrow gauge feeder direct from the Quarry into their proposed Bethesda station; needless to say, Penrhyn was not willing to place himself at the mercy of Euston. Negotiations for the L.N.W.R. Branch covered five years (1876–81); it was begun on 10th January, 1880 and with heavy works throughout, not opened until 1st July, 1884. In December 1880 they paid Penrhyn £7,000 for the land and Barber wrote 'I have not thought it necessary to push on the Conveyance very rapidly during the Shooting Season'.

More outlandish still was a Bethesda quarry's plan for a narrow gauge line to link the quarries east of the town with a new harbour on the Cegin in direct competition with the Port; worse, it was feared the Great Western Railway was behind it in retaliation for alleged humiliations inflicted by the L.N.W.R. elsewhere.

"The Bangor & Bethesda Railway (four miles two furlongs six chains in length)" authorised by 43 & 44 Vic. Cap. CXLV of 6th August, 1880 never fulfilled the ambitions of Euston – Lord Penrhyn saw to that. [J. M. Dunn's records note a 'Motor Car' was introduced on the line on 1st June, 1886.] Sizes of buildings, heights of signal posts and situations of stations etc. were limited, river flows were protected, visible telegraph posts and wires eliminated;

> Company shall not . . . in any way impede or interfere with the use of the private tramway belonging to Lord Penrhyn, and recently constructed by him for steam locomotive traffic . . . in the case of any interference during the construction of the said railway as aforesaid the Company shall pay to Lord Penrhyn the sum of four hundred pounds per diem . . . during which the use of such private tramway is impeded . . . .

The branch was an expensive one and can never have covered its costs. The slate transfer bank at Bethesda accepted some slate from the local Coetmor Quarry which arrived by cart, and a fractional amount for local use came similarly from Penrhyn Quarry, but it was 'never really used' according to Dunn.

Returning now to the new Penrhyn venture; on 9th March, 1878 the 'CARNARVON & DENBIGH HERALD' wrote:

> The contract for the construction of a two foot gauge railway extending from Port Penrhyn, Bangor to Tregarth in connection with the Penrhyn Slate Quarry has been let to Mr. Richard Parry, Menai Bridge. The contract will occupy about 2 years in execution and will give employment to a large number of men. Mr. Algeo, Menai Bridge, is the engineer in charge of the works.

Algeo's 'Draft Specification & General Conditions' survey of 3rd May, 1877 – as amended – was ready on 12th December; Parry began work on 18th March, 1878 and on 25th September, 1878 the locomotive HILDA was delivered to the Quarry, riding thence on a road wagon drawn by a team of horses and a complete departure from anything Penrhyn had bought previously from de Winton, having a horizontal boiler; it was set to work and found to be admirable. An order for another was made on 26th November and delivered to the Port on 18th August, 1879 as VIOLET.

Between March 1878 and October 1879 the old Railroad's surviving portion continued to carry out its duties witnessing its last train at midday on Thursday, 2nd October. Hectic work ensued. No trains ran after the line at the head of Dinas Incline was severed and linked to a point on the new railway 150 yards to the west. In the anxiety to complete the work an error in levelling occurred near the L.N.W.R./Penrhyn Railway viaduct over the head of Cegin Pool which resulted in a steep fall on the north side of the bridge – the steepest portion of the Railway being inadvertently created – and led to an area where flooding would become a recurring embarrassment. This mishap led to bitterness with Algeo who left in irritation.

On Monday morning, 6th October, the Daily Log entry says 'Opening of New Line of Railway', apparently without ceremony. So the Penrhyn Quarry re-emerged at the forefront of the trade with a transport system which could match the best and beat the majority, thus ensuring continuing profits for the owner; from November 1877 a fleet of newly designed slate wagons fitted with Spooner-recommended single-flanged wheels took to the rails, de Winton supplying 200 vehicles over the next four years. There was a dramatic change in the requirements expected of the Coed-y-Parc Workshops now caught up in an industrial revolution of parochial but cataclysmic proportion.

The new undertaking now settled down to an era of little outward change, with certain back-room ideas to close the undertaking altogether. (The advent of new steam locomotives, the workmen's train, the introduction of new rolling stock, track replacements, changes at the Quarry, the Port, etc. is dealt with under appropriate headings which follow.)

Captain I. Griffith, Manager in the period 1928–1946, conceived a plan 'Proposed Line, Bethesda Railway Station to Quarry Siding, 20th May, 1938' whereby the main line would be abandoned below Coed-y-Parc and a new *standard gauge* railway built linking the Works area with the L.M.S.R. Bethesda terminus; all traffic would have been carried thence by the standard gauge and if ships were to be loaded at the Port, considerable double-handling would be necessary. British Rail Estate Office Plans show a proposed interchange junction south of Coed-y-Parc Works, and running east and south thence in a complete anti-clockwise semi-circle to the north of Glan-y-Gors and entering Bethesda station yard from the southeast. The line would have been just over 800 yards long and risen 73 feet; there would have been an Ogwen bridge 23 ft high. Such portions of the Penrhyn Railway as would survive would be electrified; ruins of the first stage of the scheme can be seen today in a dam above the Douglas Hill Road, part of the supply pipe and large building with waterwheel which stands below Coed-y-Parc in the glen, beside the west bank of the Ogwen. Intended to be carried out about 1938–39, World War II delayed the idea, which lingered, unfinished to the last until late 1946. (This was not the first scheme for electrification; when E. A. Young was Manager and other quarries were being provided with electric power by the North Wales Power & Traction Co. such an idea was investigated. When Young died in 1911 nothing had been done, but a hydro-electric generating set was supplying the workshops though insufficient water was available there for an extension. Electric power from the N.W.P.&T.Co. arrived the following year.)

There was a long history of service and until 9th May, 1961 there was sufficient business to warrant a train running daily, but in 1964 the Quarry was working only to one fifth its pre-World War II capacity. Many levels had closed down and McAlpine took over the business in 1964, replacing tramways in the Quarry with conveyors and building new sheds to replace the old. Employment dropped to under 300 men. Until 1964 however average times for the latterday period were 9.30 a.m. ex Port, returning at 3.45 p.m. from the Quarry. From then onwards, trains ran 'as required' and in April 1962 traffic was found to be 'very heavy' with trains loaded to over 60 wagons; for such loads a steam engine was used but the 'Big Diesel' (No. 24) was more often to be found at work. The last steam slate train ran on 28th June following and an official date for closing the Railway was announced as 24th July. It was not until November that wagons were brought up to the Quarry end of the line, the Port being cleared of stock on the 26th and 27th of that month; even this was not to be the last working as GLYDER was taken the short journey from Coed-y-Parc to the foot of Felin-Fawr, and lifted on to Red Lion Level, using two diesel rail tractors! Felin-Fawr Incline had actually passed its last run on 16th July previously.

This final closure was factually the fourth in the period of the Railway; previous occasions were:

31st December, 1900–10th June, 1901 (exclusive) during The Big Strike

22nd December, 1939–22nd January, 1940 due to start of World War II, the cessation of building and orders, rail and shipment restrictions. (It was rebuilding on a purely emergency footing after air-raids which rekindled the business but after 22nd December many levels were closed and never worked again)

14th August–4th October, 1940 initially 'closed for the duration' (of the War) but opened to limited extent for reasons above. (Penrhyn and Dinorwic railways both given extended lives due to German bombing.)

Between then and 1943/4 the Quarry and Railway was not fully back to its pre-war extent; full re-opening anticipated but not realised.

On 14th August, 1940 'The Workmen's Train Society' was wound up.

Regular steam haulage in the Quarry survived until OGWEN ceased work on Ffridd Level in January 1965, though WINIFRED was noted at work in May following. After January no time was lost in lifting the Quarry tracks, most of which had disappeared before the end of 1965.

(Note: where Railroad and Railway shared the same sections of course, details are given in the description of the Railway route.)

The 1829 Plan shows a total length of 10,120 yds (5¾ m.) and a fall of 581 ft. ["Map & Survey of Rail Road from Penrhyn Quarries to Port Penrhyn. 1829": Library, U.C.N.W.]

THE PENRHYN RAILROAD – THE ROUTE DESCRIBED

The datum level for the Railroad was fixed on the lowest step of the Port House, Port Penrhyn. It commenced high up in the Quarry and over succeeding years its original route(s) through the workings was lost and replaced by others more convenient to the times. Nothing was allowed to prevent the good slate rock from being quarried and if the rail route was hampering the work, it disappeared. The Quarry grew to enormous proportions; up to 90% of material extracted was simply rubbish and was tipped wherever convenient; if this buried the Railroad, so be it. The immediate purpose of the Railroad was to carry quarried materials to Coed-y-Parc where after processing the re-loaded wagons would be assembled into trains for despatch down to the Port. Certain wagons contained materials for processing at Felin-Fawr Mill and when ready, wagons containing such products were introduced into the Railroad traffic at the north end of Coed-y-Parc. From the Quarry there were ultimately two routes northward to Coed-y-Parc; the original one of 1801 climbed southwest from Coed-y-Parc by incline to Ponc-y-

Level (Right). (Ponc-y-Level (Right) Incline was built to carry the wagons even higher in 1823.) Thence, by a course running generally anti-clockwise, along Ponc Sling to where at its furthermost end, Sling reached the foot of Ponc-y-Level (Left) Incline.[36] It was here the Railroad may be said to have begun: the 1829 Plan of the Railroad simply shows "Quarry Machine" (i.e. weighing machine) without surrounding detail but this point agrees with the distances quoted.

Along the flank of the mountain hereabouts, the 1801 track ran along a ledge or 'Ponc' which was inclined at 1 in 100 to assist drainage and movement of rubbish wagons. The name Ponc means 'bank' and in practice was a level or gallery. In due course new inclines carried the railroad connections to further heights, and gallery upon gallery was developed: thus the rail plan was one of continuous evolution, whole inclines being abandoned in favour of more efficient ones on better sites. In short, to describe the railroad within the Quarry precincts is to treat it as a route which all too soon was superceded by events. Ponc-y-Level (Left) Incline was probably in use by 1801 while inclines above it developed from 1811; until 1843 this was the main access to Coed-y-Parc. However, the need to reach good rock resulted in part of Ponc Sling being quarried away and so the through route between the Ponc-y-Level Inclines was broken and closed on 17th October, 1843. In place of it a new artery branched off eastward south of Coed-y-Parc and en route forked, the westerly branch becoming the Sinc Bach line whilst the more easterly, having crossed the Capel-Curig Turnpike (opened July 1803) on the level, worked clockwise round the foot of the workings in an easterly direction; it crossed Tros-y-Ffordd road and the Turnpike for a second time as it did so. (The building of this new connection was heralded by the casting of 820 cast-iron track sills at Coed-y-Parc Foundry.) Near the second Turnpike crossing the line rose by incline to make junction with the starting point of the 1801 line. Whilst the Sinc Bach branch remained in use for over a century the other had gone out of use by 1890, officially closed in 1912 and lifted for wartime scrap in 1917.

As to the 1843 truncation on Ponc Sling of the original Railroad, the length between Coed-y-Parc and the foot of Ponc-y-Level (Right) Incline remained in use until 1852 when that incline was extended downwards to the edge of Sinc Bach, here to meet a tramway built in a westerly direction off the 1843 line; thus on 1st June, 1852 the 1801 Railroad route through the Quarry had almost disappeared.

At a point just south of the Coed-y-Parc level crossing, a small yard was formed where the two arms of lines (1801 and 1843) serving the Quarry, met in a junction and on Spooner's 1873 proposals, each arm of the fork is shown to be an incline from the point of junction with adjacent yard containing Carpenter's Shop and Smithy. Here a small fan of sidings was created in 1843 as a replacement yard for that built at Coed-y-Parc in 1835; this had the advantage of space, free from the confinements of the Felin-Fawr Slab Mill area.

Features alongside this small yard were the weighing machine of 1840 (on the west side) and the digging of a shaft 100 ft deep, begun in 1843 by George Twigge as contractor. At the foot of this shaft headings were driven in opposite directions; the mouth of the northernmost opened out below Tan-ys-Gafell where a 6 ft wide stone-lined tunnel mouth provides an outfall to drain down to the 300 ft contour. The date on the keystone reads '1849': this drain emerged in the pit on Sebasto-pol Level and enabled quarrying to go down a further 60 ft. At the head of the shaft excavated material was loaded into wagons and taken by rail to the Port, being used to form a new dock alongside the original quay. The tunnel length is 1,837 yds with a fall of 4 ft. In the same period hydraulic pumps were introduced to help still further the deepening of the Quarry pits.

The Railroad passed through Coed-y-Parc, crossing the road on the level and running between buildings then serving their initial functions; Felin-Fawr Slab Mill of 1803 was on the left and another mill of 1846 to the right. There were two waterwheels (the driving stream was tunnel-led beneath the yard), the larger, also of 1846, of 20 ft diameter. Beyond the 1846 Mill was a Dressing Shed for slates, dating from 1803. The whole area was created on a plateau of rubbish, and beside its eastern flank (but on a lower level) ran the Capel-Curig Turnpike; this was ultimately diverted from a point nearby in order to avoid the encroaching rubbish tips! (This old course was finally buried.) Away to the left was a row of buildings forming the Railroad stables; here the main line formed a long loop, the Coed-y-Parc Passbye. In April 1835 the main line was moved westward towards these stables so enabling a small marshalling yard to be built, together with a point for oiling wagons but abandoned about 1843 in favour of that to the south of Coed-y-Parc.

At the north end of the yard, Felin-Fawr House was passed on the right, and a footbridge spanned the line: the track then moved in a slow curve first to the left and then returning, crossed St. Ann's Road on the level. An alteration here after 1812 enabled the line to cross the highway on a bridge suitably decked to support the horses; at this point the Railroad was double-tracked (and indeed may have so been from Coed-y-Parc since c.1830) adjacent to the summit drum of Tyn-y-Clwt Incline (121½ yds long: 46 ft 8½ in. fall at 1 in 7.8). From "Quarry Machine" to this point was 1 m. 354½ yds and the route fell 72½ ft (1 in 87½ average). At the Incline's foot there was a shallow stone-walled cutting to accommodate storage sidings; thenceforward the line ran through meadow and woodland on the hillside above the Turnpike, passing through generously-cut rock cuttings from time to time to reach Bron-Ogwen and the awkward twin-road crossing at Hen-Durnpike.

From a point almost immediately preceding the road crossing here the later Railway was laid over the site of the Railroad (see p.57 for

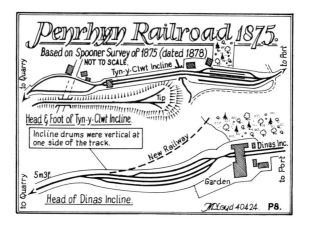

description of the route) but at the head of Dinas bluff (½ m. north of Hen-Durnpike) the two routes separated. There was a noticeable widening of the Railroad site as Dinas Incline head was reached and there were three tracks, one (the Dinas Passbye) being the longer of the loop lines. These loops converged to single line at the incline head; this was 1 m. 61 yds from Tyn-y-Clwt foot and the line had fallen 64 ft 3 in. an average of 1 in 85. The Spooner Survey suggests the buildings here were similar to those at the summit of Marchogian Incline (see below) but no evidence survives. There was certainly a cottage and adjacent garden. The Incline was 264 yds long and fell 189 ft 1 in. A gradient of 1 in 5.9 took the Railroad near Dinas Farm close by, passing under the only road bridge to cross the system initially (a stone arch carrying the Hen-Durnpike – Halfway Bridge road). At the foot the line was to continue along the west bank of the Ogwen river, then as now a pleasantly wooded setting and in such contrast with the initial stages of the route! The line lay on a shelf about 20 ft above the waters, with a stone wall between them before it turned westward and followed the left hand side of the Shrewsbury – Holyhead road (opened throughout 23rd July, 1805) and itself rebuilt on various occasions during the lifetime of the Railroad . . . whose course was also amended from time to time: in the last forty years much of the ensuing Railroad section has been obliterated by modern highway construction. The Railroad only left the side of the highway in order to retain a more regular gradient; the whole of this section was once substantially walled, either in slab or river stone, but nearer Llandegai much of it has gone. Diversions to maintain inclination were at Coch-Willan (221 ft above sea level) and more notably near Lôn-Isaf (195 ft). Road and Railroad parted company at Tyddyn-Iolyn where at a short distance northward was a passbye; by 1840 this had been moved to a site behind the Llandegai Smithy.

Here on the left was a cart road to an excavation below Cefn-y-Coed (which itself had an ironstone mine in close proximity).[37] Approaching Llandegai through meadowland on a low embankment, there was a level crossing with the Pentir – Llandegai road, then the adjacent Smithy with the Llandegai loop behind it and a few yards beyond, the site of the junction from where the erstwhile Llandegai Tramway dropped by incline to the Llwyn-On or Penrhyn Upper Mill. This stump of the old line survived until 1831.[38] After 1848, the Chester & Holyhead Railway passed under this point by Llandegai Tunnel of which the only evidence visible from the main road is a smokeshaft above to the left.

It has already been noted that the remainder of the Railroad's original course down to the Port was that built for the Llandegai Tramway, but between here and 'The Tunnel' it became necessary to build a new route when the former Tramroad course was appropriated for the rebuilding of the main road in 1819–20. This new route took the Railroad at some 30 yds distance to the west of, but parallel to the then-new road as far as a point opposite Penrhyn Home Farm where, curving to the right and falling below the level of the road, it dived under it through a construction built of huge slabs, and known as 'The Tunnel'; Ty-Newydd Cottages were alongside. This underbridge (for such it is) had slate slab walling supporting a slab roof with a clearance of 7 ft 6 in. in each dimension. The roofing slabs were 16 ft × 2½ ft × 1½ ft in size and supported modern-day traffic right up until 1975! This 'tunnel' was probably the only place in which the Railroad horses walked *between* the rails; elsewhere they walked outside to reduce damage to the sleepers.[39] Now on the east side of the road, the Railroad followed beside it for a short distance then curving to the right towards Penrhyn Park, reached the head of Marchogian Incline (known at first as Port Incline), (2 m. 1016 yds from the foot of Dinas Incline with an average of 1 in 82) which lowered it 76 ft 2 in. It had a length of 196 yds and a gradient of 1 in 7.8. The Wyatt-designed summit building took the form of a covered Gateway House with day quarters on one side and night-time on the other; on the latter side was an enclosed passage-way to contain the haulage rope which was wound around a vertical drum mounted between the building and a high wall. The space between the buildings was linked by an overall roof under which the tracks passed: in the days of the Llandegai Tramway a horse was stabled on one side here to work the incline (probably by gin) and possibly later when wagons required to ascend and there was no downhill traffic. (The building, though modified, still stands, 'Incline Cottage' having had no Railroad function for over a century.) The Incline, being the flattest on the system, caused certain operating problems and at its foot the Railroad shared the existing single-arched stone bridge over the Cegin of the old turnpike road. Now in the narrow sylvan river valley it meandered on its west bank in an 'S' curve when, turning sharply to the north, it crossed it by a low three-arched brick and stone causeway near the old wharf at the head of the Cegin creek (after 1851 it was crossed by the L.N.W.R. Port Penrhyn branch immediately before this causeway). In the short distance remaining which took the line on to the quay, (described in 1829 as Port Penrhyn pier) the tracks doubled (one line passing under each arch of the Port bridge), passed the Port oiling house and in later days, one led over the weighing machine. The 'banjo' track layout here is shown on p.63 and the Port arrangements are discussed in detail on p.62. The distance from the foot of Marchogian Incline to the end of the quay was 967 yds with a fall of 16 ft 9½ in. an average of 1 in 173. The line fell all the way save for a rise of 2 in. in 44 yds on the Cegin river bridge.

THE PENRHYN RAILROAD – OPERATING

(All double-track sections worked on right-hand-line basis.)

In a perfect world the principle by which the Railroad was worked would have been idyllic, viz. a series of inclines on which the loaded down-going wagons hauled up the empties by gravity power and, on the intermediate and more level lengths, horses hauled the trains of wagons to and fro. To make such a system as trouble-free as possible, the inclines would have to be of equal length, of equal inclination and of equal frictional loss; the levels would be the same length, all wagons would be equally free running and all horses capable of pulling the same weight . . . but the Railroad was not perfect. Despite the effects of wind, weather and wear and tear, the vagaries of loading and the peculiar traits of individual wagons being considered, the tonnages carried were remarkable and undoubtedly stemmed from the assiduous efforts of its operatives who at the start were involved in work for which no previous experience was available.

Except on inclines, at loops, and at the top and bottom of inclines, the line was single. It was an operating requirement that trains should pass each other halfway along the level lengths to feed the inclines at the length's ends simultaneously: 'Passbyes' were laid at Coed-y-Parc, Dinas Farm and Llandegai, the last-named likely to have been actually at Tyddyn-Iolyn Farm at first, but at Llandegai by 1840. A logical sequence was to build stables at the passbyes, though some at Dinas Farm already existed. At such loops hay containers were erected beside the line to enable horses to feed whilst waiting to pass another train – these rakes of wagons were called 'runs'. The location of the hay containers reveals that trains passed each other on the right . . . as they were to do on other early railways connected with the slate industry in North Wales.

The longest section between inclines was that from Dinas foot to

Marchogian head; in adverse weather trains required 1½ hours to traverse this stretch and this module became the time interval for operation: traditionally this section was said to have needed double the number of horses as elsewhere.[40] To allow for the inevitable shortcomings of working practices, a yard was built at Coed-y-Parc (initially) where wagons could be made up into runs of appointed length, the number of wagons in each run being gradually increased as technical efficiency of the inclines was improved; in this sphere the hemp haulage ropes gave way to wrought-iron chains between 4th January, 1842 and 20th September, 1850, at which last date trains were increased to fifty wagons, a very considerable rake in those times.

It was just possible to run well-oiled loaded wagons from the foot of Tyn-y-Clwt to the head of Dinas without horse power but in fact the line was not designed for such working by gravity. It was soon found that the inclines did not operate with equal facility; Marchogian was too level to work with one or two wagons, but four was ideal. However this number broke the hemp rope on Tyn-y-Clwt which had been steepened by making the Dinas Incline longer. By force of compromise the standard rake became three wagons. In early days such runs were permanently linked together in sets of three as the wagon bodies could be lifted from the frame and loaded, still with slates inside, into the holds of small ships, often bound for the Mersey. Train lengths were effected thus:

At opening or soon thereafter	18 wagons
June 1802	24
2nd April, 1838	33
4th January, 1842 reduced to	32 but in 8 sets of 4 wagons
26th November, 1842 reduced to	24 but more runs were made in sets of 4
26th April, 1843 increased to	36
July 1851	50 in sets of 5 wagons
May 1855	60 in sets of 5 wagons
14th August, 1865 reduced to	55 in sets of 5 wagons

In 1819 the Railroad was passing 24,418 tons of £58,000 value; from 1850 annual figures topped the 50,000 ton mark which were carried in trains of 50 wagons as from 1851, Monday to Friday inclusive. Saturday working was given over to moving special loads, the disposal or repair of crippled wagons, food, lime, timber, coal etc., the undertaking being the prime mover for the whole Estate besides the Quarry.

The weakest link in the rail chain was the inclines which, as mentioned, despite the experience gained since the 1750s with horizontal winding drums[41] for the ropes, were fitted with vertical drums. To maintain an even flow of traffic the inclines must pass as many wagons up as down hill; uneven working would soon fill the loops at top or bottom. Sometimes because of axle or wheel breakage, rakes of three wagons were not available and to relieve 'indigestion' in the loops, wagons were hauled singly up or down the incline, by man or horsepower. Damaged wagons were laid aside and thrown off the line if necessary. A high degree of urgency was always present, ultimately in that the quarrymen were not paid in full until the slates reached the Port!

The working of the inclines was in the hands of quarry-paid operatives but the trains were worked by contractors: of this more anon. The Railroad was operated as one unit as quite distinct from the Quarry, and its trains left their starting points every 1½ hours; in winter departure times would be spread over 9 a.m. to 4.30 p.m. (6 runs) and in summer 7 or 8 daily runs would be made according to traffic requirements, starting from 7.30 a.m.

For efficiency's sake, it was soon found advantageous to couple the slate wagons into sets of three and this was done by two chains connected between headstocks; at the one end of the set two 3 in. diameter iron rings were bolted thereon – at the other, chains and hooks. Such measures do not seem to have been applied to the slab wagons nor, (at the time the Flint Mill was operative) to the individual wagons connected with that traffic. If a single wagon failed the blacksmith was called to make it runnable 'on the spot' if possible, but always without removing it from the set. From 1842 a small number of 4 wagon sets were made up, but above this figure seems not to have been done; in general, single wagons came back into favour. A loaded wagon at one point at the beginning of the day was expected to be at the same point, duly loaded, at the same time the following day; this would include time for loading at Quarry and unloading at Port. Down journey time was about 3½ hours, the same being allowed for the empty Up return.

The capacity of the Port was limited (even though it had been enlarged in autumn 1800) and after the initial use of 'crate' slate wagons, slate was unloaded there and stacked on the ground by size in the traditional way, so necessitating double-handling when a ship arrived. This made slates open to pilferage together with other 'desirable commodities' which lay around the wharves, so preventative measures were taken to ensure the safety of coal, tar and other stores. In the case of slate, if the Port was over-crowded, loaded wagons were held at Coed-y-Parc . . . where preventative measures were no less apparent!

Overall the efficiency of the Railroad was of keen concern to those in the Quarry; apart from the matter of full payment for slates, no payment was made for broken slates delivered to the Port, so the efficiency of transport and its operatives was of concern to all. Any broken slates off-loaded at the Port were not only not paid for but were re-cut by staff directly employed by the Quarry, and offered as smaller-sized items, so giving the undertaking a second 'profit'! After the changeover from Railroad to Railway in 1879 the Railway was worked by Penrhyn employees, and the contracting scheme ended.

The undertaking contracted train working between inclines to Waggoners who supplied their own horses; it owned no horses of its own. At times of crisis working boundaries were exceeded, but this was exceptional. On 25th June, 1801 (Opening Day) John Gruffydd of Tyn-y-Clwt was Waggoner, the load being four wagons hauled by two horses: his train worked the full length of the line. By the previous February the section from Dinas Incline Foot to the Port was already open and reflected by a decrease in the road cartage rate between Quarry and Port from 4/- to 1/6d. ton.

Lord Penrhyn formally opened the Railroad on 1st July, 1801, and a reception at the Port celebrated the event, but the following day revealed that thought and care in keeping up a 'procession' of trains was yet to be developed. Additional works before-mentioned were improvements to this end. On 29th August a Railroad incline connection to the Quarry was begun. At that juncture Railroad wagons were loaded at the 'Wharf' from carts; here output from all parts of the workings, was centralized and this arrangement was not fully discontinued until 1823.

Opening Day apart, three Waggoners contracted to work the line until 25th June, 1803: their contracts were not renewed and Worthington himself provided men and horses to work the line until 31st July, 1829 when being 69, he left the scene. C. Roberts of Dolawen Farm then bought the horses to continue the service, but this being unsatisfactory, three Waggoners took contracts again shortly and thus matters continued to the end of horse haulage, a date which may have been hastened by abuse of the system by the Waggoners themselves. Williams (Survey of 1806) says of the small neighbouring farmers who worked the slate in exchange for an annual rental in pre-Railroad times . . . 'these employed their children and servants in carrying slates down to the water side with small horses and panniers . . .'. The consequent ending of quarrying leases and the coming of the Railroad might be thought to end this childhood occupation but not entirely, for the Waggoners were often little more than young boys and girls with a minimum of adult supervision.

Now to horse haulage. Until 1851 two horses (occasionally three in bad weather or some other circumstance) were attached to each 36-wagon train – an efficiency reflecting improvements in rail design. From that time, at least, three animals were used, one being attached at the rear of Down trains to assist braking, and to make a third for the Up haulage. In March 1851 some of the Quarry horses had been put to work on the main line; before then about 19 horses were in use, but afterwards the average rose to 26, these figures including horses used at the Port but not the Quarry. Though contractor-owned, it was of concern to all that the horses were suited to the arduous conditions;

careful breeding was introduced and each mare was in foal each year; the additional loading of trains was in part due to the better breed. When a Down run arrived at an incline-head a sufficient number of wagon spokes was spragged with timber baulks inserted so as to lock the wheels and hold the train; horses were then detached and moved round to head the waiting run of empties.

Bad weather hindered traffic. On 11th February, 1808 a tornado hit the district; Bangor was cut off for five days and many ships were wrecked. The quay, the main line and trains en route were damaged. The high winds (in a district well-used to gale force conditions) found a new victim in the Railroad trains (the Log entry reads 'High Wints' for over three-quarters of a century before the spelling was corrected) and if coming from a certain quarter could blow laden wagons over the top of an incline – sprags were left in wheelspokes as a precaution. The youngsters in charge of the horses might take shelter in heavy storms, but the animals were known to trudge on alone from one incline to the next, regardless of a passbye and before these lads could restrain them; discovery of such mishaps could lead to dismissal from the contract. So, heedless of the weather, the Waggoners were obliged to keep order on the line, even though this meant they were often out all night to contain the effects of it. A different hazard was frost which froze the slates together in the wagons, making unloading at the Port very slow – in such conditions there was soon a shortage of wagons to keep the flow of traffic moving.

However, the principal problem at the Port was one of storage space – an entry on 27th August, 1814 reads: 'Not work because ther is no room at the Port' referring not to ships but to ground area, for never at any time did the Port seem large enough to stock slates ahead of orders; only about 7 days' work could be stacked there at a time. Another hazard: loads might be sold and lying at the Port, but a delay to shipping, and therefore the loading, might block the Railroad. Facilities at the Quarry end for keeping wagons standing under load were equally limited: the attractions of pilfering slate lying on the quay were obvious and the attitude of management towards greater storage space was mixed!

For reasons unknown, traffic was almost stopped in the first three months of 1817 either by dispute or through horses 'Work at the Mill'; quarrymen pushed some trains along the line. Matters were resolved after coming to a head on 29th March.

On 25th March, 1824 'Repairs to Tynclwyd Incline' emphasises that all was not well with the drums on the three main line inclines (most of the Quarry drums were horizontal). This was but one breakdown of many, usually connected with the lower bearing of the drum. Elsewhere in North Wales the drum was horizontal and straddled the track at the incline head and ropes/cables from ground to drum might interfere with the movement of wagons; with a vertical drum on the

Penrhyn method the rope passed under the track at ground level and brought it out at the side of the line where the drum was located at the side of a brakesman's hut. However, whereas the simple handbrake on a horizontal drum can be worked by downward weight of a man's body on a long operating lever, a similar brake on a vertical drum can be more complex and less efficient . . . thus limiting the number of wagons in a set.

THE PENRHYN RAILWAY – THE ROUTE DESCRIBED

(Note: where the Railroad course was embodied in the newer Railway route, the Railroad course is described hereunder.)

Even allowing that it was a private railway, the Penrhyn Railway was shy to the eye and little-known outside its neighbourhood. It did not convey the public, did its work in the environment of a private estate and its day-to-day activities were not publicised (reference to it in contemporary newspapers is rare). How much in contrast with the Festiniog Railway – not too distant – trumpeting its achievements under the Spooners, yet unable to conceal its defects from print, always a physical showpiece yet continually angering slate quarries which perforce had to use it! Here then another narrow gauge railway, born one third of a century earlier and seventy years later emulating the pioneer work done on the Festiniog; both narrow gauge slate carriers but how different, the one a common carrier and the other the servant of an owner-occupier.

The route of the Railway, here hidden by woodland, now deep in cuttings, or snaking snugly down the sylvan side of Cegin was but scant known except to those who operated it. There was extreme contrast along the way, from the man made confusion of the Quarry, through the many contrasting mountain and softer rural environs of the middle journey where the train often ran like some nocturnal creature, hidden from sight as it threaded the valley bottom, and then, after passing through the parklike edge of the Penrhyn demesne, ending abruptly alongside the fresh, mud-smelling shore of the Straits debauching on to a drab quay in such contrast to the sparkle of the sea beyond, the wooded coastline of Anglesey and the ordered lands of Penrhyn Castle adjacently.

Unlike its Railroad predecessor, the Railway was judged to commence at the foot of the Felin-Fawr Incline on the north-west edge of the Quarry, and not within the Quarry itself. This Incline was completed in August 1874 and two extra staff were taken on for the purpose; it formed part of a first stage in improvements right along the Quarry – Port link, some five years before the old Railroad itself was discontinued. Oddly, the Ordnance Map printers working on the

1886–88 survey for the First Edition of the 25 inch/1 mile sheets, produced the pre-1874 access route and, showing the track layout already at least eleven years out of date, provided posterity with a false record. From the Incline foot two tracks struck off northwards at differing levels to enable empty wagons to run on to the foot of the Incline by gravity. Beyond the foot the main line began, flanked by various parallel tracks; that to the extreme east being once a siding (post 1912) but having the 1933 Ponc Sling access route branching off it. Before abandonment in 1873 this east line formed the site of the former 1843–1874 access to Sinc Bach. These form part of that same marshalling yard which was first a feature of the Railroad and had been moved from Coed-y-Parc. The yard ended at its northern edge in a single line passing under Coed-y-Parc road bridge, this being a level crossing with adjacent gatekeeper's cottage until 1900.

Looking northward from halfway up the Felin-Fawr Incline, and viewing this scene below, it might be noted how the arms of the rubbish tips embraced the land on either side. To the left was the long single-line stone shed built in 1903 to house the Workmen's Train carriages, but marked as 'Engine Shed' on the 1912 O.S. Maps. This definition may be a 'hang-over' from the time beginning in 1879 when two main line engines were kept at Felin-Fawr overnight; in earlier times the Workmen's Train was kept in a shed below the Quarry (and possibly not transferred to this shed immediately it was built in 1903 – the precise date of this transfer is not known). It could be that the two main line engines were squeezed out and down to the Port shed when the Workmen's Train increased to 13 vehicles, for that train had latterly grown too long for the shed so the south end was taken down and the carriages poked out of it. Alongside was the 6th milepost. Beyond on the same side was (correctly) a small Engine Shed, which in due course acquired the nickname 'The Baldwin Shed', after the purchase of three ex-War Department locomotives from that American builder in 1924 had proved fruitless and they were stored inside. There was a water standpipe for main line engines on the wall outside. In much earlier days the building housed the little private saloon carriage which in later years was kept in the Port Engine Shed.

This yard was always full of stock, lines of slate wagons loaded and waiting the next run to the Port, with empties alongside making their way slowly to be hauled up by the endless chain incline at Felin-Fawr, with perhaps another row of Quarry Flats standing with huge lumps of slab on them, waiting to be run down into the Felin-Fawr Mill in the Coed-y-Parc complex. Other odd wagons found a home there month by month – there was not much spare accommodation elsewhere. Wagon loads of coal waiting to go up into Quarry Departments and the wooden-bodied 'Fullersite' wagons could be easily distinguished too.

Away to the right might be discerned the course of the abandoned 1843 line (i.e. that shown on the First Edition before-mentioned) but, ere its grassgrown course had gone many yards, the foot of the waste tips buried it. Beyond and behind this there was a drop of some 20 ft with a supporting wall and, running along near its top the course of the 1933-built link line, a second generation (so to speak) of the 1843 access and intended to bring Sling Level into easy communication with Coed-y-Parc independently of the Felin-Fawr Incline . . . but doomed to operational failure on account of its sharp curves.

In the distance (and across the middle of the scene), the abutments and road bridge at Coed-y-Parc marked the boundary of the area, the bridge itself with ornamental railings to the road and a pair of wooden gates beneath it; these were shut to prevent unlawful access to the workshop area at all but working hours. Beyond the bridge might be seen the huddled roofs of the mills and workshops and moving to the left, the row of houses bordering the line to the west, formerly the stables (Tai'r-stablau) for the Railroad but now converted into domestic dwellings. It was a rural setting for this early nineteenth century industrial centre, the wooded Ogwen valley stretching away behind the works until the hills beside it merged with those of Anglesey beyond the waters of the Menai. From no point on the Railway itself was such a view obtainable.

Coming down-incline into the yard, there was formerly an island platform between the running line where the daily Workmen's Train terminated: during working days, its stock was shunted into the long shed out of the way. Almost under Coed-y-Parc road bridge the line was single for a few yards, only to branch out beyond and make its way, curving slightly to the right and following a tall wall on the left with other lines alongside: the trackwork was particularly interesting, especially the severely-curved pointwork leading into the Erecting Shop. On the right hand various buildings which made up the Felin-Fawr complex stretched alongside, many of them employed latterly for purposes quite different from their origins. Nothing today can recall the intense activity of bygone days, for not only did these workshops serve the Quarry and Railway, but the whole Estate; at first the Galedffrwd river was utilised to drive two water wheels which supplied all the power required; this stream was not readily seen as it tunnelled under the ground hereabouts.

The main line summit lay adjacent and there was a second standpipe in the tall wall for the engine to take water whilst the loaded slate train was prepared; here too was the Oil House where wagons were oiled for the downward run. The first of four gradient posts showed a fall of 1 in 60 started here – these posts were not marked in any way but simply indicated a rise, fall or level. At the north end the yard tapered between Mill Cottage and Felin-Fawr House and here both old and new lines passed under a footbridge built by John Foulkes in 1823; beneath this hung another pair of protective wooden gates. Looking back from this bridge emphasised the enormity of the Quarry area across the face of the mountain, and the vast piles of useless rubbish would be immediately apparent. The slope of Carnedd-y-Filiast was completely terraced with man-made "steps" of which only the upper ones were visible, the lower masked by the spoil tips at this nearer side of the workings. The size of these spoil banks made the tips of the largest coal mine seem like molehills in comparison. The backcloth reached up the craggy Nant Ffrancon to the peaks of the Carneddau, for much of the year snow-covered. What might have been taken for patches of snow in the gallery area would grow and fade, then prove to be the exhaust steam of locomotives which themselves were almost invisible, dwarfed by the scale of the place.

On the Railway, there began a long fall of 550 ft to the Port; here at Cilgeraint the tipping of rubbish from the Felin-Fawr Mill had completely buried the old Railroad site and in fact, to prevent this unwanted material from falling down on to the adjacent road and dwellings, high 30 ft fortress-like walls were built up in slab and the material tipped behind; in such fashion the road up Douglas Hill was reached. It was obliged to pass through these tips in a 12 ft wide man-made "chasm" formed between walls across which both Railroad (latterly) and Railway were given bridges; immediately to the left and outside this rubbish walling the course of the Railroad towards the Tyn-y-Clwt Incline head, forms a driveway today. However, Tyn-y-Clwt Incline and all its ancillary works have long been buried, and the new Railway (this section being part of the Tyn-y-Clwt Incline avoiding line built 1876) cut down westward of these tips, supported on a slab embankment. It had originally crossed the Douglas Hill road on a level crossing, but clearly this temporary arrangement (shown on some maps) was ended when an overbridge spanning the "chasm" soon followed; it was known as St. Ann's or Cilgeraint (New Bridge) and was alongside the Railroad bridge – but east of it. A solid wooden paling hid the train from the view from the roadway, and whilst the Railroad bridge had been decked to support the horses, the Railway bridge was formed in the 'standard' method used elsewhere viz. a square-section timber beam supported on slab piers, 4-hole chairs being used thereon to carry each rail. And this was not all, as an adjacent tip line also had its own bridge over the road until the site was full and the tip abandoned. Here too a junction in the tipping system had once thrown off a spur line which passed off the top of the 'fortress walling' and crossed the old turnpike road by a wooden span; it led on to further spoil banks on the east side of this road, which at a later date were linked by an incline which dropped a tramway into the Ogwen Tile Works.

On a point level with the foot of the old Tyn-y-Clwt Incline the new Railway (still on its stone-walled embankment) passed over the Pen-y-Friddoedd footpath by a 5 ft span, unusually built in rolled-iron joists; the civil engineering here showed the contemporary Spooner influence,

the Railway carried on a stone-slab and earth-fill causeway 18 ft high ×
10 ft wide. Now in a most pleasant woodland on the Mynydd Llandegai
hillside, all traces of industrial origins were soon forgotten as the views
of the Ogwen valley unfolded below on the right and the course of the
Railroad down there could be picked out from time to time. The
Railway passed through a number of rock cuttings, one being only 8 ft
wide at formation level, and through meadowland which began to fall
more steeply down to the stony Ogwen; beyond the river, bare uplands
rise to the slopes of Moel Faban, with straggling dwellings and an
occasional slate quarry breaking the regular curves of the grasslands.
Another causeway section with a bridge spanning a footpath brought
the line to the back gardens of Bron-Ogwen and here old and new
systems came together again and the steepest 'intended' grade (1 in
36)[42] of any length flattened somewhat as Hen-Durnpike Crossing was
reached; this was a close-walled road and rail intersection with protective tall semaphore signal (its signal hut perched on the walling, the
enceinte of successive Mrs. Parry – gatekeepers) and twin road gates,
made all the more risky as several roads met hereabouts. The hut,
wooden walled and slate roofed, survived the closure. Here the line was
420 ft above sea level, and there were 'Whistle' boards on each side of
the gates; this was a most dangerous and narrow place, more especially
for the road-user! The position of the approaching train could be
determined quite exactly by long forewarning of its steam hooter, each
main line engine having an individual tone.

After slowing severely, the Down train would accelerate along the
straight length ahead, running over a section of route which was once
that of the Railroad. Below to the right the road drops, sharply and
curving, to the Pont Coetmor bridge and the river, boulder-strewn and
tree lined with escarpment below the Railway, is especially picturesque
here; however, most of this view is masked from the line by a tall
intervening wall on the right hand, and the steep slope on the left
leading up towards the houses on Pen-Dinas. A staircase footpath
crossed the line here, the 5th milepost was passed, and the line carried
for some distance along a stone shelf – again a Spooner feature. Parallel
and below the Old Road to the Quarry kept company before falling
down beside the river; the Railway passed a former ballast quarry on
the left which must have been thus used in Railroad days, and then
emerged from behind this narrow walled section, high up on the Dinas
bluff, with meadowland on either side . . . a sudden transformation.
The L.N.W.R. branch to Bethesda which emerged from a tunnel down
below on the right and crossed the Ogwen immediately on a stone
arched viaduct, would also pass unseen from the Port-bound train, as
would the levels of a small copper mine in the wooded slope between
Railway and river below.

The Railway now began a long left hand curve round the Pen-Dinas
hill, itself an ancient hill fort. A last and pleasant view down the Ogwen

valley to Anglesey beyond was glimpsed as the line turned very sharply round its most acute curve (85 ft radius: it was here the Baldwin engines might occasionally derail), the line supported on low walls and passing through a copse. Here the Railroad passed the head of Dinas Incline and its course can be discerned falling steeply into the river valley; just before this point the widening of the right-of-way earmarks the former stabling loops at its summit. Now followed a complete contrast in surroundings once more; running due southwest and now falling at 1 in 93 and on the 400 ft contour there was a short length of shallow causeway followed by an equally shallow cutting with gates in the iron railings at its end to mark the Workmen's Train halt at Corrig-Llwydion (often spelled Cerrig) and immediately the line was bridged over the Tal-y-Cae to Hen-Durnpike road which climbed up steeply beneath it. The original timbers had been replaced with steel spans, and the stone supporting walls gave a roadway 25 ft in width; it was here that the contractors began building the new Railway in 1878. On the west side of the road there followed a short embankment and here the L.N.W.R. was crossed for a second time, being in deep cutting below after it had emerged from the west mouth of the Dinas Tunnel. The Penrhyn Railway's skew overbridge was single arched, in brick and of course, provided at Euston's expense. At this bridge the two lines were at 31 ft difference in level. Now side-by-side but preserving their levels the two railways made for Tregarth, there being a station for each concern, though that for the narrow gauge was at the foot of the 1 in 60 and only sited here out of spite in 1902! Still in cutting but now almost level at 1 in 2867, the Penrhyn line passed under what might be called the 'standard' form of road overbridge, stone with brick facings; in a cutting behind the Shiloh Chapel was the Workmen's Train platform, linked with the nearby road by footpath and wicket gate. No trains ever seemed actually to stand there, for it was sufficient for the Workmen's rake to run slowly past as the men jumped on or off! Here was the 4th milepost and the slopes of Moel-y-Ci are a feature on the left hand, with the Railway passing on through meadowland: along this stretch the standard gauge was adjacent, parallel but unseen, being in deep cutting.

For the next 250 yds a loop was formed together with a long siding on its north side – trains passed each other on the right. Unusually, iron railings fenced the route here, whereas elsewhere the ubiquitous estate fence made of slabs stuck into the ground on edge and wired together near the top, was (and is) a feature of the district.[43] Until the reduction in trade made the running of but one train (from 4th May, 1928) sufficient to move stocks, trains passed here regularly. There was a water tank used by Up trains which stopped if required. Beyond the loop came an occupation crossing. There was no signalling. The loop, Pandy (or sometimes Tyn-y-Lon) was an original stopping point for the Workmen's Train and boasted one of the four Waiting Huts, but a stone throwing incident during the Great Strike so displeased His Lordship that the stop was removed to Tregarth as punishment: so along a straight length, under a bridge leading to Moel-y-Ci Farm, (having passed the third gradient post) and falling at 1 in 43, leaving the temporary level of the passing loop the Railway began a long right hand curve, falling deeper into cutting as it did so; shortly the cutting became heavily wooded (Pant-y-Cyff or Rhydau-Duon), the 3rd milepost was passed and a short siding alongside on the right without permanent track connection was reached. By now the line was running north again, having made something like the shape of a 'Z' on the map since leaving Hen-Durnpike in order to sustain an even gradient for steam working. The siding now running parallel with it served a small gravel pit and connection was made as required – and probably since 1881 – by a set of portable Spoon Points which were lifted off after use. On Mondays a wagon was manhandled down to here from Coed-y-Parc, pushed through the narrow curved cutting into the working and loaded up as required; output was small being only about 150 tons a year, with 1912–14 being the best period. An embarrassing accident occurred to the Up Workmen's Train here one Monday morning, when, the Spoon Points having been inadvertently left in position, the train engine tried to enter the gravel pit and was derailed. The Engineer's diary records the date, 3rd February, 1941, that the engine was CEGIN – an unusual choice – and that the train 'Arrived Mill 10.30 a.m.'.

Quitting the woodland on embankment, and passing another stopping point, Felin-Hen, the line crossed the Pentir – Bethesda road on a 17 ft span in lattice ironwork, and still curving to the right, dropped from the embankment on the far side of the road and reversed direction slightly to run through the edge of Coed-Wern-Ty-Gwyn. The L.N.W.R., by now somewhat transposed and so above the narrow gauge, also had a station (Felin-Hen) on the south side of the road here, where there was a pair of unmistakable 'Crewe' cottages; this line also crossed the road and entered the same wood; the two systems slowly converged, the Penrhyn to fall into a steeply-sided 15 ft deep cutting and pass under L.N.W.R. Bridge No. 8 by means of an acutely-skewed bridge. This bridge had served elsewhere and been cut down to 31 ft span for re-use here; it formed a 'tunnel' almost 43 ft long for the narrow gauge and gave generous vertical clearance of 14 ft and 14 ft horizontal! The civil engineering demanded for the standard gauge here was considerable, with occupation bridges to serve the nearby Coed-Hywel-Uchaf Farm and after wooded embankment there was a costly and impressive eight-arched viaduct over the Cegin with a height of some 55 ft from the river. Once, a siding for the nearby mill had existed too.

Following this the narrow gauge left the woodland (its cutting passing the farm immediately on the right) also the 2nd milepost, and traversed Glas-yn-Fryn embankment to begin to thread its way along the narrow coppice which fringed the east bank of the Cegin – a much smaller stream than the Ogwen alongside which the first part of the route had run. Ultimately this long wooded northbound run brought it to another overbridge – once just a footbridge – where the Workmen's Train made its last stop before the Port. It was variously dubbed Llandegai (which was certainly the most adjacent place) but locally Tyddyn-Mynyddig ('Mountain Smallholding'). The road here crosses the Cegin by ford and then climbs steeply to pass under the L.N.W.R. Bethesda branch as it climbed steeply northward to meet the main line at the east portal of Bangor Tunnel: there is however, a footbridge for pedestrians and the site is locally called The White Bridge, the Welsh name being seldom used.

The Railway, now only 70 ft above sea level, continued under the umbrella of trees to where the river was diverted to keep it to the left side of the track, and in consequence the municipal boundary comes billowing out across the metals and back again. Now looms ahead through the trees the fine Chester & Holyhead Railway's Cegin Viaduct, 59 miles from Chester with seven semi-circular arches each of 35 ft span – it has masonry piers but the stone arches are faced with brick. (Ref: Public Record Office, M.T. 27/49.) Down in the valley below it, Railway and river passed through adjacent arches and the former followed the river bank, over the occupation crossing to Felin-Esgob (the 1st milepost just passed), the gradient easing to about 1 in 209, and entered the Nant Maes-y-Geirchen gorge, a former beauty spot now somewhat tarnished. The line found a foothold on the rocky bank in the form of a shelf above the river and almost unnoticed the L.N.W.R.'s Port Penrhyn branch came in from above and beside it from the right, this stealthy incomer keeping company with the Quarry line all the way on to the wharves. The Shrewsbury – Holyhead road being reached, each line passed through individual bores in a tall stone embankment carrying it across the valley, the Penrhyn bore being 36 ft long and of its basic loading gauge viz. 15 ft wide and 11 ft 10 in. height from rail to top of arch with 7 ft horizontal clearance at the foot of the walls.

The first plan for this bore by Algeo is dated February 1877 entitled 'Port Penrhyn and Bethesda Railway' with a limited clearance of under 10 ft from rail level to roof – this would have passed the later 'Port' type engines (such as WINIFRED) with vertical height of almost 9 ft with chimney of length as delivered. Between that date and February 1878 a revised vertical dimension of 11 ft 10 in. from formation level was adopted. A letter of application[44] (16th February, 1877) from H. Barber, Solicitor and Notary, Bangor, to The Commissioners of Public Works refers to it:

> The tramway which will be of very narrow gauge (2 ft only) is intended for the conveyance of slate by miniature locomotives from his Lordship's quarries etc. . . . in substitution for a tramway worked by horses which passes by a tunnel under the turnpike road very near to the situation of the works now proposed and which last

mentioned tramway will be discontinued when the new one is formed. As the tramway will be confined to Lord Penrhyn's own lands and be used for his own purposes only it is not prepared to apply for an act of Parliament for its formation.

On 28th February, 1877 Barber added it would be necessary to interfere with the surface of the road but this would be done by digging up half of the road at a time and continued:

I may mention that the tramway already referred to as being now in use was constructed in the manner proposed (taking down half the road in width at a time) under the Shrewsbury and Holyhead road about the year 1852 or 1853 . . .

[The reference may refer to the Railroad 'tunnel' but the date is misleading.] On 8th March, 1877 he wrote to the Office of Works:

. . . it now appears that owing to the necessity of executing other works previously to carrying out those sanctioned . . . these latter cannot advantageously be commenced for some months at least.

On 9th February, 1878 Barber submitted a revised plan signed 'Robt. Algeo 1878' entitled 'Penrhyn Quarry Railway – Bridge under turnpike road'.

Now alongside one another, the two lines crossed the Cegin by a common bridge (L.N.W.R. No. 3) formed of wrought-iron beams on stone supporting piers and open timberwork; on the far bank the walls of the estate converged towards the lineside and there was an occupation crossing ('The Nursery Crossing') with gates in the wall on either hand. The L.N.W.R. 1st milepost (from the main line) survives here. Both lines were instructed by suitable Whistle Boards to sound their approach to this narrow bottleneck between the walling; there was only a 21 ft clearance to accommodate both lines. From here the Penrhyn Nursery wall continued on the left hand with the Cegin winding below to the right; all this was set in a narrow valley, heavily wooded and lush. Suddenly the walling ended and both lines were projected across the Cegin for the last time: the river passed beneath them into the head of Cegin Pool where in times past there was a wharf. (Before Richard Pennant's work here, the river was tidal to this place.) This was L.N.W.R. Bridge No. 4, between 1851 and 1879 a wooden trestle of eight 17 ft 6 in. spans and perhaps the only wooden structure over which locomotives passed on that Railway? (The old Railroad was severely curved here and passed under the first span of this bridge, as noted previously.) The later bridge still remains; it is of steel spans 46 ft 6 in., 53 ft and 43 ft, girders 4 ft 2 in. deep carried on 5 ft stone piers giving an average clearance above the river of 10 ft, the width is 24 ft 6 in. and wooden handrails are fitted: here the track is 'level' at 1 in 580.

Returning momentarily to the occupation crossing at the Nursery, from this point down to the Port the old and new Penrhyn lines were on the same alignment save for those places just mentioned. Although divergent under Bridge No. 4 the courses were alongside again at its north end and thereafter used the same site. Due to haste in constructing the new Railway and the desired level not being achieved there was a section at the north end of this bridge which marked the steepest inclination on the line, 1 in 33. This created a permanent flooding problem and the crisis with Robert Algeo who walked out in consequence.

For the remaining short distance to the Port the two gauges, being side by side, took on the appearance of a dual driveway in a setting bounded by water, trees and parkland: herons once abounded in the Pool. The Penrhyn line now doubled and all three lines passed under the Port road bridge, an imposing two-arched Regency-style overbridge which had superceded a more basic design: on the coming of the L.N.W.R. the individual Railroad tracks which had occupied each arch, were placed in the westerly one and the L.N.W.R. took the easterly arch. As at Coed-y-Parc, these arches contained wooden gates, normally closed save at working hours. Under the 'Penrhyn arch' was a watering point for locomotives and on the further side the Oil House where the last employee charged with lubricating wagons served until he was 87!

On the south side of the bridge a semaphore signal for Penrhyn trains stood between the archways to indicate the position of the mixed-gauge level crossing of tracks on the quay beyond. Alongside came the fourth and last of the gradient posts.

Distances were measured from the Port House steps and sometime after 1833 a slab post on the west side of the line and standing about 2 ft 6 in. out of the ground was erected every mile: the appropriate figure was chiselled into the east face. Not all posts survived to closure.

From Port steps to the Oil Store at Coed-y-Parc (the summit of the 1 in 60 climb) the length was 5 m. 7 fur. 9 ch. with an average rise of 1 in 64½; extended to the foot of Felin-Fawr Incline the length was 6 m. 0 fur. 5½ ch., the final length rising at 1 in 300. From Port to Coed-y-Parc the railway climbed 492 ft.

THE PORT AND SHIPS

Seen from the air the Port projected unnaturally into the slob of the Straits. It was a thumb-and-finger outline, the thumb being the older portion and the crooked finger to the east being the newer arm; the inner basin or New Dock of 1855 included a 'stepped wall' on the east side of the 'thumb'. Before 1803 the works projected little beyond the High Water Mark and even when fully developed the works dried out at low water. Prominent behind the east side was the spoil which had been tipped into the mud in a large flat tongue of rubble.

The extension of 1803 took the original (west) wharf far enough to allow ships to berth on either side – previously this had only been

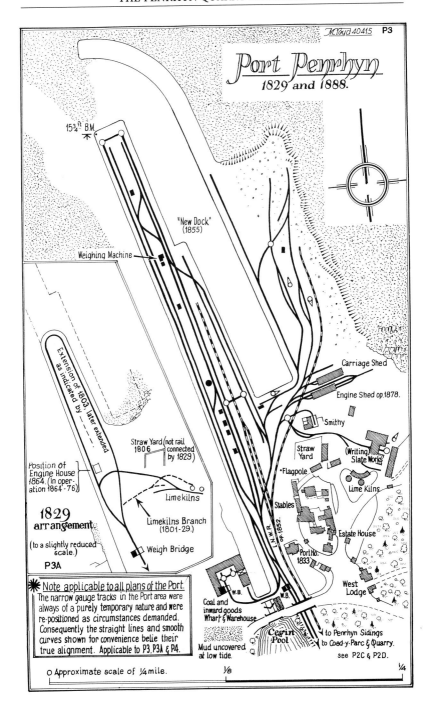

M.J.C.Lloyd 40415 P3

Port Penrhyn
1829 and 1888.

153¾ ft BM

"New Dock" (1855)

Weighing Machine

Extension of 1803, later extended as indicated by ---

Carriage Shed

Engine Shed op.1878.

Smithy

Straw Yard (not rail 1806 connected by 1829)

Position of Engine House 1864. (In operation 1864-76)

Straw Yard

(Writing) Slate Works

Flagpole

Limekilns

Lime Kilns

1829 arrangement.
(to a slightly reduced scale.)

Limekilns Branch (1801-29.)

Stables

L.N.W.R. op. 1852.

Estate House

P3A

Weigh Bridge

Port Ho. 1833

West Lodge

✳ Note applicable to all plans of the Port.
The narrow gauge tracks in the Port area were always of a purely temporary nature and were re-positioned as circumstances demanded. Consequently the straight lines and smooth curves shown for convenience belie their true alignment. Applicable to P3, P3A & P4.

W.B.

Coal and inward goods Wharf & Warehouse

W.B.

Cegin Pool

Mud uncovered at low tide.

to Penrhyn Sidings to Coed-y-Parc & Quarry. see P2C & P2D.

0 Approximate scale of ¼mile.

⅛

¼

possible on the west or river face of the wharf. The Railroad tracks were taken round the end of the pier formed by this additional length and when an even longer mole was extended to the present length of the works, the same form of track layout was taken round the end of what had now become a full jetty. This main track was taken along each side of the jetty so as to bring wagons as near the ships as possible. A number of parallel 'ladder rung' tracks ran at right angles joining these outer lines from side to side; in the middle of each 'rung' was a wagon turntable allowing vehicles to be rotated so as to bring the brakehandle on to the desired side.

Dawkins-Pennant (inherited 1816) used his influence at the Office of Woods & Forests to support renewals of his Crown lease and block applications for renewal on neighbouring competitors' quays but, after a Public Enquiry ventilated complaints to no avail, enlargement continued! The easterly portion was developed, mainly out of rubble brought down from the Quarry and tipped into a large plateau.

The track layout development at the Port was complex and frequently changed; this was due not only to the additions to the wharves but the coming of, and extensions to, the standard gauge. Only the Spooner surveys have remained to record what the arrangements were in the 1860s, and detail of trackage before then is not known though basic formation is recorded; this served the extensive slate yards which were laid on the ground, there being more area for stocks here than elsewhere.

Among the features which still remain are the handsome Port House of 1833, (the administration centre of the undertaking) and the two-road engine shed attractively designed with 'tunnel mouth' doors to each of the two single roads. The extension to the carriage shed alongside in timber to accommodate the extra carriages of the Workmen's Train is unusual. On the old jetty stands the circular privy for use of slate loaders, allowing 13 men 'to engage in conversation' simultaneously.

The crossings of standard and narrow gauge on the level, the confusion of rail tracks and the extent of this man-made delta of rubble provide fitting complementary features to the vast quarry which created them.

Chronological Summary of Port Development

1780	By this date an established shipping point with recorded tonnages
1786	Leased from Bishop of Bangor for 21 years (20th December)
1790	'Commodious Harbour' in existence but Pennant says (1796) Port too small and ships have to be served in rotation
1797	Writing Slate Factory established
1800	Improvements to accommodate 50 vessels at once

1801	Slate Mill built. Siding into Flint-reducing Kilns laid
1802	Further lease from Bishop of Bangor (1st November)
1803	Wharf on east bank of Cegin extended northwards
1806	Straw Yard provided for packing slates more securely (August)
1820	Stone bridge over Cegin replaces wooden one
1829	Flint kilns converted to lime kilns; siding closed. Writing Slate Factory passes from Worthington to Quarry
1829–30	Further extension of wharf on east bank Cegin making it '1,000 ft long and able to accommodate 100 vessels'. This wharf was given a 'ladder pattern' of sidings, each 'upright' lying along the edge of the quay on either hand
1833	Port House built – designed by Benjamin Wyatt (II)
1835	Decorative iron bridge between Cegin Pool and Port replaces older stone structure, which itself replaced the original road ford
1847	Writing Slate Factory enlarged
1849	Materials from Quarry drainage adit deposited at Port – east side
1852	Standard gauge branch from L.N.W.R. main line opened (January)
1855	New mole on east side with New (or Inner) Dock between it and existing wharf made using slate rubbish as material. River diverted. Floor of new dock paved with slab
1863	Lime kilns closed down – stone from Penmaenmawr in future
1864	Steam-operated system for towing wagons over weighbridge installed with Engine House. (Stationary boiler and winch draw slowly-moving train over weightable without stopping.) First 'driver' on payroll
1871	L.N.W.R. extended on to east side wharf and breakwater around New Dock (after approval given 29th May). Dubbed 'The Beaumaris Siding', a skit on its orientation. Note this line ran to the east side of the narrow gauge tramways on this portion of the Port, so that eastward branches off the narrow gauge required to cross the standard gauge on the level . . . a clumsy arrangement
1876	Steam haulage over weighing machine ceased
1877	By this time Straw Yard has renewed rail connection. Two shunting engines by de Winton & Co. delivered to Port for use on the quays, but initially sent to Quarry for trials there
1878	Engine Shed built (at a later date this was converted into a 'through shed' by extending the tracks through the end wall)
[1879	New Railway opened (6th October)]
1880	Carriage Shed for workmen's coaches provided (two roads)

1881	Further extensions to L.N.W.R. on east side
1888	Even further extensions to L.N.W.R. on both arms of the Port, and line on east side (built 1881) re-aligned to allow narrow gauge to run on extreme east of site and permit the discontinuance of a number of standard gauge/narrow gauge crossings on the level. (A portion of this relaying took place alongside the flagstaff which stood prominently upon a 'tump' by this date)
1891	Standard gauge/narrow gauge interchange sidings and platform provided at north end of Beaumaris Siding
1900	Overhead gantry crane erected over interchange of 1891
1903	Carriage Shed extended
1906	L.N.W.R. siding extended into Writing Slate Factory
1924	Grout Plant in connection with 'Fullersite' business established on east quay (this became a warehouse in 1943). Writing Slate Factory became Dixon's 'Eureka' Works (ceased early 1930s)
1925	Weighing machine provided on Coal Wharf, west quay
1927	Lines extending behind Engine Shed taken up (at later date shed divided internally) Carriage Shed given four tracks
1934	Fitting Shop erected

Tonnages Shipped[45]

	tons per annum		tons per annum
1780	1,800	1809	20,000
1792	12,000	1826	46,000
1794	15,000	1844	41,000
1796	8,000	1859	120,000

Employment

The Inspector of Mines Report for 1906 states 102 men were employed at the Port, (but only 14 on the Railway).

THE PORT PENRHYN BRANCH: MINERAL TRAINS ONLY

This standard gauge branch from the Chester & Holyhead section was opened in January 1852; the last working was on 2nd March, 1963 and official closure at 30th June, 1965. At the main line the junction and yard was controlled by Penrhyn Sidings Box, having a Saxby & Co. (Patent 1722) 12-lever frame of 1870, removed after closing of the box on 23rd August, 1954 (and now in the National Railway Museum at York). Built over Penrhyn Estate as single line, provision was made for double where physically possible; it fell mainly into the Port at 1 in 50

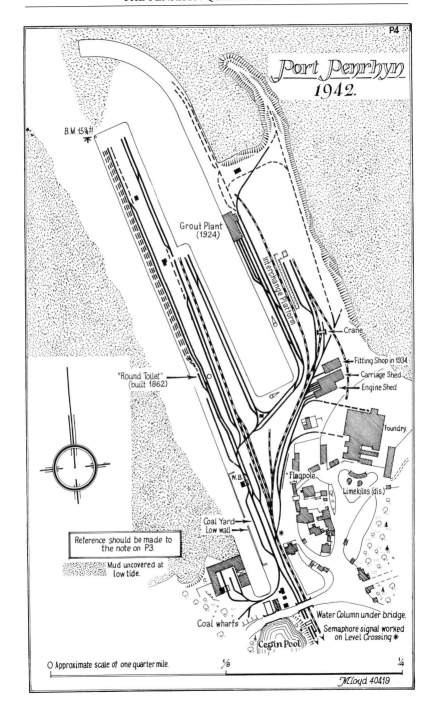

P4

Port Penrhyn
1942.

B.M. 153 ft

Grout Plant
(1924)

Interchange Platform

Crane

Fitting Shop in 1934

Carriage Shed

Engine Shed

"Round Toilet"
(built 1862)

Foundry

W.B.

Flagpole

Limekilns (dis.)

Coal Yard
Low wall

Reference should be made to
the note on P3.

Mud uncovered at
low tide.

Coal wharfs

Cegin Pool

Water Column under bridge.

Semaphore signal worked
on Level Crossing ✳

O Approximate scale of one quarter mile.   ⅛   ¼

M.Lloyd 40419

and 1 in 64 for its 1½ miles. Where the Penrhyn Railway and the standard gauge came side-by-side near the Cegin bridge below the A5 road, there was insufficient clearance to pass a Penrhyn locomotive and a standard gauge wagon! Further, the water pick-up scoop on standard gauge engines would foul the standard gauge/narrow gauge crossings on the Port, at least until the narrow gauge was lowered to give more clearance in 1924.

The operating method was to propel the train down-grade to the quays, sounding the whistle most of the way; before starting all brakes would be pinned down. The goods guard would ride on the leading wagon carrying a flag or lamp; until 1960 one train Mondays to Fridays was worked daily and in that year 2,860 standard gauge wagons of slate or 'Fullersite' were brought out. The track was lifted in 1965/6; it had been classed as a siding since 22nd August, 1954.

The Appendix to the L.N.W.R. Working Timetable August 1919 refers to 'One Engine in Steam' (or two together) working; that trains must propel down and stop with leading wagon clear of Port bridge, thence work to directions of guard; whistle sounded all the time from 'Penrhyn Junction'. If it was known that the loop at the Port was clear, the engine might precede the wagons down the Siding. (No Down trains called at Penrhyn Sidings yard; they had to proceed to Menai Bridge and collect on the Up run.)

Miscellaneous Notes

A steam crane was bought for use at the Port but little use was found for it – W. W. Vivian, Manager of Dinorwic Quarries offered to hire it for use at Port Dinorwic at 5/- per week, where it was found to be very satisfactory and ultimately Dinorwic bought it; it remained in use there until the dock was closed.

To keep the Inner Dock clear of mud, lighters or 'flats' were loaded by hand and towed out into the Straits at the same period every year to take advantage of the Spring Tides. The dumping was done off Beaumaris, and again unloading was by hand! The steam tug used for this annual event was the SYLPH completed in 1881 by W. Allsup & Son, Preston and purchased by the Marquis of Anglesey (Henry Paget) of Plas Newydd in 1891. This tug was sold in 1894 but other vessels continued on the duty.

The Anglesey Shipping Co. (the operating body of 1891) – being W. W. Vivian of Vaenol and the Dinorwic Quarries, E. A. Young of Penrhyn and Lord Penrhyn – included a dredger in their fleet; in truth it was more like a hulk which was dragged up and down the Port but was never strictly sea-going. It had once done duty as a 'Royal Yacht' on the occasion of the visit of the Prince and Princess of Wales in 1894 but clearly fell short of the desirable as the following day an offer was accepted from Vivian for the royal party to use his steam pinnace!

Plate XXVII   Loaded train about to leave Felin-Fawr; the last three wagons have their brakes pinned down. (From a publicity booklet of the late 1920s.)

Gwynedd Archives

Plate XXVIII   As business fell away, the slate train grew shorter.

Maid Marian Fund

Plate XXIX   In July 1952 GLYDER was the Port shunting engine. *J.I.C. Boyd*

Plate XXX   BLANCHE and WINIFRED line up at the Port – a customary photographic courtesy shown on family visits: July 1947.   *J.I.C. Boyd*

Plate XXXI   Conversation piece. LINDA and 78058 exchange pleasantries down on the quay: April 1962.

D.L. Chatfield

Plate XXXII   The Up empties have just passed under the North Wales main line viaduct and crash noisily on towards The White Bridge in the spring sunshine.   *J.I.C. Boyd*

Plate XXXIII   LINDA simmers in Pant-y-Cyff cutting near Milepost Three. The 'fireboy' has been despatched to a farm for a saw to remove a fallen tree which blocks the line: April 1962. *J.I.C. Boyd*

Plate XXXIV   LINDA pulls clear of Coed-y-Parc bridge at the end of the Up journey. *J.I.C. Boyd*

Plate XXXV   Double Summer Time is still operative so the morning Workmen's Train – still as yet to pick up a customer – catches a roseate sunrise.
J.I.C. Boyd

Plate XXXVI 'Incline Cottage', the Wyatt-designed house at the head of Marchogian Incline. The Railroad passed between the two gabled ends: January 1966. *J.I.C. Boyd*

Plate XXXVII The Collection of various track materials (here shown laid out beside the Engineer's Office at Coed-y-Parc in 1945) has not survived. *J.I.C. Boyd*

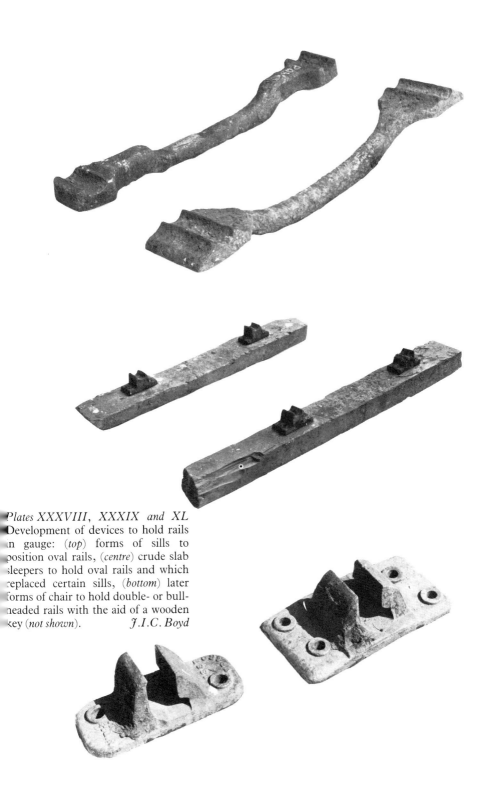

Plates XXXVIII, XXXIX and XL Development of devices to hold rails in gauge: (*top*) forms of sills to position oval rails, (*centre*) crude slab sleepers to hold oval rails and which replaced certain sills, (*bottom*) later forms of chair to hold double- or bull-headed rails with the aid of a wooden key (*not shown*). *J.I.C. Boyd*

Plate XLI   Water-balances PRINCESS MAY and LAD
Headframes were supplied by de Winton & Co. EDW,
shyly from behind one of the bridge uprights: 1896.

connected Sinc Bach Level below with Red Lion.
LTO, a horizontally-boilered de Winton engine peeps
Gwynedd Archives

Plate XLII 'The Knitting', a nice piece of track geometry in flatbottomed and chaired 'T' rails in the Quarry's Red Lion Level: 1956. *J.I.C. Boyd*

Plate XLIII The headframe of PRINCESS MAY water-balance showing counter-balanced double shaft and water tanks behind structure: c 1925.
National Museum of Wales

Plate XLIV MARCHLYN, now the only wisp of steam in a desert of rubbish. By June 1960 only five engines remained at work in the Quarry. *D.L. Chatfield*

Plate XLV A solitary NESTA sits patiently awaiting the end of the dinner hour: April 1962. *D.L. Chatfield*

Plate XLVI   'Right Side' rubbish wagons descend to the Quarry floor from Red Lion Level.   *J.I.C. Boyd*

Plate XLVII   Levels which unhelpfully occurred part-way up an incline were served by junctions such as this.   *D.L. Chatfield*

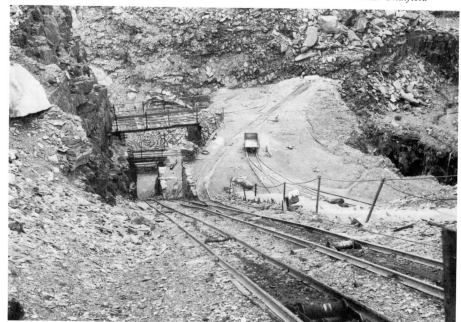

Plate XLVIII   In the top galleries NESTA (her driver, 'Will Coch') draws a train of rubbish wagons along Ponc William Parry.   *D.L. Chatfield*

Plate XLIX   Bird's eye view of Ponc Ffrith and the eastern side of the Quarry beyond and below. WINIFRED and MARCHLYN were then at work on this Level.
D.L. Chatfield

Plate L   Winter stone-scape in the Quarry; GLYDER's driver has interrupted his dinner and driven her from the snug shed for the benefit of the camera.

D.L. Chatfield

Plate LI   Home-going time for men and machines; ELIN and GWYNEDD return to their shed at the day's end; mid-1930s.

B. Roberts

Plate LII ALAN GEORGE with runner wagon attached puffs under a creeper-covered arch on Sinc Bach. Sanding gear is still fitted: c 1912.
Loco Publ. Co.

Plate LIII Line-up outside Coed-y-Parc Workshop. BLANCHE, CHARLES and LILLA perch drunkenly on some extraordinary trackwork.
J.I.C. Boyd

Plate LIV A trainload of slates is weighed on Twlldyndwr Level, each wagon stopping momentarily on the weigh table. *Gwynedd Archives*

Plate LV A run of slates descends the chain-hauled Felin-Fawr Incline whilst LINDA waits below to take the next run to the Port. *Gwynedd Archives*

From earlier times shipment was made by local schooners, a method which almost spanned a century. Under E. A. Young a policy to build a fleet of ships expressly designed for slate cargoes created The Anglesey Shipping Co., the principal shareholders being Wm. Preston of Lleiniog Castle, Samuel Chadwick, Sir R. H. Williams-Bulkeley of Baron Hill, Beaumaris, S. J. Millar (a London stock broker) with O. T. Jones, Manager. The loading of ships at the Port was done by men employed by the Quarry, but elsewhere unloading might be done by the crew; about 300 tons of slate could be handled by then per day, the slate merchant giving each man 3/6d. for his pains.

Some shipping records were discovered in 1976 by builders working in the former Quarry Office at the Port. (These have been salved and together with personal notes, have been placed with other Penrhyn documents at the U.C.N.W. by Mr. Edmund H. Douglas Pennant through whose courtesy they have been made available to the author.) The Anglesey Shipping Co. managed the fleet on behalf of the Penrhyn Quarry (later Penrhyn Quarry Ltd., Bethesda), on behalf of the owners, the Penrhyn family: by 1930 five steam coasters survived, all registered at Beaumaris and having black hulls with white line, cream funnels with black top with a rampant Red Dragon on the cream portion. By 1935 only four ships were left, in 1940 three, 1945 two and by the 1950s only SYBIL MARY remained. Instructions were given in the 1950s to destroy all records and much, including full and half models of ships was lost. Some models saved are now in the Penrhyn Castle Museum.

SHIPPING FLEET

Ships were registered under successive names of owners and managers, the details being:

Owner	Manager	Period	Note
Anglesey Shipping Co.	O. T. Jones	1891–1911	In 1898 all ships
William M. Preston	O. T. Jones	1892–1919	registered under
Rt. Hon. Baron Penrhyn	O. T. Jones	1911–1920	Emilius A. Young
Rt. Hon. Baron Penrhyn	T. J. W. Humphreys	1920–1937	(Penrhyn's
Rt. Hon. Baron Penrhyn	R. J. Lewis	1937–1938	Agent).
Anglesey Shipping Co.	R. J. Lewis	1938–1951	When Young died
(title revived)			(1911) registration
Penrhyn Quarries Ltd.	R. J. Lewis	1951–1955	passed to Baron
			Penrhyn.

All ships were steamers save one; all had engines aft.
Crews were mainly from Bangor and Port Dinorwic.

Name as Operated	Tonnage Gross Net	Period Operated	Dimensions (Ft. & ins.) Length × Beam × Depth	Builder	Date Built	Disposal
ANGLESEY	117	1891–1894	91.5 × 17.9 × 8.3	Paul Rodgers & Co., Carrickfergus	February 1891	Sold 1894
MARY B. MITCHELL	227 195	1893–1919	129.7 × 24.4 × 10.8	" "	April 1892	" 1919
HARRIER	207 69	1894–1926	120.0 × 20.1 × 9.4	Scott & Co., Bowling	September 1892	" 1926
BANGOR	340 120	1894–1933	145.0 × 24.0 × 9.0	Scott & Sons, Bowling	August 1894	" 1933
PENRHYN	355 127	1895–1937	145.0 × 24.0 × 11.7	" "	August 1895	" 1937
PENNANT	650 266	1897–1925	180.0 × 29.1 × 10.7	" "	September 1897	" 1925
PANDORA	203 76	1903–1941	116.0 × 23.1 × 8.7	Schleisinger, Davis & Co., Wallsend	January 1893	" 1941 to Admiralty
LINDA BLANCHE	530 369	1914–1915	180.4 × 28.1 × 13.9	Scott & Sons, Bowling	July 1914	Sunk 1915
PAMELA	408 147	1921–1944	150.3 × 25.1 × 9.2	" "	September 1921	Lost 1944
SYBIL MARY	270 96	1921–1954	130.1 × 22.1 × 7.9	" "	November 1921	Sold 1954

Ship details

ANGLESEY

Built for A. S. Co. Last owner Grecian Marbles (Marmor) Ltd. 1912. Foundered off Guira. Her builders were better known for their steel schooners (the second Penrhyn ship being one of them).

MARY B. MITCHELL

Registered in Preston's name, and took name of an old lady he knew, Mary Brasier Mitchell; owned jointly with Chadwick. In 1911 registered owner became O. T. Jones. Legend has it she was intended as a yacht for Lord Penrhyn but this seems very unlikely. Worked regularly between the Penrhyn wharf on the Thames, and also to Hamburg. Became Submarine Decoy 'Q9' after requisition by the Admiralty in 1916. Fitted paraffin auxiliary engine 1916, after being grounded and refloated 'on the Ushant'. Sold to Tyrul family of Arklow, 1919. Last owner Dowds of Dublin, foundered in 1944 after being wrecked off Kirkcudbright coast; no loss of life. Three-masted topsail schooner since conversion in 1893 from private yacht built 1892. (Was not restored to A. S. Co. service, post war.)

HARRIER

Apparently swopped for the vessel of this name having a larger capacity and built for C. H. Pile of London in exchange for the ANGLESEY in 1894 when purchased by A. S. Co.: proposal to re-name ANGLESEY but this never done. "A fine little ship built as a fish-carrier and good turn of speed compared with coasters of that era." Last owner Thesen Steamship Co. (Cape Town) 1936. Lost without trace 1943.

BANGOR

For A. S. Co. A year after being sold to Alexander Johnston, Belfast, she foundered off South Rock Light Vessel 1st March, 1934, with a cargo of stone; there is a Scott drawing of 1915 suggesting a rebuild.

PENRHYN

For A. S. Co. Sister ship to BANGOR. Went to Port Dinorwic for repairs in 1933. Last owner Tennants Tar Distillers and Engineers Supplies, Belfast. Broken up by Hammond Lane Foundries Ltd. at Dublin 1951.

PENNANT

For A. S. Co. Sunk off Southend pier in 1925 after being run down in thick fog; probably on general cargo duties by then, indicating falling-off in slate trade. Largest ship in fleet; the flagship. Used mainly on continental runs, especially to Hamburg. Re-floated but sold for breaking up almost at once. "A very fine ship."

PANDORA

Built for Leith & Montrose Shipping Co. and after other owners acquired by A. S. Co. in 1903. Was on west Irish coast duties at times. "No raised forecastle like the other boats." "BANGOR was similar to the PANDORA." Foundered off Whitby, 22nd October, 1951.

LINDA BLANCHE

For Baron Penrhyn. Sunk by German U boat off Liverpool, 1915 – crew allowed off first.

PAMELA

For Baron Penrhyn. Lost without trace between Sharpness and Liverpool, 1944; "probably capsized with cargo of grain. Old cautious captain had retired, mate in charge of her – a hard case." Lost funnel on one trip, fell over side.

SYBIL MARY   For Baron Penrhyn. Unconfirmed sale to Dinorwic Quarries
               1954. Sold 1954 for breaking up. Arrived Dublin 12th March,
               1955 for breaking up by Hammond Lane Metal Co. Ltd.
               Carried 80 tons water ballast – only 9 ft difference loaded or
               empty. "Not renowned for her sea-worthiness . . . 1949–52
               on slate runs Dublin–Bangor . . . half crew were from the
               village . . . only coaster afloat with the Red Dragon on the
               funnel." Wartime service November 1942–August 1945.

All ships built by Scott of Bowling were designed by James Maxton, Belfast.

Note: Ships built to carry stone, slate etc. were stoutly constructed to withstand loading
shocks and sea passages; ships built for such cargoes can always be determined
where gross and net tonnages are available, the actual net tonnage being low
compared with the gross tonnage e.g. PENRHYN 365 gross and 77 net tons; where
the ratio was 1 net to 4.74 gross tons. However, the last five ships were not so
stoutly built averaging 1 net to 2.716 gross tons. "All boats built for slate carrying
were deadly with a light cargo." Only the smaller ships could berth up to the Port
bridge, the rest normally berthing in the 'Dock'.

COED-Y-PARC AND FELIN-FAWR

The untidy cluster of slab-built buildings forming the Coed-y-Parc
and Felin-Fawr workshop community did not make for efficiency;
grown from the early nerve-centre of the Railroad, Estate and Quarry,
it was at first a centre for processing the stone. The first Slab Mill
(named Felin-Fawr) here was opened 2nd July, 1803; it may have been
the earliest in the Principality; the Railroad passed along the east side of
it. To its west were the stables, an earlier structure of June 1801,
latterly becoming a row of cottages (the roof having been raised) behind
a tall slab wall. Of all the buildings the Workshops in the south-east
corner were the largest, and the Foundry of 1832 with its stumpy,
tapering square chimney stack stood to the west of it. Unseen and
underground beneath it, flowed the Afon Galedffrwd which drove two
waterwheels, (the smaller installed in 1906). The 1907–1912 extended
apron of ground – surrounded by a high slab wall – to the north-east of
the workshop buried the Capel Curig Turnpike Trust's road which ran
under the east wall of the Workshop; the 1906 waterwheel is almost
over the site of that highway which was diverted to north and east to
accommodate the growth of the Works.

The other waterwheel, erected in 1846 and extant 1985, is against the
east wall of Felin-Fawr Mill, being 20 ft diameter and overshot from
the same underground river, fed by pipes whose entry is upstream from
the Works. There was a second Slab Mill called Felin-Fach opened in
March 1846 between this wheel and the west side of the Workshops, to
deal with the increased flow of slabs from the new Quarry pits. This
huddle could not be compared with the military-style workshop complex at Dinorwic Quarry (Gilfach-Ddu) and it is curious that no attempt

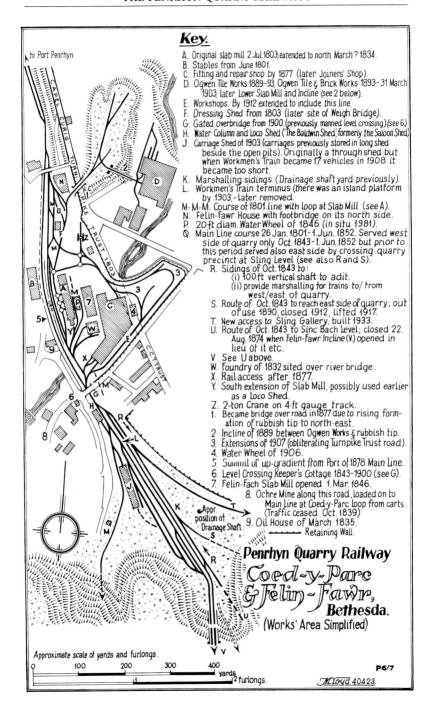

to Port Penrhyn

Key.

A. Original slab mill 2.Jul.1803; extended to north March? 1834.
B. Stables from June 1801.
C. Fitting and repair shop by 1877 (later Joiners' Shop).
D. Ogwen Tile Works 1889-93, Ogwen Tile & Brick Works 1893-31 March 1903, later Lower Slab Mill and Incline (see 2 below).
E. Workshops. By 1912 extended to include this line.
F. Dressing Shed from 1803 (later site of Weigh Bridge).
G. Gated overbridge from 1900. (previously manned level crossing)(see 6.)
H. Water Column and Loco Shed ('The Baldwin Shed', formerly the Saloon Shed.)
J. Carriage Shed of 1903 (carriages previously stored in long shed beside the open pits). Originally a through shed but when Workmen's Train became 17 vehicles in 1908 it became too short.
K. Marshalling sidings. (Drainage shaft yard previously).
L. Workmen's Train terminus (there was an island platform by 1903, - later removed.
M-M-M. Course of 1801 line with loop at Slab Mill (see A).
N. Felin-Fawr House with footbridge on its north side.
P. 20ft diam. Water Wheel of 1846 (in situ 1981).
Q. Main Line course 26 Jan.1801-1.Jun.1852. Served west side of quarry only Oct.1843-1.Jun.1852 but prior to this period served also east side by crossing quarry precinct at Sling Level (see also R and S).
R. Sidings of Oct.1843 to:
   (i) 100ft vertical shaft to adit.
   (ii) provide marshalling for trains to/from west/east of quarry.
S. Route of Oct.1843 to reach east side of quarry; out of use 1890, closed 1912, lifted 1917.
T. New access to Sling Gallery, built 1933.
U. Route of Oct.1843 to Sinc Bach level; closed 22. Aug.1874 when Felin-Fawr Incline (V.) opened in lieu of it etc..
V See U above.
W. Foundry of 1832 sited over river bridge.
X. Rail access after 1877.
Y. South extension of Slab Mill, possibly used earlier as a Loco Shed.
Z. 2-ton Crane on 4-ft gauge track.
1. Became bridge over road in 1877 due to rising formation of rubbish tip to north-east.
2. Incline of 1889 between Ogwen Works & rubbish tip.
3. Extensions of 1907 (obliterating Turnpike Trust road).
4. Water Wheel of 1906.
5. Summit of up-gradient from Port of 1878 Main Line.
6. Level Crossing Keeper's Cottage 1843-1900 (see G).
7. Felin-Fach Slab Mill opened 1. Mar. 1846.
8. Ochre Mine along this road, loaded on to Main Line at Coed-y-Parc loop from carts. (Traffic ceased Oct.1839)
9. Oil House of March 1835.
———— Retaining Wall.

Appr. position of Drainage Shaft

Penrhyn Quarry Railway
Coed~y~Parc
& Felin~Fawr,
Bethesda.
(Works' Area Simplified)

Approximate scale of yards and furlongs.

0   100   200   300   400

yards. 2 furlongs.

P6/7

M.Lloyd 40423.

succeeded to replace it, this being due to the ability to carry out some Quarry and railway repair work at the locomotive sheds on Red Lion Level where limited workshop facilities were available. It is a comment on the commanding position of Penrhyn in the trade that the elementary surroundings in which all estate construction and mainten- ance was carried out, was sufficient unto the day.

The foregoing was a yard criss-crossed by Works tramlines, a weighbridge near the main line on the west side, a lifting 2-ton gantry crane of 1912 on 4 ft gauge rails to the east, all on a site where in earlier times the Railroad had its buildings and business. Whilst the Railroad had driven almost due south-to-north over the area and buildings were to arise on either side, their extent was limited by rising ground to the west and the turnpike at a lower level on the east – the later Railway was taken in a slow right hand curve between the stables and the 1803 Mill, much to the west of the old line.

This was an oasis of industry for almost three-quarters of a century before it was matched by similar facilities coming into that part of the county: in a fire in 1952 the Fitting and Joiners' Shops were destroyed.

The water-powered weighing machine of 1840–76 was a conven- tional weighing table but incorporated a device which drew a train forward a wagon-length each time and paused whilst each wagon stood on the weigh-plate. (The 1864 Port machine was similar, but employed steam in place of water power.)

THE QUARRY

"Five or six terraces of great extent rise above one another on the side of the mountain; along these swarm men, machines, trains of an hundred waggons attached together and rolling rapidly along the iron railways . . ."

So wrote an early spectator whilst almost a full century later came:

"There is no likelihood of slipping by the Penrhyn slate quarries without ample evidence of their existence. Half the side of the mountain seems to have been sliced away and robbed, with mammoth terraces along which men and trucks go crawling like a host of busy ants . . ."

The Penrhyn Quarry has ever been a spectacle, (its many forms of railway use, motive power and civil engineering spanning the whole era of railways) a stadium where first, temporary portable lines allowed sleds carrying perhaps only one immense slab – loaded thereon by simple three-legged derrick – to be hand-propelled from quarry face. Then, according to situation, overhead wire hoists ('Blondins') or incline or hydraulic hoist might lift vehicles – containing either good rock or rubbish – to a higher level to reach the Mills or the rubbish tip according to load. Slab won from upper levels might descend by incline to join such vehicles at the Mills from whence emerged the finished

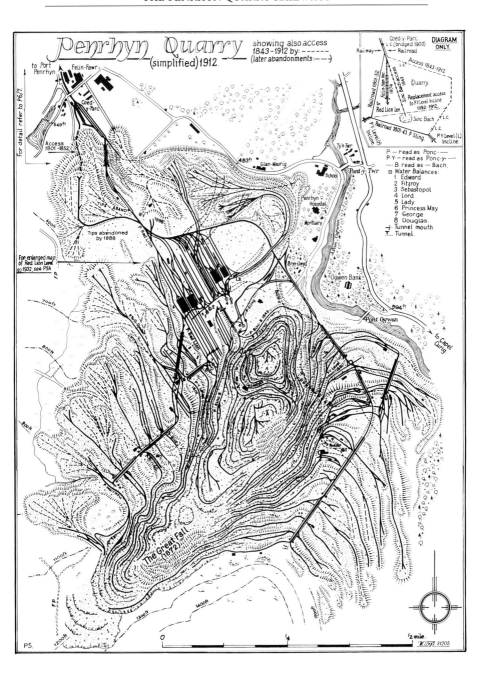

Penrhyn Quarry (simplified) 1912.
showing also access
1843-1912 by: ------
(later abandonments:----->)

DIAGRAM ONLY

Coed-y-Parc
L.C (bridged 1900)
Railway ----> Railroad
Access 1843-1912
Railroad 1801-52
Felin-fawr Inc.
1874
Sinc Bach Access
1843
Quarry.
Replacement access
to P.Y. Level Incline
1852-1912.
to
Red Lion Lev
P.Y. Level
Incline (1)
Railroad 1801-43 P. Sling
Sinc Bach
L.C.
L.C.
P.Y. Level (L)
Incline.

P. – read as Ponc –
P.Y.– read as Ponc-y-
B – read as Bach.
Water Balances:
1 Edward
2 Fitzroy
3 Sebastopol
4 Lord
5 Lady
6 Princess May
7 George
8 Douglas.
Tunnel mouth.
T... Tunnel.

to Port Penrhyn
Felin-Fawr
Coed-y-Parc
For detail refer to P6/7.
549 ft
Access 1801-1852

483 ft
Glan-Meurig
Ty'n-Twr
School
Pont-y-Twr
Penrhyn Hospital
Mortuary
Tips abandoned by 1888
Bryn-Llwyd
For enlarged map of Red Lion Level (c) 1932, see P5A
Ogwen Bank
394 ft
Pont Ogwen
to Capel Curig
600 ft
700 ft
800 ft
800 ft
The Great Fall (1872)
1100 ft
1300 ft
1400 ft
1200 ft
FP

P.5.

0   1/4   1/2 mile.
M.J.T.Lewis 31205

product, again on the railway; slates loaded in slate wagons destined for the head of Felin-Fawr Incline would be lowered to the Railway and thence to be taken to the Port; rubbish carried away for disposal, either on the edge of Red Lion Level or up by incline to a convenient upper floor for tipping there. Geology and geography combined to make the location a pertinent factor in the viability of the undertaking.

Rubbish wagons lifted by incline would be made up into trains at the required Level, and after passing over a weighing table en route, hauled to the end of the tip where there was a release loop for the locomotive; then by individual man-handling, each wagon was pushed against a stop block to shoot its contents through its open end, and down the tip – occasionally the wagon followed its contents. Re-assembled, the train returned empty to the incline head and wagons descended to their proper Departments, each marked with identification to that end.

Over the decades the Quarry worked downwards into pits below the true ground level, or upwards in terraces or galleries to form an amphitheatre round the mountainside, but the pits could only be extended downwards, for to work outwards would invite collapse of the workings above; drainage of the lowest workings was by tunnel. The depth of the Quarry was usually given as 1,140 ft with 19 galleries. Above, each Level might be extended into a working face at the one end, perhaps with clearly defined galleries as the Level matured; at its other end it would debouch on to a tip. Levels were linked by inclines, but their pattern was spasmodic and labour-intensive. Each Level had its own railway system, almost independent except for coal supplies which came from the Port and thence up the attendant inclines: the Level's rail system would extend, if need be, from Quarry face to tip-end. As rubbish grew nine times faster than the end-product, most of the railway system was required simply to clear it away. Rubbish tips grew to immense size and their tramways ever longer whilst an increased number of locomotives was allocated to it. Some Levels had their own small Mill but the large cluster of Mills on Red Lion was the nerve-centre of this work. Where steam locomotives worked there was an engine shed, slab water tank (inside the shed to keep it frost free), facilities for small repairs, including a pit and lifting beam, and the inevitable weigh house out on the tip. There would also be a 'Caban' or Mess Room; coal to warm these buildings came up with the locomotive supply.

Following World War I, motive power on some Levels was of considerable variety working in close proximity: there might be found man-power, horse (up to 1928), steam, petrol or diesel traction. Before May 1828 horses were employed 'unofficially' but then about 24 were used to haul rubbish: there were 32 by 1851 then some were taken away to work the Railroad. In the 1890s only 8 remained but they hauled complete trains on Red Lion until 20th November, 1900. On the Levels the horses were owned by the men who worked the rubbish; for this they were given a special allowance for food and grooming, and charged a reduced rate at the Quarry's blacksmith's shops. Before steam was brought in to work the rubbish banks, man-power was intensive; pictures taken before World War I show four men to a rubbish wagon (obviously worked individually as there were no couplings), tilting it sideways off the line to discharge the load.

In this vast crater all the customary features of railways were crammed together: as the giant hole moved slowly southwards and clawed into the mountain, so behind it on the north side its excreta buried the earlier works.

Steam first came into the Quarry in 1876, and petrol-engined rail tractors in 1932 being light enough for new working faces and weak galleries; diesel tractors replaced these Coed-y-Parc-built petrol units during World War II when part of the Quarry was taken over by the Ministry of Supply.

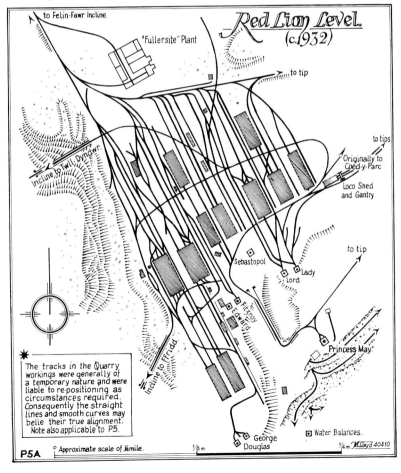

to Felin-Fawr Incline.

"Fullersite" Plant

Red Lion Level
(c.1932)

to tip

to tips

Incline to Twll Dyndwr

Originally to Coed-y-Parc

Loco Shed and Gantry

to tip

Sebastopol

Lady

Lord

Fitzroy Edward

Incline to Ffridd.

Princess May.

The tracks in the Quarry workings were generally of a temporary nature and were liable to re-positioning as circumstances required. Consequently the straight lines and smooth curves may belie their true alignment. Note also applicable to P5.

Water Balances.

George Douglas

P5A Approximate scale of ⅛mile. ⅛ m ¼ m M.Lloyd 40410

The Railroad, in a final 'pincer' movement, had gained the Quarry from both west and east; from 1801–52 the first route served Ponc Sling Level by incline and the foot of Ponc-y-Level (Right and Left) Inclines.

Next, in 1843, a line was brought round the east side from Coed-y-Parc and again by incline reached the same height. It enjoyed diminishing importance as the Quarry evolved and was disused before closure in 1912, and lifting in 1917, whilst sixty years before, the last part of the western access had been abandoned (1852); its farthest extremeties had gone as early as 1843, when made redundant by the new eastern approach of that year, and much good slate was lying beneath its course. A new access to an extended foot of the Ponc-y-Level (Right) Incline existed 1852–1912, taken off that same eastern approach. All these sites are long lost. In 1843 a direct, then all-level, route into Hen-Waelod (Sinc Bach), to re-open old pits was created and ultimately served the several pits in the core of the excavation. Sinc Bach Level opened 1843 in consequence. From 1865 came the creation of a basic plateau Level (Red Lion) formed from the rubbish from the pits on which mills, offices, workshops, apprentices' sheds, engine sheds and so on, would rise – at first it was linked by bridge to the hydraulic hoists: this Level had no actual quarrying sites, and a new railway linked its mills to the head of the new direct Felin-Fawr Incline with 70 ft fall (not counter-balanced but worked by a continuous chain) which dropped to the head of what soon became the new Railway. It could be said that the Red Lion link was a Quarry-extension of the main line; it rose by 10 ft from the mills to the incline head (so it was said) to prevent runaway vehicles going over the top of Felin-Fawr. This new Red Lion Level swept away the small 'Richard Pennant' Quarrymen's Chapel of 1812; buried too, was the comparatively young Sinc Bach access line of 1843 and by 1874 this plateau had, like a lava stream, crept northwards to reach the back gardens of households at Coed-y-Parc.

It remains to mention a scheme commenced in 1933 with great optimism to ease the loadings on Felin-Fawr Incline and bring the trains from Ponc Sling round to Felin-Fawr without using Red Lion Level: this new route was brought round the eastern and northern edges of the rubbish tips to join the main line at the foot of Felin-Fawr Incline and it helped to employ labour during the depression of the early 1930s, but it never proved an operating success for even with considerable clearance the route was too sharply curved and trains frequently left the rails.

Levels' names reflected dates, humour, marriages or characters: Ceiling (once the highest Level), Garret (the once penultimate Level), Sebastopol (dated 1854), Agor Boni (after Napoleon at the time of the French Wars), Twlldyndwr ('Thunder Water Hole') – a name found in many quarries – or William Parry. Inclines took their names from

Levels: formerly balance-worked, many became electrically-driven when in 1912 The North Wales Power & Traction Co. reached the district. A consequence of 'The Great Fall' was that many Levels were severed thereafter.

The eight hydraulic hoists on Red Lion Level (the first of 1852) were counter-balanced by an ever-abundant water supply, and like the inclines/levels, took names from contemporary Levels. The nearby hydraulic inclines of Ponc-Twrch and Ponc-Twlldyndwr (on the Left Side) carried rubbish wagons upwards yet further from the hoists.

There were approximately 23 miles of 'main line' on the Levels and a possible total Quarry mileage of 50; how some physical rail connections where inclines on slab embankments bridged Levels were made is not known. Unproven too are sites of many former landmarks and buildings in the Quarry. Initially, galleries were begun at vertical distances 30 ft apart; this was later amended to 60 ft.

Confusingly, 'The Quarry' meant the whole site except Red Lion, but if the Works (with a language of its own) sent a 'loco to the Quarry' it might mean it was sent to Red Lion (for work, or storage)! Until 1912 the Quarry was divided into nine Districts (District 10 was the Port), a District being an area of rock face usually incorporating three Levels: for further complication, certain Levels might have four names, depending on age and location.

Figures issued in 1933 illustrated the convincing economy of steam haulage: (the terms are as published).

Plant & Machinery	Performance per ton/mile	Wage Cost per ton/mile	Power & Maintenance per ton/mile	Total Cost per ton/mile
Loco – steam	117 tons	.007d	.039d	.046d
Loco – petrol	40 tons	.032d	.019d	.051d
Inclined Plane	60 tons	.016d	.037d	.053d
Hydraulic Shaft	71 tons	.121d	.203d	.324d
Aerial Ropeway	11 tons	.247d	.261d	.508d

TRACKWORK: FROM RAILROAD TO RAILWAY

All the older, isolated Welsh railways had their own vernacular, adopting English words created by the industrial revolution.

The variety of pointwork both on the main line and inside the Quarry was notable; the switch-bladed turnout found on railways all over the world was almost non-existent there being only half a dozen examples on the main line. Most turnouts were of the movable stock rail type, or stub-switch operated by a single lever, and dubbed a 'Shifting Set'. Occasionally a fixed turnout was sufficient if vehicles trailed over it;

this was a 'Dumb Set': a 'Passbye' allowed vehicles to pass each other on a loop.

In the Quarry, unique to Penrhyn, portable tracks which ran up to the working face and built in 1½ in. diam. round bar were known as 'T. H. Rails' after Thomas Hughes, the inventor and the foreman platelayer. A primitive turnout found in the Quarry was a pair of lifting rails the ends of which could be laid over the adjacent lines; 'ears' or 'spoons' projecting downwards at the loose end, secured them to the fixed track. Such crude equipment would only support a wagon: these were 'Spoon Points'.

Such were the gradients on the system that gradients of less than 1 in 100 were ignored and deemed to be 'Level'!

Concerning the track itself, it is convenient to separate the main line from the Quarry, never overlooking that (for instance) odd survivals of track at the Quarry might be obsolete equipment taken from the main line: some materials were peculiar to the Quarry and never served the main line.

The Tyn-y-Clwt Deviation of 1870 – the first portion of Railroad to be converted to Railway – was worked by locomotive from the first, but the adjacent lengths of old Railroad were also a part of that locomotive-worked line and embodied Railroad materials of 1801. Their strength might have been sufficient for the short period in which this era lived (1876–79) and for light engines acquired initially, but not to later motive power. The Railroad materials (developed as from 1801 to 1879) continued to suffice for the horse section between Dinas Incline foot and the Port which remained a tramroad until abandonment in 1879.

Phase I (to 1832)

The short elliptically-sectioned rails were first supplied from Coalbrookdale Foundry [William Fawcett (Lydia Ann Street, Liverpool)] per Samuel Worthington (The Coalbrookdale Co. (of Abram Darby) had sold this business to Fawcett in 1790.) in cast-iron, later to be replaced by wrought-iron; later, a wrought-iron rail of 'T' section with a flange or bulb along one side of the foot to give strength, commonly found in other parts of North Wales displaced it; this in turn gave way to the familiar flat-bottomed or Vignoles rail, albeit of some curious sections but still in wrought-iron. Then, (outside the period of this phase) came the new Railway with steel rails. The first rails were 4 ft 6 in. long and according to Wyatt's contemporary account, were carried on wooden sleepers; these were replaced by cast-iron sills which in due course gave way to slate-slab. Both wooden and slab sleepers had primitive chairs affixed to them; thus the elliptical rails were supported by three generations of sleeper, each with shortcomings. The 'T' rails which followed were laid in a cast-iron sleeper combined with chairs and this form lasted in the Quarry until closure and was the last to use

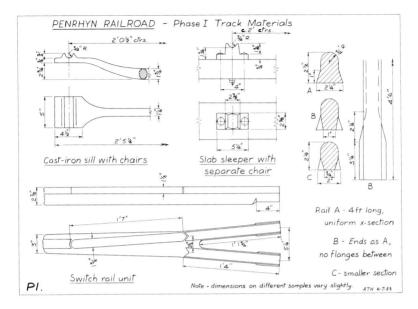

iron sleepers, all subsequent trackwork being laid on wood.

Certain small details of the early days have never been explained. Some or all of the first rails were cast with an iron 'foot' at each end which was 'dovetailed' into the original wooden sleepers by pushing it into the slot and there abutting with the adjacent rail, the joint being formed inside the timbering: this is the usual interpretation given to the drawing in Tredgold (pp.24–25). Weaknesses must have been apparent, for cast-iron sills began to appear in 1803, the 'foot' being slid into a light 'jaw' or chair to receive it in the same way as the wooden sleeper.[46] However, the sleeper was formed by a tiebar of flat 'U' section which could be buried beneath the earth, only the outer ends appearing above the surface to carry the rails, and these had the appearance of 'pads' at each end: there were several forms of this sill. The foot cast on the rail end was 3 in. long but before long the rail was redesigned with the foot extending the full length of the rail, so giving increased strength. These sills were not an innovation but only new to North Wales – they were already in use in the Blaenavon area of Monmouthshire and in Glamorganshire before 1790; here they often carried plate rather than edge rails, due to the influence of Benjamin Outram.

The principle of the rounded rail was long known, but not in the Penrhyn form: in earlier times tree trunks provided 'round rails' upon which crude wheels with double flanges could be run and which showed much mechanical advantage over road wheels. This system was widely used on logging railways and to obtain further adhesion by a

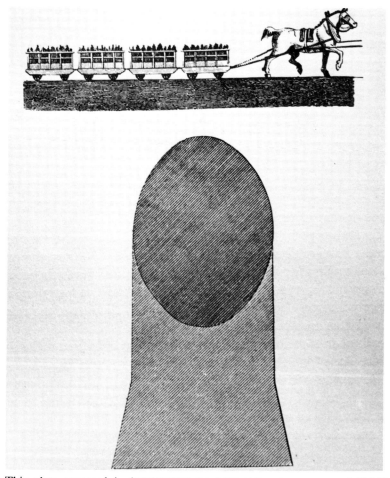

This plate appeared in 'REPERTORY OF ARTS AND MANUFACTURES' Vol.iii (Second Series) of 1803 and shows 'Artist's Impression' of First Phase slate wagons and oval rail in chair.

steam locomotive running over it, the inside of the wheel surface was cleated! Furthermore the rounded rail (as opposed to a square section bar often found in Monmouthshire) produced less friction, and if used by wagons with double-flanged wheels which ran loosely on their axles, strict adherence to gauge was a secondary matter and track maintenance costs were reduced.

The drawbacks of the Penrhyn system were not then known i.e. that in time the wear inside the concave rims would cause the wheels to fit more tightly on to the rail heads, and to bind. However, these rails served until the end of the 1820s and were ultimately cast in several lengths viz: 2 ft, 2 ft 3 in., 3 ft, 3 ft 6 in., 4 ft, and 6 ft (such have been found) the last-named requiring an intermediate supporting sleeper. To counteract this wear a flat top to the elliptical-sectioned rail was introduced in 1807 – all these rails weighed about 23 lb./yard – laid in cast-iron sills (which had replaced the wooden dovetailed-joint sleepers); the sills however only weighed about 12 lb. and were comparatively weak, possibly accounting for the three variations in pattern discovered. A variety of wider 'chair' was used for butt-jointing where 6 ft rail lengths were used.

A number of sills was unearthed by the writer in the 1940s and each was found to have a small slab inserted under each end to increase the bearing surface, and recessed along three edges to receive the sill end. These sills proved wanting, for by 1820 they were being replaced by a heavy sleeper cut in one piece from slate slab and roughly dressed along the edges, the upper surface being left as won from the rock but recessed at each end to carry a separate cast-iron chair. The chairs[47] were shaped as a saddle into which the rail was dropped fairly loosely, a feature of the design which is as yet not fully clear but the method was clearly sufficient unto the day. The chair base was usually 5¼ in. × 3 in. (with 2½ in. height) but there was a variety with wider saddle presumably to accept butt-jointing in which case the rails could have had the end of the foot removed (certain survivals suggest this was done). A countersunk bolt projected downwards from the chair, passed through a clearance hole in the slab sleeper and was provided with a threaded end of mongrel dimensions and secured by a nut ("Whitworth" was as yet unknown!). Projecting downwards also and flanking this bolt were two shorter lugs (occasionally loose dowels were used; such pattern had a chair width of 2½ in.) which engaged roughly in matching holes in the sleeper to hold the chair 'squarely'. The sleepers were crudely smashed to suitable lengths but were of average cross-section 7 in. × 3 in. In April 1952 a point casting was discovered which fitted these old cast-iron rails.

The gauge of Phase I track cannot be stated precisely; it was approximately 24½ in. measured over the rail centres and this dimension is given in records dated 1806. However, slab sleepers checked in the writer's 1943–6 fieldwork showed a centre-centre variance from less than 24 in. to a full 24 in. – and no more. Of course with the system in use dimensional exactitude in materials was not necessary and the gauge was determined in the first place by the use of the 'cart' type wagons' bodies which were placed on chassis between the wheels . . . a legacy of the Llandegai Tramway period about whose track there is no certainty.

It is fortunate that like the Dinorwic Railway, Penrhyn also was visited by two Prussian mining engineers in 1826–27, Messrs Carl Von Oyenhausen and Heinrich Von Dechem. They were not impressed!

'RAILWAYS IN ENGLAND – Observations made on a journey in the years 1826 and 1827' (Berlin 1829) had this to say:

> The railway is neither well laid nor specially well maintained, but is used only for the transport of slate, the loads of which cannot be very great and involves no costly outlay.
>
> The gauge of the railway is 24 in. The rails are 3 ft long, and differ from any of those previously described, but are of much poorer construction; the cross-section is an ellipse 1¾ in. high and 1¼ in. wide. At each end is a 4 in. long piece of the rail 2¼ in. high and at the bottom straight and 1¾ in. wide, which is inserted in a cast-iron chair. These chairs are 8 in. long, 6 in. wide, the baseplate is 1¼ in. thick, and the side walls are 1 in. high: they are joined by cast-iron sleepers. The rails are not fixed very carefully into these; some are merely placed in, but others are fixed by spikes. The cross-sleepers rest on stone sleepers. In the quarry, however, where the railway must often be relaid or lengthened, the rails merely rest on wooden sleepers, in which they are either sunk, or fastened by spikes driven in on both sides of the rail. *[One is bound to ask why the authors do not mention the slab sleepers which are known to have been introduced five years beforehand.]*

Phase II (1832–1849)

Though the weaknesses of Phase I track were soon manifest, it was 1832 before steps were taken to replace it; perhaps the repeal of Slate Tax with consequent increased business led to improvements or perhaps the shortcomings of the materials were not as great as suggested, for the neighbouring Dinorwic Railway built about 1825 used a very similar track from the outset (including the elliptical rails).

In 1832 management placed a bulk order for 'T' section wrought-iron rails in 15 ft lengths; the head resembled a round bar in section, with a flat flange attached, that flange having a rib along one bottom edge and there were several variations in the section; the rails were parallel not fishbellied, and the weight was almost the same as the elliptical rails replaced. Ten years later a further order was given, but in 24 ft lengths; this latter not only found its way into the main line but was used in the Quarry for the first time. The Railroad inclines however, remained unrelaid to the end and certain lines in the Port also. This new rail was carried on a development of the earlier sills, being a flat cast unit with chairs cast integrally having the jaws outlined to receive the 'T' rail with the lower flange facing inwards and having an iron key driven in on the outer face to secure the rail inside the chair. Most of these were supplied by outside foundries but one lot was cast at Coed-y-Parc. There were several patterns of the combination and many survived in the Quarry to the end . . . it was a popular form of track; a wider unit (4½ in. across) did duty for butt-joints and weighed 62 lb., the carrying equivalent being narrower weighed 40 lb. There were clearly problems where rails of differing section were jointed in differing profiles of chair and many surviving rail ends have been chamfered for 2 in. to make them fit. (In 1939 the author was told that long after this track was outdated on the main line it was eagerly sought for in the Quarry, and probably all the main line material once discarded found a second home in the workings. For the latter purpose a chair was cast and widely used in the Quarry to hold the 'T' rail to wooden sleepers.)

Phase III (1849–1883)

The 'T' rail of Phase II was best suited to horse-drawn lines and also to be found on the Croesor, Gorseddau, feeder lines of the Festiniog, the Cedryn Tramway and in many other places in North Wales where the narrow gauge had a footing. At Penrhyn its life on the main line was comparatively short for in 1849 the first of five weights of flat-bottomed rail was introduced.[48] The first four sections were in wrought-iron and the last in rolled steel viz:

1849	18 lb./yd.	Length 21 ft.		Used in partial relaying of main line
1876	30 "	"	21 ?	Used on Tyn-y-Clwt Deviation but may have been laid earlier between Felin-Fawr Incline top and along Red Lion Level into the Quarry
c1877	28 "	"	21 ?	Laid into new Penrhyn Railway but proved too light
1878	44 "	"	24	Laid in new Penrhyn Railway below Dinas Incline top
1883	43 "	"	?	Probably used only in Quarry

All the foregoing was laid on wooden sleepers approximately 4 ft 6 in. long × 10 in. × 5 in. deep and was dogspiked thereto.

Phase IV (from 1887)

When CHARLES, the first of the main line locomotives specially designed for the Railway, arrived in 1883, its weight was almost double that of the introductory types, being 12¼ tons in working order; ten years it later was followed by two more locomotives of the same weight and pattern. From this time singly-flanged wheels were adopted for locomotives and wagons: the existing line, laid in 28 lb./yd flat-bottomed rails, was wholly inadequate to bear the weight of such stock. It is a measure of the profitability of the undertaking that locomotives, stock and replacement track were all funded within a short time; the metamorphosis was completed by orders for double-headed steel rails (50 lb./yd) placed in 1887, 1891 and 1909, sufficient material to replace all the flat-bottomed rail in the main line and leave enough surplus for rail renewals. The chairs weighed 31 lb. each having 2-fixing holes (1887), the 1891 pattern being heavier at 42 lb. with 4 holes; these were pinned to wooden sleepers originally 4 ft 6 in. long (but later 4 ft 3 in.) × 10 in. × 5 in. deep. Rails were secured in chairs with elm keys (3 lb. each) driven from the outside according to the best main line practice of the day. The securing pins had chisel ends and were driven in by hammer: in due course many of these were replaced by coach screws. Rails and chairs were bought through agents but in later years Coed-y-Parc cast its own chairs. There was an odd batch of 3-hole chairs; these were to be found in the Tregarth passing loop and were untypical; some survive in the display at the Penrhyn Castle Museum.

The Felin-Fawr Incline which linked the Quarry with the south end of the main line had British Standard 3066 flat-bottomed rails laid on longitudinal sleepers 9 in. × 4½ in. secured to cross members by flanging plates – an unique arrangement.

A summary table of rails (dimensions, where known, in inches) collates all the foregoing:

Rail		Weight lb./yd	Height in.	Head Width in.	Base Width in.
1800	Elliptical (cast-iron)	23	1¾ (later batches 2 in. & 2¼ in.)	1¼ (later batches 1½ in.)	—
1807–9	Elliptical flat top (cast-iron)	20–23			
1832 &	'T' bulb (wrought-iron)	22	2½	1½	¾
1842		(some only	2	1¼	½)
1849	Flat-bottom (wrought-iron)	18	2½	1½	2
1876	″ ″	30	2½	1½	3
c1877	″ ″	28	3	1½	3
1878	″ ″	44	3	1½	3
1883	Flat-bottom (steel)	43	(used in Quarry only)		
?	Flat-bottom (wrought-iron)	c16	2	1	1¼
	found at Quarry Outfall – original place of usage uncertain. (Does not conform to any known order.)				
From 1887 Double or Bullhead (steel)		50	4½	2⅛	1¾

Sleepers as just described; these were at first wooden, then a sill type in cast-iron incorporating the chair, then (1820) made in slab to carry separate cast chairs. Next Coed-y-Parc cast sleepers incorporating the style of separate chair used on the slabs of 1820-on of which a wider pattern carried the butt-jointed rails. For a long period the main line was carried on slab or these cast sleeper combinations so that when 'T' rails came in 1832 Coed-y-Parc cast a new pattern of sill with chairs to accommodate them. In due course all the main line (save inclines) was laid in 'T' rail on these sills (inclines remained in elliptical rails with slab sleepers, as before-stated).

There was no sophisticated method of joining rails until 1878 when with the introduction of heavier flat-bottomed rails the four-bolt fish-plates came; before that rail ends were simply butted together.[49] Fishplates were either flat plate or, (with the double-headed rail) Spooner & Huddart flanged type . . . Spooner influence was obvious on the eventual track! By 1878 creosoted wooden sleepers were spaced at 2 ft 7 in. centres (i.e. 9 per rail length) one being sited under the joint; with bull-head rails the joint sleeper of earlier rail forms was discarded, sleepers shortened by 3 in. and laid at 2 ft 9 in. centres – they were 'sawn to L.N.W.R. section'.

The purchasing agents were wholesalers Benjamin Gibson of Liverpool and the first four miles of the new Railway materials came through them: the characters cast on the first batch of (2 hole) chairs were 'WP & Co 1887' and may be William Preston & Co. of Birkenhead. Coed-y-Parc supplied subsequent chair requirements.

Ballast was obtained from small screen slate chippings, boiler ash or from the gravel pit at Felin-Hen. In the Festiniog Railway archives is an undated drawing by J. S. Hughes for an oak former to set out super-elevation on P.Q.R. curves.

Instances of specific major trackwork

The replacement with flat-topped elliptical rails from 1809 until Coed-y-Parc made the last batch in 1832 must be regarded as having postponed the day for wholesale replacement of the Wyatt track. The original oval rails were found further use as fencing posts and slab wall re-inforcement where specimens still survive, but one with the significant 'dovetail' does not (though there were samples in the Battersby Collection built up with the writer in the mid-1940s).

The light 18 lb. flat-bottomed rails of 1849 were put into the main line between Tyn-y-Clwt and Coed-y-Parc – a short distance; the almost twice-heavier following batch went into the new Tyn-y-Clwt Deviation of 1876 – there is a hint that this came from the short Red Lion Level length in the Quarry leading to Felin-Fawr Incline top; if so credit must go to the Quarry for having the first instalment of modern material! The next batch of c. 1877 weighing 27 lb. went into the main line but was hopelessly light, so 350 tons of 44 lb. were ordered through Gibson on 9th March, 1878 to the Railway's own special section, being delivered the following October from (and made at), Newport, Monmouthshire . . . the same foundry had sent a small quantity of 30 lb. the previous May. The 44 lb. rails formed the new Railway then building west from near Dinas Incline top, but Tregarth passing loop and Felin-Hen gravel pit sidings were laid in 30 lb. If the Red Lion Level had in fact been robbed of its heavy rails in 1876 (see above) their replacements were short-lived as this section was now relaid using some of the 44 lb. rail of 1878, but around and within the cutting sheds 30 lb. sufficed. Actual deliveries from Newport proved to be 380 tons and 31 tons of each. As locomotives were taking over from horses within the Quarry, in 1883 the last flat-bottomed rails (in rolled steel) ordered were destined for use there; they were the heaviest yet at 43 lb.

In 1887 Gibsons received an order for 314 tons of double-headed steel rails, nominally 50 lb. but actually 48 lb., which were delivered in May to replace worn flat-bottomed rail in the main line; the latter was placed both at the Port (where the layout was being revised) and between Coed-y-Parc and the foot of Coed-y-Parc Incline; on the main line they were first laid where curves and gradients were most adverse. In the period 26th May–26th October, 1887 the permanent way gang under Thomas Roberts laid 8,113 yards of this new material, involving an entirely new technique for them. This was done mainly at weekends and in evenings so as not to interfere with the traffic and covering over 4½ miles of the total 6 miles 5½ chains of main line. In July 1891 200 tons of bull-head rails came from The Darlington Iron & Steel Co. Ltd. of Middlesbrough for the main line and the last of the flat-bottomed rail disappeared. The Red Lion Level main line – a regular victim of change – lost its four-year-laid flat-bottomed rails too when this material replaced it – this was the first chaired track in the Quarry. So a fine railway with modern track from Port right into the Mills in the Quarry came into being.

A further delivery in May 1909 of the 1891 section was made by Guest, Keen & Nettlefold Ltd., Newport costing £1,064 12s. 11d. but not paid for until 9th November – nice credit terms for the purchaser! This was principally for a length of line approaching the Port which was not only worn but flood damaged; it was laid in after overhaul of the Afon Cegin bridge (L.N.W.R. No. 4) in July–August 1911. Within four years this batch was exhausted.

The foregoing comprise the major relaying works, but take no account of the continuing renewals on a casual basis; these would tend to decrease as traffic slackened with the fall in trade. There was a wholesale renewal of sleepers 1923–24, many replacements of standard gauge (L.M.S.R.) sources together with redundant material from the Point of Air (sometimes Ayr) Colliery, Flintshire – such sleepers can be cut in half-length. Heavier patterns of chair from Coed-y-Parc replaced the smaller ones as they broke. (In 1945, for example, in the vicinity of Cegin Pool the standard gauge rails were 'Crewe 1903 Steel' while the Penrhyn also used standard gauge rails carried in chairs of L.N.W.R. or 'C.L.C. 1937' pattern! Hereabouts P.Q.R. rails were mostly double-headed 'Dowlais Steel 1887', with clasp fishplates.)

Pointwork on the main line

The use of wagons with double flanges from the outset made it impossible to use the conventional turnout embodying one or two blades to guide single-flanged vehicles into a new direction; instead the method was to move a section of the track bodily from side to side . . . theoretically to any number of desired positions. To achieve this a pair of rails was not connected to the adjoining track at the chosen point of divergence; instead, the loose ends were moved across, pivoted by varying methods at their other ends, until they were clear of the rail ends opposite which they had begun their movement. Another pair of rails received them and vehicles could be thus run off in a new direction by means of the adjoining pair of rails. If the switch rails were short the sideways movement might be over something of a 'dog leg' at the pivoting position, but longer switch rails provided a better path; however this form of point, sometimes known as 'Fothergill'[50] or 'stub' pattern as opposed to 'blade' pattern was basically somewhat crude and only suitable for low speeds. This point could be made up in any rail section and though suited to both single- and double-flanged wheels, is seldom found where single-flanged wheels predominate. At the crossing of rails (erroneously, the 'frog') there was a movable loose rail; a more sophisticated pattern embodied a base casting and a loose rail – the casting included a pair of sockets at each end made in the form of a 'V' to receive the short rail end – similar castings allowed a pair of individually pivoted switch rails to match up to the turnout rails. On the main line and on principal quarry tracks the 'Fothergill' point was developed so that a single point lever – often moving inside a simple framework into which it might be pinned and padlocked in position – could operate both switch and crossing rails with one set of rodding. The rodding was carried on the end of the sleepers which were secured from movement by bolting disused 'T' rails side-down in the form of tiebars along the sleeper ends to hold them rigidly.

At Tregarth loop and siding, at the first point approaching the Port and within the Port (on the flagstaff loop), some conventional blade-type pointwork was installed, supplied by The Isca Foundry, Newport; for Tregarth this firm also supplied point-levers. To assist the maker a quantity of the bull-head rail delivered on 11th August, 1891 was sent to Newport and made into six turnouts later that year. Woe betide thereafter should any double-flanged wagons come down from the Quarry . . . derailment on these Isca points was inevitable!

TRACKWORK IN THE QUARRY

Portable lines

Within the vicinity of the working faces on the galleries a light track which could be moved forward as required was used. Its most predominant form was the 'Hughes track' contrived by Thomas Hughes the foreman platelayer in the Quarry and first used in August 1852 (Hughes was killed in 1887), consisting of wrought-iron bars 1½–1¾ in. diameter and roughly round in section. The bar was elbowed in a short right-angled 'drop' at each end; the downward projection so formed could be pushed down into a wooden or cast-iron 'pad' formed with two adjacent holes for that purpose; thus the end of one bar pushed into the pad would be brought close to the end of the next bar, also having an end in the second hole of the same pad. Not only did this form a crude joint – the space between the bars was short enough to be jumped – but so long as the 'curve' was not excessive, the bars could be laid in a series of doglegs to form a crude curve. This simple form of track was sufficient for hand-operating at the rock face. Some pads had a triangular outline and three holes; by moving the end of a bar across into an empty hole a simple switch was created and a short bar which could be lifted out and placed in a second position, formed the crossing. It was simple but ingenious and may have originated with rough wooden or slab sleepers suitably drilled, which could also maintain the gauge. No intermediate support was given to the bars, many of which were the same elliptical section as the earliest rails, perhaps redundant from the main line. (There is a nice reference in 'THE BANGOR SLATE QUARRIES' (Samuel Hughes) Weales' Quarterly Papers on Engineering Vol. III 1845 p.5.) Early prints of the workings show that barrows were widely used at the rock face and that timber was used for portable track sections.

At some situations 'Hughes' track was joined to 'T' rails; for this purpose some pads were cast having one hole and one slot to take the foot of the 'T' rail.

Other tracks in the Quarry

Where steam engines required it, 50 lb. chaired rail as on the main line was used, but elsewhere bridge and flat-bottomed rails of various weights abounded, further extensive use was made of 'T' rails carried in the combined sleeper and chair sill from Coed-y-Parc; joints were made in the chair and wooden keys secured the rail in all chairs – in its first form iron keys were used – it was widely used throughout the Quarry. Occasionally rails were carried in separate chairs (supplied by the Foundry) pinned to wooden sleepers.

Pointwork was very mixed, having regard to the double-flanged wheels in use. Many patterns of switches and crossings were cast in the Foundry, and most pointwork of this type used only one moving blade in the outer rail – as on street tramways. At crossings the castings might have sections of rail slotted so as to pass the double-flanges, others used the loose short rail before-mentioned and some embodied a tall guide to lead the wheels. A complicated piece of pointwork on Red Lion was dubbed 'The Knitting'; there were thirteen 3-way stub and one bladed point in an area 125 yds × 7 yds with curves of about 6 ft radius!

On the more permanent lines pointwork was of stub pattern built up in 28 lb. flat-bottomed rails in the same manner as those described for the main line.

Flat-bottomed rails were ordered for the Quarry long after they were discarded on the main line, for instance, from Benjamin Gibson (who supplied rails from 1883), and Messrs Henderson & Glass of Glasgow from 1912; contemporarily with the latter Messrs Leslie & Hall of Glasgow supplied from 1906, a second time in 1924 and from then until the ultimate catharsis in 1965.

An undated list of track materials found on certain Levels has survived:–

Gallery Name	Flat-Bottomed Rails	"Thomas Hughes" Rails	Round Rails	Bridge Rails	Wooden Sleepers	Cast-iron Chairs/ Sleepers	Mute Castings	Points
Ponc Smith	0	1813	976	15	–	–	125	1
	789	400	600	38		(and 1 Shifting Set)		
Ponc Blue	200	1862	2212	–	–	–	8	94
	965	422	600					
Twlldyndwr	–	1136	–	–	–	–	–	–
Ponc Level	46	2128	1772	–	–	–	2	86
	0	1136	395					

The lower figure is termed 'Scrap Rail': all rail figures are yardages.

SEMAPHORE SIGNALS

The two semaphores previously described were to be found one at Hen-Durnpike (on a very tall post) and one in front of the central pier of the two-arched road bridge at the Port to face Port-bound trains to assist shunting when the engine had drawn up the main line; this latter signal warned when the level crossing rails of the Penrhyn Railway were not positioned to cross the standard gauge siding – their 'normal' position. Signal posts were painted white, with a black section at the foot; the arms were not identical. The face of the semaphore was formerly divided equally into two colours, red (left hand) and white (right hand) with the metal parts on the right hand end in black. Later, whilst the metal parts remained the same, the face was all white save for a black wide stripe vertically down it in the position conventional for such stripes on main line signals. However, the stripe itself was bordered originally each side by a narrow yellow band; colours from left to right were therefore: white, yellow, black, yellow, white. Latterly the yellow bands were discarded. The arm at Hen-Durnpike was painted the same on both faces and pointed westwards from the post, but the rear of the Port arm was plain white.

LOCOMOTIVES & RAIL TRACTORS

Although the Penrhyn Railroad was, by almost a quarter of a century, earlier than any neighbouring narrow gauge railway, it was comparatively a late comer to introduce locomotives in late 1875. When steam was first tried, some North Wales narrow gauge lines already had steam haulage; among the more notable were Festiniog Railway (July 1863), Talyllyn Railway (1864), Festiniog & Blaenau Railway (1868), Dinorwic Quarry (1870), Gorseddau Junction & Portmadoc Railways Co. (September 1875) the last named owning a de Winton product, others of which had appeared in several quarries before 1875.

A change from horses to steam was urgent and variations of requirement could be read into the three departments to which locomotives were allocated viz: Port, Main Line, Quarry. Above all was the need for greater efficiency of the main line (then a Railroad), for improved methods in the Quarry, to reduce unrest among employees, to meet competition in the industry and also the growing pressures from standard gauge railway companies to tap all quarry areas of North Wales; the time and cost of resistance was considerable.

'The Great Fall' in the Quarry (1872) produced a decision to (a) introduce more efficient methods in the Quarry, and (b) replace the Railroad; the first step was an 1874 order for locomotives for haulage between the Cutting Sheds and the weighing machine at the head of the new Felin-Fawr Incline outlet (opened November 1874).

The decision to use engines was encouraged by C. E. Spooner; to ignore his advice would imperil the viability of the Quarry. It was to be 1875 before the order to Augustus Beatson for GEORGE SHOLTO NO. 3 became reality in the shipment of a more conventional locomotive to the Port on 21st December with trials at Coed-y-Parc ensuing: soon the engine was working between Felin-Fawr Incline foot and the head of Dinas Incline on the first portion of the new Railway to be opened (15th October, 1876). When No. 4 EDWARD SHOLTO was delivered on 16th December, 1876, it replaced No. 3. By this time vertical-boilered engines LORD PENRHYN and LADY PENRHYN had been working the main line Red Lion Level since May and October 1876 respectively and when in May and June 1877 respectively the vertical-boilered GEORGE HENRY and KATIE were delivered for use at the Port (although not initially used there), all departments had been provided with steam power.

BRONLLWYD (formerly COETMOR)

Richard Parry began work on the Tyn-y-Clwt Deviation on 9th March, 1876 and on the new Railway on 18th March, 1878, and a vertical-boilered steam locomotive was used by him. There are no references to this engine in the Penrhyn records, but the insurance record of 1892 refers to it as 'Y ffronllwyd'. It may have been built by Hughes at the Valley Foundry, on Anglesey. Battersby's records state the engine was at first COCTINOR and that earlier reports of it being fitted with a cross-tubed boiler are untrue, but there were syphons to improve the water circulation. When outclassed on the Railway, it was sent to the Quarry as a stationary engine to drive slate-sawing tables. It was scrapped in 1906.

A theory that this may be the same engine, suitably re-gauged, which Brundrit & Co. Ltd.'s granite quarries at Penmaenmawr ran as MONA (but may have found to be too light and returned to de Winton in part-exchange in 1878) requires confirmation, and the dates would require a slight adjustment. Further, the same source suggests the engine may have begun life at Peel Harbour works, I.O.M., 1865–1872.

No. 3 GEORGE SHOLTO

The acquisition of this engine may stem from an enquiry by Mr Augustus Beatson who wrote to Penrhyn saying he was delivering an engine to Dinorwic on 28th July, 1875 and could he come and see them about it? 'Yes', came the reply. On 5th October, 1875, following his visit to Penrhyn he received an order for a locomotive which was delivered on 21st December to Port Penrhyn.

When John Francis (the Manager) ordered two engines for the Quarry from de Winton & Co. of Caernarvon his instructions were quite unknown to the owner; there had been strikes at the Quarry (31st July and 9th November, 1874) and Francis' intention was to reduce a restive labour force by introducing steam locomotives there.[51]

In due course de Winton advised that the first of the two Francis-ordered engines was ready and the second well-advanced (19th August, 1875), so catching the owners (who were unaware of the order) off their guard that they declined to take delivery. However, this did not prevent Beatson receiving his order on 5th October following (the strike still then in force), a decision which suggests that the new main line would be given an engine no matter what troubles there were elsewhere!

How the engine came to Coed-y-Parc is not known, possibly along the Railroad. On arrival the Engineer (J. J. Evans) reported:

> I find the chimney is 2 feet higher than the Dinorwic engine. I hope we can manage with the bridges. I see one of the 'Plugs' of the Water Tank is not with the Engine.

On 28th December he wrote to Arthur Wyatt:

> We had a trial just now on the Engine in the prescence of Hundreds of Men,

> Women and Boys – from the Mill to Cilgeraint empty, and from Cilgeraint with 23 Wagons. These were brought up with 90 lb. pressure – and this is the most hard step of the whole line . . .

The next day:

> We had the Engine to work this afternoon and it is alright, but unfortunately the Guard had an accident, he broke his arm. What a job. I would not for £10.

Beatson's wrote:

> . . . new patterns and castings had delayed the locomotive . . .

The origins of this engine are not on record; it is not described and its builder is not directly given save that it was made 'in the South of England'. It left Poole on 15th December, 1875, suggesting Stephen Lewin & Co. of that town as builders. 'ENGINEERING' of 5th November, 1875 p.327, has an engraving of a narrow gauge 0–4–2 well tank built during that year by Lewin:

> . . . a very neat little engine . . . with two tanks between the wheels and one in front. The arrangement of the valve gear is novel . . . there are several features about this little engine worthy of attention. Six wheels, for example, are seldom fitted to so small an engine.

The article says it was built for mineral traffic, had outside cylinders 9 in. × 18 in. and was narrow gauge. 'THE CHRONICLES OF BOULTON'S SIDING' (Alfred Rosling Bennett) contains a reference to an engine dubbed LEWIN when acquired by Boulton which was then for sale or hire. The dimensions agree, and the driving wheels were 2 ft 6 in. diameter; Bennett gives a side elevation based on photographic sources. John Beatson confirms the engine was a well tank.

A suggestion that a Lewin engine delivered earlier to Dinorwic was PERIS is unproven, as the cost of an engine of this name supplied from de Winton & Co. is recorded at Dinorwic . . . one of few facts surviving! The Dinorwic Lewin engine may have been disposed of quite soon. The published Works photograph shows an engine with outside frames, Stephenson valve gear driving off the leading axle and connected to overhead valves by means of rocker arms. The steam feed pipes came from a large dome on the leading ring of the boiler and carried outside the steam chests. There were clearly short side tanks in addition to the well tanks, all the wheels (unusually) were of one diameter, the frame and gear outside and the footplate cabless. In Lewin style the smokebox was short with stovepipe chimney. The firebox was of tall raised pattern later widely adopted by Hunslet for this and other slate etc. quarry engines. The handbrake operated on the rear axle and there was a large sandpot on top of the boiler, a Salter safety valve on top of the dome and as to Battersby's records, the engine might have appeared to be a side tank at first glance; the spiral springs are clearly there. Two features of the illustration suggest the engine(s) was built speculatively, for the buffer beams are nearly four feet from rail level and the long wheelbase with its limited flexibility would hardly be suited to any quarry.[52]

Two years later the trading name was John Beatson & Co., 7E, Irongate, Derby: "Iron and steel rails, all sections 10–86 lbs. per yard . . . fishplates, chairs etc. etc. . . . locomotive engines etc. . . . Delivered at all Railway Stations and Ports in Great Britain."

The price quoted to Penrhyn was £850, or an extra £15 if six-coupled. Later, Beatson wrote to Penrhyn on 1st April, 1876:

> I am very pleased to have a good report of the Engine. Everything was done that could be to keep the centre of gravity low as I think shown by the position of the Water Tank, which is placed under instead of over the boiler. I hope it will become 'steady' as it becomes older.

Accompanying was a receipt for £828; (de Winton engines for Penrhyn were then costing about £300 each.)

So it may be that Lewin engines 'broke the first ground' at both Dinorwic and Penrhyn: the familiar high position of cylinders and outside gear in the later engines supplied by Hunslet to both concerns may well have originated with the Lewin design . . . it was clearly not provided for North Wales, as Lewin featured it earlier. When in the early 1880s Penrhyn was looking for additional engines for the main line they referred The Hunslet Engine Co. to one 'with steeply inclined cylinders working at Penrhyn very satisfactorily'. A letter from Lord Penrhyn to Hunslet regarding the proposed CHARLES may refer to the Lewin engine:

> I presume you have taken every care in balancing the engine . . . one of ours was not rightly balanced and the front wheels would not bite properly and were obliged to add weight in front to effect this.

(It could be that the Lewin, with full tanks and bunker, might tend to see-saw on the centre axle with consequent lack of traction on the leading wheels; when a heavy train was attached at the rear end, this fault would be accentuated.)

The engine carried an oval brass plate 12 in. × 9 in. with raised lettering reading in the upper half 'GEORGE SHOLTO NO. 3' and in the lower 'John Beatson Derby Contractor' which may infer that until the engine was proved satisfactory, Penrhyn would delay purchase. Beatson received instructions to name and number the engine dated 6th October, 1875.

Locomotives for Quarry and Port by de Winton & Co., Caernarvon (Vertical-boilered)

The building of the new main Red Lion Level and the carrying of stone from the lip of the pit craters (to which it was raised by water balances), via new Cutting Sheds and thence taking the finished work to the weighing machine at the top of the new Felin-Fawr Incline – a total distance of about ½ mile – was completed by autumn 1874. By this date the anticipated Quarry strike was in force: Francis' order for two locomotives @ £300 each has already been noticed. One, the first of the two, found an owner at Pen-y-Bryn Quarry, Nantlle on 6th September following, where it was named RHYMNEY. It was sold in August 1891 to Pen-yr-Orsedd Quarry (the advertisement confirming a cylinder diameter of 6 in.) where it had a wonderful reputation:

> Best engine we ever had: very sharp beat and the smallest . . . only engine in the quarry capable of starting 20 two-ton wagons from rest . . .

remarked the driver.[53] The smokebox and chimney thereon were offset, built this way it was said, to prevent rain etc. going down the chimney and corroding the top tubeplate. The second engine of similar type to Francis' order was ultimately taken for delivery on 1st March, 1876 as No. 1 LORD PENRHYN, instructions being given to the makers to this effect on 7th September, 1875, the day after the first engine was sold elsewhere. (This may have had significant psychological effect at Penrhyn!)

These delivery instructions were accompanied by an order for a second engine. No. 1, late in delivery (11th May, 1876) was then found to be of wrong gauge! de Winton wrote on 19th May 'we will alter our No. 4 Engine (LADY PENRHYN) to your gauge of 1 ft 11 in.' No. 2 LADY PENRHYN followed on 3rd October. No. 1 and No. 2 were not the same, LORD PENRHYN having the offset smokebox (as RHYMNEY) but LADY PENRHYN having an all-in-line smokebox and boiler. LORD PENRHYN was the last of that type at Penrhyn; the style of LADY PENRHYN was new to Penrhyn but had been sold already elsewhere.

> A new and improved design of Equal Strength but about 7 cwt. less weight . . . and with an improved boiler. (de Winton: 9th February, 1876).

Both LORD PENRHYN and LADY PENRHYN were fitted with a low speed device for shunting over the ordinary tables so allowing the special ones at Coed-y-Parc and the Port to be superceded.

On 6th August, 1876 (i.e. with LORD PENRHYN the only de Winton in use) two "shunting" engines "of larger design & construction than previous" were ordered for the Port, though initially, these two engines went to the Quarry for a short period, presumably for evaluation against Nos. 1 and 2. These were to be GEORGE HENRY, delivered May 1877 and KATIE (later KATHLEEN) delivered June 1877. Up to now, the first four engines delivered for main line or Quarry had carried numbers and names; henceforward, only names were borne. In November 1877 KATIE – at the Port since 15th July – became the first item of rolling stock to have central buffers fitted.

On 5th December, 1876 (again, with only two engines as yet at work) another order was given for a Port shunting engine GEORGINA, delivered 1st October, 1877, and for ALICE 'one engine, same as LADY PENRHYN' delivered in (spring?) 1877, perhaps in advance of GEORGINA? ALICE was likely to be destined for the Quarry; on 12th December 1877 de Winton fitted central buffers to it at the Quarry – as for KATIE.

On 11th October, 1878 de Winton delivered their last vertical-boilered engine; this was INA of the same size as KATIE. GEORGINA had been built with a 'flat' frame (as opposed to the curved frame) as used on No. 2, but carried the larger boiler on a 4 ft 4 in. wheelbase as used on KATIE; it was a type on its own. The four main types can be summarized thus:

Type Name	Boiler	Frame	Cylinders	Suspension	Wheel Diameter	Wheel-base
1) LORD PENRHYN	Large – offset smokebox	Curved	6 in. × 10 in.	None – pedestal bearings	1 ft 8 in.	4 ft
2) LADY PENRHYN	Small – in-line smokebox	Flat	6 in. × 10 in.	None – pedestal bearings	1 ft 8 in.	4 ft
3) GEORGINA	Large – in-line smokebox	Flat	6 in. × 12 in.	Sprung horns under footplate only	1 ft 8 in.	4 ft 4 in.
4) KATIE	Large – in-line smokebox	Curved	6 in. × 12 in.	Sprung horns under footplate only	1 ft 8 in.	4 ft 4 in.

Boiler pressure was 120 lb.

Engines in each type were:

1) LORD PENRHYN
2) LADY PENRHYN and ALICE
3) GEORGINA
4) KATIE, GEORGE HENRY and INA

making seven vertical-boilered engines in all; LORD PENRHYN (1876), LADY PENRHYN (1876), ALICE (1877) at the Quarry and, (up to 1883) KATIE (1877), GEORGE HENRY (1877), GEORGINA (1877), INA (1878) at the Port: GEORGINA and INA to Quarry from 1883. These engines were approximately of 1530 lb. (small,) and 1836 lb. (large,) tractive effort.

GEORGE HENRY (now in The Narrow Gauge Railway Museum, Tywyn) is 10 ft 10 in. overall, 7 ft 11 in. to top of chimney, 3 ft 4 in. wide over frame with overall boiler diameter of 3 ft 1 in., height footplate from rail 2 ft.

GEORGINA was irreparably damaged in a rock fall at Sebastopol Level in 1904.

Locomotives for the main line by de Winton & Co., Caernarvon (Horizontal-boilered)

(The de Winton correspondence for January–June in 1877–79 has not been traced.)

By 9th February, 1876 for use on the forthcoming new main line and 'capable of hauling 70 to 80 empty wagons up 1 in 40' de Winton & Co. had designed a more conventional locomotive with horizontal boiler. The next month the firm was sent an order for one engine to this design, to cost £800.

It would work the Tyn-y-Clwt Deviation which began with a steep climb of 1 in 36 from Hen-Durnpike to a summit at Cilgeraint (New) Bridge. Six days later (19th March) Parry began building and it opened on 15th October; GEORGE SHOLTO was the first engine to work along it. On 16th December No. 4 EDWARD SHOLTO arrived – the first main line design from de Winton – GEORGE SHOLTO was then displaced.

There was more traffic offering than one locomotive could handle, for the Log Book of 30th November, 1876 has 'Run lost at Cilgeraint. Horses stopped by Police'. The engine had failed the previous day 'Cylinder Cover thrown out'. There is some doubt as to how, by then, horses would have crossed the new summit bridge which had no decking – as had the older bridge.

EDWARD SHOLTO was a four-wheeled saddle-tank with outside frame but inside cylinders; these were 9½ in. diameter but space was limited; outside rods connected the driving wheels. The boiler may have had a circular firebox to allow the eccentrics clearance on the back axle. The engine was delivered by road to the Quarry and served until 1907. A similar engine followed on 25th September, 1878 in the form of HILDA (also delivered to the Quarry) but having side, instead of a saddle, tanks which should have made it less unsteady. An open-backed cab was fitted (not unlike those fitted to the later L.N.W.R. 'Claughton' class!). The engine cost £800 plus £10 for horses to drag it from Caernarvon. The slightly-inclined cylinders had a long opening in the frames for access. It weighed about 10 tons and was quite a large engine for this manufacturer.

The previous 5th November, train lengths had had to be reduced to 50 wagons as longer ones derailed EDWARD SHOLTO. HILDA and the next, VIOLET (delivered to the Port on 18th August, 1879, work being started on it on 26th November, 1878) had circular fireboxes, outside frames and cranks with a marked row of rivet heads showing the placing of the inside cylinders. Again, a long hole in the frame allowed access to the motion and each had a vertical opening in the rear of the bunker. When the new Railway opened on 6th October, 1879 three engines were available: their appearance is somewhat in doubt but the outline is recalled as having strong Crewe-like features, with an upswept frame under each end, and a curved L.N.W.R.-type cab, curved bunker top and square-base pattern chimney; one suggestion made is the designer had Crewe training or was strongly influenced! By having a circular firebox the eccentrics could be on the rear axle and Joy's valve gear fitted.

A Quarry photograph of 1896 partially reveals EDWARD SHOLTO, working on Sinc Bach Level. VIOLET was the first engine to finish (1902) with HILDA the last in 1911.

The nominal tractive effort – accepting the dimensions of these engines are not all available – cannot have been more than approximately 3850 lb. and it is remarkable that such units could have tackled the 50 wagon empty trains up 1 in 36 – their pace must have been slow. When three Hunslet main line engines were available (by 1893) they were used as standby, but all had found employment in the Quarry by the end of 1900.

Locomotives for the main line by The Hunslet Engine Co. Ltd., Leeds

(Maker's patterns confirm engines built to 1 ft 10¾ in. gauge to suit official gauge of 1 ft 11 in.)

All locomotives supplied by this firm designed to traverse 21 ft radius curves. Length 18 ft 6 in. over buffers. Width 5 ft 8 in. Height 8 ft.

With 9½ in. × 12 in. cylinders and the usual 20 or 24 inch diameter wheels the de Winton main line engines would be fully worked to keep traffic moving on the new Railway; judged against RHYMNEY's performance on the rough quarry tracks at Pen-yr-Orsedd (20 2-ton wagons) the boiler might have limited the steaming rate. This is only speculation, as is a lack of adhesion in bad weather, nonetheless after VIOLET had been delivered in August 1879 less than three years would pass before a special main line design had been prepared by Hunslet, and took shape as CHARLES (Works No. 283) which left Leeds for Penrhyn on 27th May, 1882. Battersby's notes reflect that this, the first Hunslet at Penrhyn (Dinorwic had had a four-coupled saddle tank from Hunslet as early as 1870) was both efficient and a welcome addition to the existing motive power! The outside cylinders were raised steeply at 1 in 6, so positioned as to enable the crossheads to clear the leading outside crankpins, allowing the connecting rods to lie behind the coupling rods (the Midland Railway 4–4–0 compounds were similarly fitted), so that the cylinders were placed unusually high up beside the smokebox sides. Thus placed the cylinder centres were kept close together and the overall width of the motion reduced but if the intent

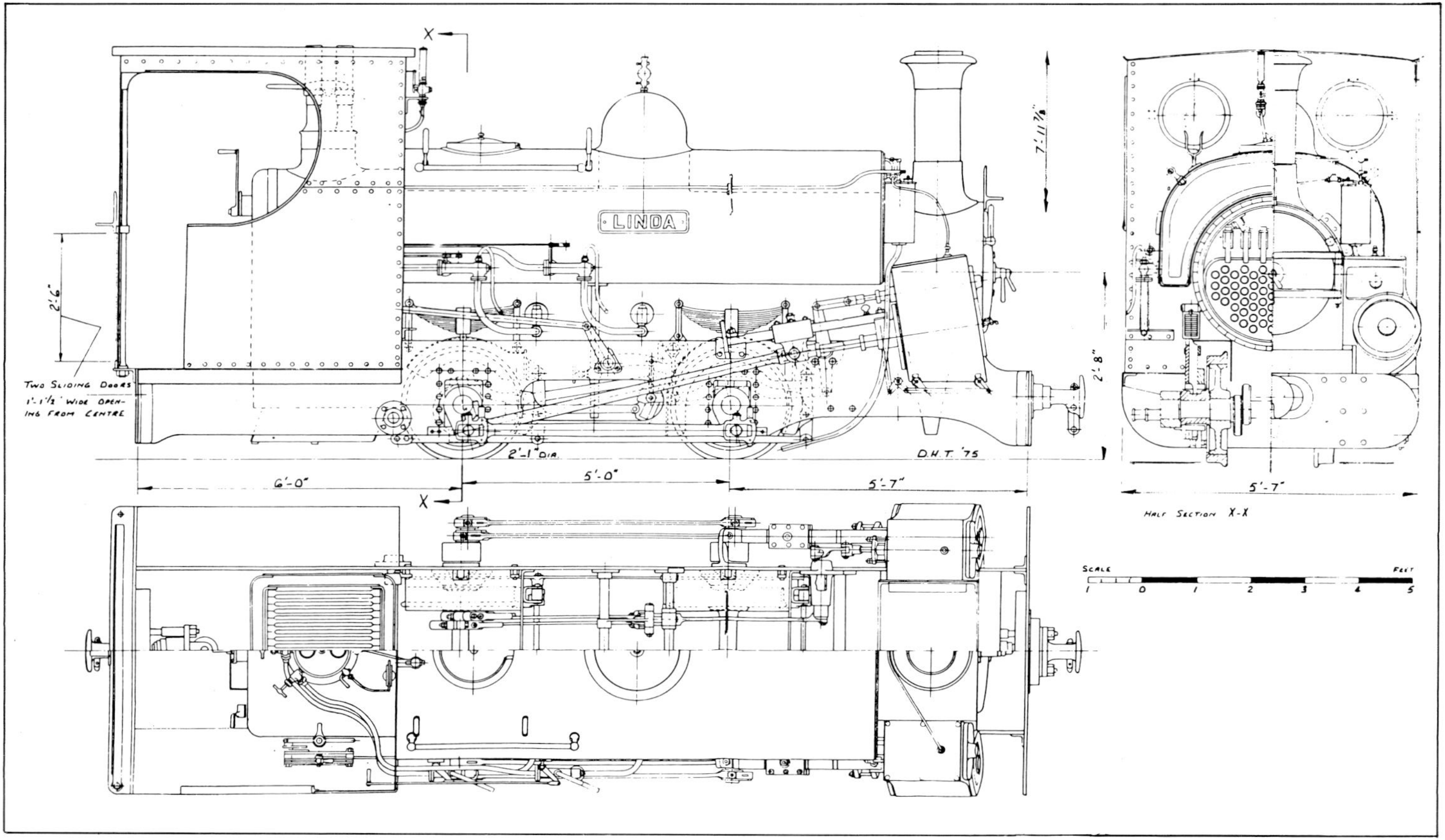

Half Section X.X

LINDA

7′ 11½″

2′ 8″

DWT '75

5′ 7″

5′ 0″

2′ 1 DIA.

6′ 0″

X

X

Two Sliding Doors
1′ 1½″ Wide Open-
ing from Centre.

2′ 6″

5′ 7″

Scale   Feet
1 0   1   2   3   4   5

Drawing: Don. H. Townsley

LINDA, one of the three main line engines by The Hunslet Engine Co. Ltd.

Plate LVI Is this the mysterious GEORGE SHOLTO No. 3, pictured before delivery in the Poole Foundry yard? *Loco. Publ. Co.*

Plate LVII There is no mystery about the surviving plate off the above. *Narrow Gauge Railway Museum Trust*

Plate LVIII The unacceptable de Winton locomotive which became RHYMNEY at Pen-yr-Orsedd Quarry lies derelict after a full life: 1936. *W.H. Whitworth*

Plate LIX Reputed to be LORD PENRHYN (a 'sister' engine of RHYMNEY!) it appears similar in most respects save that of having a curved main frame; it survived until 1909 in the Quarry. *J.H. Battersby*

Plate LX GEORGE HENRY outside The Baldwin Shed, the last de Winton to survive (most had gone by the mid-1920s) and now in the Museum at Tywyn. *J.I.C. Boyd*

Plate LXI The first of the Port Class, GWYNEDD of 1883, working in the Quarry in May 1951.   *J.I.C. Boyd*

Plate LXII LILIAN was the second Port Class engine, seen here in the Quarry in 1936. (In 1985 it is working in Cornwall.)   *W.H. Whitworth*

Plate LXIII   The original flat smokebox door was still in place on WINIFRED in the early 1930s.
per J.I.C. Boyd

Plate LXIV   NESTA of 1899 was the third of the Small Quarry Class, here working on Ponc William Parry in 1962.
J.I.C. Boyd

Plate LXV   ELIN differed latterly from the remainder of the Class, having a larger boiler (fitted in 1945) and Ramsbottom safety valves.   *J.I.C. Boyd*

Plate LXVI   HUGH NAPIER, first of the Large Quarry Class in 1904.
per C.C. Green

Plate LXVII The rebuilt PAMELA emerges from the Workshop: July 1952.

J.I.C. Boyd

Plate LXVIII SYBIL MARY (the name also carried by the ship) was a regular performer on Red Lion Level: 1936. *per C.C. Green*

Plate LXIX   As in the previous illustration, GEORGE SHOLTO also worked on Red Lion in the same period.   *W.H. Whitworth*

Plate LXX   EDWARD SHOLTO, last of the Class, was on Twlldyndwr in Juiy 1950.   *J.I.C. Boyd*

Plate LXXI LINDA waits for the 'right-away' to take
bucket prominent 'up front'. : July 1950.

t Up run of the day from the Port, the sand-
J.I.C. Boyd

Plate LXXII   CHARLES, less cab backsheet, with the later Saloon used for the weekly pay train (at Coed-y-Parc).   *Loco Publ. Co.*

Plate LXXIII   With the earlier Saloon attached, BLANCHE waits at the foot of Felin-Fawr Incline.   *Loco Publ. Co.*

Plate LXXIV   Still almost intact, TREGARTH – abandoned after her last run on 24th April 1929 – begins to be clothed in a mass of thicket.   *per J.I.C. Boyd*

Plate LXXV   The rebuilt Kerr Stuart with boiler lowered, is out of use on Red Lion Level by 1947, with firebox trouble.   *J.I.C. Boyd*

Plate LXXVI (opposite top) LILLA proved a useful engine for the heavy work required on Red Lion: 1950. *J.I.C. Boyd*

Plate LXXVII (opposite middle) JUBILEE 1897 was also very suited to Red Lion Level work: July 1947. *J.I.C. Boyd*

Plate LXXVIII (opposite bottom) Three little maids with no work stand outside Red Lion shed; EIGIAU (stove-pipe chimney replaced), GERTRUDE and ALAN GEORGE. *J.I.C. Boyd*

Plate LXXIX SANFORD was abandoned by the mid-1930s and slowly fossilised in Coed-y-Parc yard.

per J.I.C. Boyd

Plate LXXX SKINNER was still on Quarry duties, seen here in the mid-1930s.

W.H. Whitworth

Plate LXXXI (below) There were only two six-coupled engines on the roster; BRONLLWYD (here on Red Lion) has flangeless centre wheels: May 1951.

J.I.C. Boyd

Plate LXXXII   STANHOPE seems to have acquired a runner wagon both front and rear . . . and that at the front appears to contain a tea urn!

Maid Marian Fund

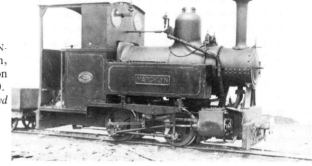

Plate LXXXIII   After STAN-HOPE had been withdrawn, MARCHLYN remained alone on Twlldyndwr Level: July 1950.

J.I.C. Boyd

Plate LXXXIV   GLYDER was one of the last steam engines to work in the Quarry; it first came into use in May 1952, at the Port.   *J.I.C. Boyd*

Plate LXXXV One of the Coed-y-Parc converted Morris cars, still with 'bull-nose' radiator. These worked on less-stable Levels.   *per B. Roberts*

Plate LXXXVI Six-cylindered Morris car conversion of 1937, as then in service.

W.H. Whitworth

Plate LXXXVII (below) The author leans on No. 1, possibly an ex-Ogwen Tile Works wagon then in use for 'Loco Coal' traffic (according to chalked message!) The origins of No. 8 alongside are also obscure: June 1945.

J.I.C. Boyd

Plate LXXXVIII 'Fifth Phase' slate wagon with handbrake removed (left) with No. 104 of 'Fourth Phase' (right) at the Port. Workmen's Train Carriage Shed and Loco Shed stand behind. By this date origins of well-modified slate wagons were deceptive! October 1953.   *J.I.C. Boyd*

Plate LXXXIX   To run between Red Lion and Levels up to Ponc Holywell these man-riding cars were reminiscent of fairground amusements! 1960.   *D.L. Chatfield*

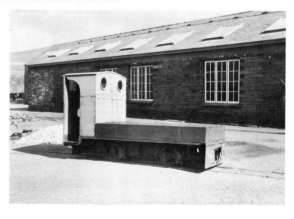

Plate XC This latter-day brake van for use on slate trains was once the locomotive SANFORD: 1962.   *D.L. Chatfield*

was to reduce oscillation, then it failed miserably!

The cylinders were 10 in. diam. × 12 in. stroke with driving wheel diameter 2 ft 1 in. on a 5 ft wheelbase; overhangs were considerable, 5 ft 7 in. at the front and 6 ft at the rear. Boiler pressure was 140 lb.; the saddle tank held 500 gallons (the tank might require 'topping up' at Tregarth loop on the Up journey); tractive effort was 5050 lb. The slide valves above the cylinders were worked by Stephenson's Link Motion inside the frames, the movement being brought outside by rocking shafts and levers. As delivered the cab was open at the back above the waist, there were sliding doors in the back-sheet to allow coaling-up from a following wagon, and the spectacles were square. To cover the open back all engines of this class had a roll-down canvas blind; dates of backsheet fitting were: LINDA 1905, CHARLES 1929, BLANCHE 1934. Before construction began Penrhyn had asked for brass axleboxes (rather than gunmetal), had specified the type of injectors, that the dome cover should be brass, that the safety valves and whistle should be mounted outside the cab. Penrhyn was clearly influenced by L.N.W.R. practice, for they referred Hunslet to the Crewe method of placing safety valves on saddle tank engines "outside the shelter cover". They wanted the footplate 6 inches wider

> . . . the shelter cover you have not got quite right, it is bigger than ours, it should be more this shape (enclosing sketch). Please look at the L.N.&W. engines.

In the event, Penrhyn's engine had two 'harmonic whistles' outside the weatherboard fitted shortly after delivery, but the safety valves were inside the cab, the waste steam carried up through the cab roof in a funnel. There was a sandbox between the frames delivering in front of the leading wheels, and below it a tapered chute to empty smokebox ash. A hand brake, but no steam brake, was fitted. There was no footplating round the engine and it was eleven years later before two more similar machines were sent from Leeds on 29th June and 6th July 1893, named BLANCHE and LINDA (Works Nos. 589 and 590). Care was to be taken that these three engines had sufficient adhesion on the leading wheels.

The last two Hunslets had the cylinder bore enlarged to 10½ in. and the grate area became 5.2 sq. ft against 4.5 sq. ft on CHARLES, giving them a tractive effort of 5550 lb., and allowing train length to be increased to a maximum of 60 wagons at which it remained (officially) to closure. The rear frame was extended by 3 in. and again no full rear weatherboard was fitted until Coed-y-Parc made them. Their circular spectacles distinguished them, and each had a different note of hooter, making each member of the class audibly distinguishable. Within the dome CHARLES had a valve regulator, but the others had slide valves for which an oil reservoir was placed on top of the cover. Unlike CHARLES, sanding gear was not fitted but a specially-shaped lidded bucket was hung on the smokebox door and it was part of the 'fireman's' duty to sprinkle sand on the rails by hand *en route*, as required. In working order CHARLES was 12 tons 5 cwt., the other two just 1 cwt. more. Although many engines in the Quarry had a small tender (or 'runner') attached, the main line engines never had; nor were they ever seen to work off the main line at the Port.

These engines took their names from:

CHARLES   Lieut. Hon. Charles Douglas-Pennant (1877 – 1914), son of G.S.G. Douglas-Pennant.

BLANCHE   Blanche Georgina Fitzroy (1865–1944) who married Edward Sholto Douglas-Pennant, 3rd Baron Penrhyn.

LINDA   Linda Blanche Douglas-Pennant (1889–1965) daughter of Blanche (above).

During the mid-1950s Hunslet used these engines in an advertising campaign with an artist's sketch of a quarry scene with BLANCHE. The point was made that engines supplied over half a century before were still capable or doing the work: (that is not to say they were infallible, for an entry of 20–3rd October, 1925 reads: "3½ days of overtime using Port engine on the main line."!)

CHARLES had a new firebox in October 1900 and April 1923 and carried the boiler off BLANCHE (with a welded water tank) December 1940 to July 1942 when boilers were impossible to obtain: its old boiler (repaired) was then restored. For over two years the engine was out of use after a fire in the cab in April 1933; a driving axle broke in April 1948 and the boiler was condemned in October 1955; however the engine worked a last 'special' three years later before going into the Castle Museum on 21st May, 1963. It seems to have had a nasty habit of leaving the track – 'Llew's engine off line' (November 1925) and again February 1926.

BLANCHE cost £800 new: it had a new firebox in July 1920, 'new boiler – off a week' 1st August, 1925, and the boiler off LINDA in October 1939 and new firebox; the driving axle broke in June 1937 and a welded tank was fitted in September 1949. It, too, occasionally left the rails and worked the very last steam trip over the main line on 27th July, 1962, being sold to the Festiniog Railway on 17th December 1963.[54]

LINDA also cost £800 and had new fireboxes in 1905 and 1920 (fitted 1921 at Leeds), and a new boiler in April 1936 (back to traffic 1937). A new cab back was provided in 1905, the driving axle straightened in 1931; it was then to break twice – in 1934 (replaced by that off BLANCHE) and 1953 respectively (larger axle fitted March 1954). It was stored at the Port shed 24th August, 1940 to 18th May, 1950 – during part of this period CHARLES was stored at Bethesda – and received a welded tank in January 1951. The records note 'Collision with old lady' at Hen-Durnpike level crossing 11th July, 1958 (the lady was only bruised, thankfully) and a derailment 8th October, 1958. The engine was rented to the Festiniog Railway and arrived at Minffordd via B.R. on 14th July, 1962;[54] it had worked its last Penrhyn trip on 11th July, 1962 and broke down at Felin-Hen. The F.R. purchased her along with BLANCHE in December 1963.

(There are extensive records of the usage of these engines.)

They received the 'new livery' in April 1936 (LINDA), June 1936 (BLANCHE) and November 1945 (CHARLES).

Locomotives – The Port Class by The Hunslet Engine Co. Ltd., Leeds

Length 13 ft 10 in. over buffers. Width 5 ft 4 in. Height 7 ft 8 in.

The year after CHARLES was delivered Hunslet was again called upon to supply more conventional shunting engines for the Port, (and so replace the de Wintons GEORGINA and INA which were sent to the Quarry when GWYNEDD and LILIAN were delivered in 1883). The third and last was WINIFRED of 1885. For almost the whole history of the railway thereafter, at least one was stationed at the Port: they were maker's numbers 316, 317 and 364.

They were cabless four-coupled saddle tanks with outside cylinders 7 in. × 10 in. outside frames and inside Stephenson valve gear, heavily framed with raised fireboxes. Polished brass domes and safety valve trumpets; Salter safety valves were prominent; the footplates were dropped slightly on the frames and coal contained in a bunker within the side sheets. A low rear footplate sheet with sliding doors enabled coal to be taken from an attached end-door wagon. Driving wheels were 1 ft 8¼ in.; wheelbase 4 ft; boiler pressure was 120 lb. and weight in working order 7½ tons. Tractive effort at 75% B.P. was 2205 lb. Water capacity 150 gallons.

A photograph of the Port in 1894 shows LILIAN and WINIFRED at work on the quay with the wrench-type handles prominent on the flat smokebox doors as originally fitted, a large wooden tool box on the left hand running plate over the beam (duly painted and lined out), conspicuous oil reservoirs on the dome tops to lubricate the regulators inside and both, as seemingly customary over the whole period, with their chimneys to the south.

Name and date new livery	Date delivered	Fireboxes and boilers	Laid up	Sold (or)
GWYNEDD June 1945	July 1883	1908 fb. April 1929 fb.	August 1954[a]	1965
LILIAN August 1937	August 1883	1908 fb. October 1929 fb. Br. off WINIFRED July 1952: cond. 1955. Had larger firebox than GWYNEDD.	August 1956[b]	1964
WINIFRED[c] June 1937	April 1885	1920 fb. br.off July 1936 New fb. June 1937. Br. to LILIAN; off January 1952. Given LILIAN br. with new barrel & back- plate, and new firebox June 1953.	July 1936 – June 1937	20 July 1965[d] (in working order) for £400.

(a) Last situation Ponc Holywell with MARCHLYN (by 1950). "Boiler scrapped" January 1955, lying at Coed-y-Parc.
(b) On scrap road by December 1956 but described as "working . . . good" in January 1955.
(c) Reputed to be last steam engine to work in quarry (18th May, 1965) but regular use of steam had ceased in January 1965 (OGWEN on Ffridd Level).
(d) MANCHESTER PROGRESS sailed to Norfolk, Va. carrying this and five other Penrhyn engines.

Locomotives – The Small Quarry Class by The Hunslet Engine Co. Ltd., Leeds

Length 11 ft 6½ in. over buffers.   Width 5 ft 4 in.   Height 7 ft 3 in.

The original purpose of the class was to replace the aging de Wintons in use at the Quarry. The design was similar in many respects to the Gallery class engines supplied to Dinorwic Quarries from 1886 and it is interesting to compare some dimensions:

	Penrhyn Small Types	Dinorwic 'Alice' Class
Introduced	1894	1886
Boiler Pressure	140 lb.	160 lb.
Outside Cylinders	7 in. × 10 in.	7 in. × 10 in.
Wheel diameter	1 ft 8¼ in.	1 ft 8 in.
Wheelbase	3 ft 3 in.	3 ft 3 in.
Weight in working order	6 tons	6 tons 14 cwt.
Tractive Effort	2540 lb.	2940 lb.

There were four engines in the batch: MARGARET (605 of 1894), ALAN GEORGE (606 of 1894) with two to follow five years later; NESTA (704 of 1899) and ELIN (705 of 1899). The whole appearance of the last-named was altered when fitted with a larger boiler in February 1939, supplied by Marshall Sons & Co. Ltd.; these engines were smaller than the Port class and had domeless boilers. Whilst the earlier engines for Dinorwic had Ramsbottom safety valves, Hunslet remained faithful to the older Salter variety though ELIN's bigger boiler had a Ramsbottom type. These engines gave a very good account of themselves on the exposed rough quarry tracks, and were to be found among the higher levels at times. ALAN GEORGE was allocated to Sinc Bach when new, had sandboxes fitted to the centre of the tank sides and a wooden tool box on the leading left hand running plate. A photograph shows the engine, new, on the level and surrounded by men with paper and string lying on the running plate! [55]

Name and date new livery (if applied)	Date delivered	Cost £	Fireboxes and boilers	Laid up	Sold (or)
MARGARET	May 1894	500	1908 fb. 1920 fb.	1939–August 1948. From 8th November, 1958 at Coed-y-Parc.[(a)]	1967
ALAN GEORGE	May 1894	500	1908 fb. 1921 br. and fb. June 1932 fb.	5th November, 1953 at Coed-y-Parc.[(a)]	1965
NESTA October 1941	December 1899	575	1911 fb. October 1926 fb. 1928 br. welded Port Dinorwic? October 1941 fb.	—	20th July, 1965[(b)]

Name and date new livery (if applied)	Date delivered	Cost £	Fireboxes and boilers	Laid up	Sold (or)
ELIN February 1939	January 1900	575	1911 fb. August 1927 fb. Br. condemned 9th February, 1938. New br. ex Marshall Sons & Co. Ltd. February 1939. Re-tubing September 1945.	17 November 1954 at Coed-y-Parc.[a]	July 1962

(a) "Laid up at Workshops – boilers scrapped." (January 1955).
(b) Date of sale with five other Penrhyn engines to U.S.A.

Locomotives – The Large Quarry Class by The Hunslet Engine Co. Ltd., Leeds

Length 13 ft 10 in. over buffers.   Width 5 ft 4½ in.   Height 8 ft 3 in. original chimney.

In 1912 Hunslet had offered the Penmaenmawr & Welsh Granite Co. Ltd. a heavy 3 ft gauge four-coupled saddle tank for use on the levels of this granite quarry. It was not taken up, but a small-gauged version had been in use in Penrhyn Quarry since HUGH NAPIER had left the Leeds Works on 29th August, 1904 (Works No. 855). This was to be the first of six engines for haulage of heavy rubbish and slab-slate loads along the working levels, trains which at their best were made up of unsophisticated wagons running somewhat crudely on – at times – indifferent track. They weighed 7 tons 12 cwt. in working order, and for this reason there were certain galleries on the south edge of the Quarry (in the vicinity of The Great Fall) from which they were debarred. In general appearance the familiar outlines of Hunslet related them at once to the Port and Small Quarry classes, save the immediate difference of the Ramsbottom safety valves distinguished them. As built they had four sandboxes (2 on each side of the saddle tank) which in common with most others were removed as it was impossible to store sand dry enough to prevent clogging in one of the wettest regions of the British Isles. The cost was £640, thus confirming the oft-told Penrhyn rule-of-thumb on costs . . . before World War I an engine cost about £80 per ton. PAMELA (Works

No. 920) and SYBIL MARY (Works No. 921) left Leeds on 17th November, 1906; the joint cost was £1,232. Oddly, whilst HUGH NAPIER had the usual two injectors, these two only had one; this had to be remedied quickly. With great foresight, three more engines at £600 each were ordered to complete the class, GEORGE SHOLTO, GERTRUDE, and EDWARD SHOLTO (Works Nos. 994–6), the foremost ex-works 11th May and the other two 27th May, 1909. Initially, the first-named was dubbed IN MEMORY OF GEORGE SHOLTO but altered quite shortly. Confirming that Penrhyn was not immune from trouble with injectors, these engines ultimately enjoyed the luxury of three!

Name and date new livery	Date purchased	Cost £	Fireboxes and boilers	Laid up	Sold (or)
HUGH NAPIER September 1938	October 1904	640	1922 br. September 1938 fb.	20th December 1954 at Coed-y-Parc (br. gone.)	To Penrhyn Castle Museum November 1966
PAMELA[a] March 1938	November 1906	616	April 1926 fb. Br. removed May 1951. BRONLLWYD br. fitted January 1952. April 1958 fb. condemned.	1946 (rebuilt later)	October 1966 (as rebuilt)
SYBIL MARY August 1936	November 1906	616	December 1920 fb.[b] August 1936 fb.	6th March, 1955	April 1966
GEORGE SHOLTO November 1942, (partly lined out only.)	May 1909	600	December 1920 fb.[b]	1947 at Coed-y-Parc. (Br. gone).	February 1966
GERTRUDE November 1943, (partly painted.)	July 1909	600	April 1927 fb.	February 1955	October 1961
EDWARD SHOLTO February 1938	July 1909	600	April 1928 br. repaired at Port Dinorwic. February 1938 fb.	June 1956	June 1961

(a) See separate account for rebuild of this engine 1951–52.
(b) Hunslet order dated 21st December, 1920.

Boiler pressure on this class was 140 lb., driving wheels 20¼ in. diameter, wheelbase 4 ft, width at cylinders 5 ft 4½ in., cylinders 10 in. stroke × 7½ in. diameter giving a tractive effort of 2953 lb. at 75% boiler pressure.

General Notes on Hunslet Port and Quarry Class Engines

As built these engines were given 10 leaf springs to each axle box, but due to the thrust of the outside cylinders, they were replaced with eleven on the rear axle. As supplied, there would seem to have been a wooden toolbox for each engine, lamp bracket at foot of chimney (but nothing at the rear) and sanding gear; some (possibly all) had a regulator lubricator reservoir on top of the brass dome – ALAN GEORGE was possibly one of the exceptions. All these refinements disappeared, the sand proving more nuisance than useful as it was difficult to keep it dry in the store by the engine sheds up in the Quarry.

Access to the front brake blocks was by a large opening in the frame behind the slide bars, and there was a chute under the smokebox for emptying clinker and ash drawn through the tubes. Alterations to superstructure could be picked out where welded components took the place of the former rivetted ones. It will also be noted that chimneys were of differing outline and length.

It was company policy to renew fireboxes rather than boilers; instead, the practice of reducing working pressure to a figure of 100–120 lb. began in the late 1920s, but when it was clear that even then the boilers would not meet a hydraulic test of double the working pressure, engines had to be removed from service in the middle 1950s. This was intended to be a temporary storage awaiting renewals, but with the slackening in demand and a general run-down of the railway system, together with a diminishing use of the Port, attractive cash offers were accepted for some of these locomotives.

Other than the main line engines, each foregoing engine (and some of the Quarry engines yet to be described) was attached to a 'runner wagon', a form of 'tender' made up like a sled wagon but having a 6 in. deep heavy plate beam: this carried all forms of emergency gear, re-railing ramps, the steel rope used for hauling wagons over weighing tables (locomotives could not pass over these), chains, hooks and spare couplings. Some drivers took a pessimistic view of their territory – no doubt after experience – even to carrying track repairing materials and push-bike thereon!

Second-hand Locomotives for Main Line and Quarry

Following the First War came a 'boom period' 1918–21 when the Quarry produced 25% of all British slates (Dinorwic and Blaenau Ffestiniog also produced 25% each), but exports fell away and only 3%

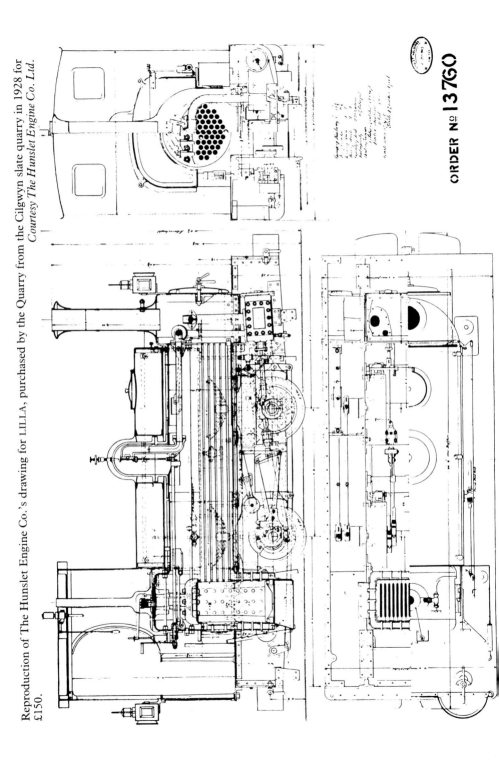

Reproduction of The Hunslet Engine Co.'s drawing for LILLA, purchased by the Quarry from the Cilgwyn slate quarry in 1928 for £150. *Courtesy The Hunslet Engine Co. Ltd.*

ORDER No 13760

of output was shipped from the Port. Many overseas customers preferred Ffestiniog slates, and in 1934 Glasgow was taking all Irish slate production; Eire only took 1.1% of Penrhyn production due to a 1934 tariff. This was the economic backcloth to the details which follow.

The interval and problems of World War I brought a change to a policy which bought engines from only one manufacturer, and there was no more direct buying. Manufacturers of engineering equipment who had been directed on to wartime products did not immediately resume their normal routine, and customers prudent enough to place orders early were the first to be supplied. The Quarry found itself flooded with orders for slate as a spate of domestic housing began, and along with other quarries enjoyed a short-lived boom; but its railway system was starved of maintenance and the order book for slates could not be met. First evidence of need was the purchase of what became SERGEANT MURPHY – a decision made when it was clear that only CHARLES of the locomotive fleet had had a thorough overhaul. No record appears of the purchase date, but it was probably among two lots of machinery bought in 1921; there is a note that patterns for firebars were made in October 1922. It was the last of the HAIG type built by its makers and the first six-coupled engine at Penrhyn: it was nameless on arrival but nicknamed SERGEANT MURPHY after the contemporary hurdler – the gait of the engine was said to be reminiscent of that gentleman in action! Battersby in due course, had nameplates made, thus according official acceptance of the title.

Next came three engines for use on the main line, the purchase date being 15th August, 1924 and the supplier Hardinge & Co. of London who had contracted to provide the new 'Fullersite' plant, of which these engines would form a part: they were American and reputed to have been bought on the strength of a photograph which also gave authority for payment . . . a change of Quarry Engineer followed soon after, J.H. Battersby taking over!! The 'Fullersite' works was hardly more successful than the American engines; an output of 1,000 tons weekly was expected but was seldom more than 200 tons a month. The American engines were expected to handle this extra traffic.

Larger engines, LILLA and JUBILEE 1897, were bought in something of a panic when the American engines began to show their weaknesses; they were large enough to work alongside the Hunslet main line engines and share the duties; 'Fullersite' traffic remained to be proved as yet, however. SANFORD, SKINNER, and EIGIAU came and were the smallest of the second-hand flock; they were intended for haulage on Ponc Garret and Ponc Twrch where the galleries could not support larger engines,[56] and it was for use in such places that a petrol rail-tractor fleet was conceived . . . though in typical Penrhyn fashion the first of these was to find use at the Port.

BRONLLWYD and STANHOPE were for the specific purpose of rubbish clearance below the tips on the Sinc Bach Level, along which the new

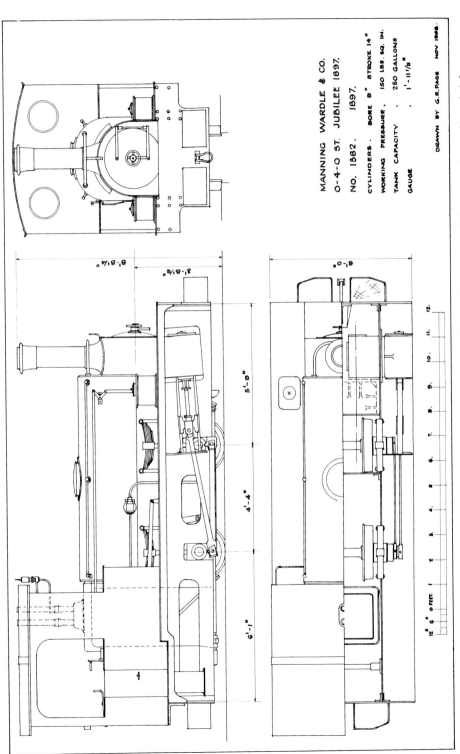

MANNING WARDLE & CO.

0-4-0 ST. JUBILEE 1897.

NO. 1382.   1897.

CYLINDERS . BORE 8" STROKE 14"

WORKING PRESSURE . 150 LBS. SQ. IN.

TANK CAPACITY . 250 GALLONS

GAUGE . 1' - 11½"

DRAWN BY G.R.PAGE   NOV 1968.

JUBILEE 1897 was the second engine to pass to the Quarry in 1928 from the Cilgwyn slate quarry. Like LILLA, it was intended for main line haulage.

Drawing: G.R. Page

exit tramway was to be laid. STANHOPE was the earlier in service, initially at the Port for about nine months where it displaced petrol tractors Nos. 1 & 2.

The much later batch of CEGIN, OGWEN, MARCHLYN was intended for a water supply contract for the neighbouring rural district council but never used on it, being left to stand at the Port, covered by distinctive green tarpaulins! (A secondary usage would have found them work in the Griffith Railway Scheme. The last engine GLYDER would also have found work there.) Also, an enquiry was made of the Festiniog Railway in November 1934, had they locomotives for disposal? Portmadoc offered their two ex-War Department units, both the 4–6–0 tank (then working on the Welsh Highland system) and the 'Simplex' rail tractor, but these were too heavy.

Some manufacturer's products stood the test of Penrhyn needs reasonably well, whilst others – noticeably cheap to buy – did not always prove to be a good bargain.

Main line engines from The Baldwin Locomotive Works, Philadelphia, U.S.A.

Length over couplers 22 ft 1½ in. Width overall 6 ft 9 in. Height rail to chimney 8 ft 10½ in.

The three engines obtained through the Surplus Government Property Disposal Board had been built for the United States Government use rather than the British War Office. They were the only three of this type to be purchased "from France (for) £887 2s. 10d." and had the advantage over their very similar counterparts with 4–6–0 wheel arrangement in that they were 2–6–2 and more steady running bunker-first. They were built to Class 10–12–¼–D,5 commencing with 'Road No. 5001'. With a gauge of 1 ft 11⅝ in. they had to be regauged at Penrhyn;[57] they had inside bar frames, outside cylinders 9 in. × 12 in. with slide valves on top, Walschaert's valve gear, driving wheels 23½ in. diameter, 16 in. diameter 'truck wheels', a rigid wheelbase 5 ft 10 in. and total wheelbase 15 ft 7 in. Total weight in working order was 18 tons 9 cwt. (Imperial), tank capacity 476 gallons (American). The boiler and firebox were of steel, the boiler being pressed at 178 lb. (a high figure for Penrhyn). Tractive effort was 5249 lb. Total heating surface was 291.9 sq. ft of which the firebox contributed 5.6 sq. ft.[58] Some of these 'American Side Tanks' [*sic*] were built by The American Locomotive Co. in 1917 with slightly different dimensions and some had been rebuilt in 1918 by W.G. Bagnall Ltd., Stafford.

> Works No. 46764/1917   No. 3 TREGARTH
> Works No. 46828/1917   No. 2 FELIN-HEN
> Works No. 47143/1917   No. 1 LLANDEGAI

From a Wages Book oddments of information come through about
the Baldwins, thus: 12th September, 1924 "Unloading new engine from
truck". It was to be 12th October the next year before another mention
is made: "Baldwin Engines firing Monday" (note the plural). By the
fifth of the next month we learn TREGARTH's driver is David Jones and
twenty days later the "Foundry" is working overtime on TREGARTH's
boiler. In March 1926 FELIN-HEN and TREGARTH are both at work; on
the fifth of that month FELIN-HEN appears for the first time, (boiler
washout) and in April David Jones has the TREGARTH "on week-end
work". On 30th April LLANDEGAI first appears, for washout and the
next day Richard Roberts spends "Halfday firing Baldwin engines"
again suggesting two were out.

There is now a gap until February 1927 when TREGARTH and
LLANDEGAI are both at work; the next month TREGARTH and FELIN-
HEN are in use and "kept alight on Sundays". There is a curt note on
2nd July "No Baldwins out"; one returns to work a week later and
LLANDEGAI has a washout on 16th July. On 25th July two Baldwins are
out; as their stokers (the Penrhyn term) were both actually drivers they
were given an extra halfday's pay each time – does this suggest they
were trying to overcome firing troubles with more experienced men?
August must have been a high spot in the life of the Baldwins for all
three were used, David Jones back on TREGARTH (he usually had
BLANCHE) and Richard Roberts on LLANDEGAI (usually LINDA) but on
20th August comes the note "Hunslets back on main line" . . . there is
an air of relief about this entry! On 3rd September David Jones is given
the shovel again "firing Baldwin" and in mid-month LLANDEGAI and
TREGARTH were in steam again on the same days; it is clear these
engines were being given every opportunity to give an account of
themselves.

In mid October it was TREGARTH on washout with the other two at
work and they must have continued thus for TREGARTH is on washout
again on 12th November: this is the last entry for a Baldwin until 28th
April, 1928 when TREGARTH is again on washout – the other two must
have been laid off; . . . worse follows, for TREGARTH does not seem to
have been put into steam again until 19th March, 1929 and the last
entries for a Baldwin occur: 22nd April, when the same engine is given
a "Sunday run", and on 24th April "Engine (TREGARTH) failed – leaky
tubes". Then comes the Parthian Shot: "Loading engine into LMS
truck" 10th March, 1940, heralding the departure of FELIN-HEN for
Liverpool.

Against these scrappy entries it is known from the records that
LLANDEGAI arrived in August 1924 but subsequent entries are too
complex to re-tell. In short there was a series of repairs to the motion
and on 15th November, 1927 a piston rod and cylinder cover were
broken; in March the engine was stripped down and converted into a
stationary unit; it drove the Llandegai Saw Mill May 1929 to July 1931

when that Mill closed. What was left was scrapped in January 1940, having lain at the Port since the Mill closed.

FELIN-HEN was last used on 29th June, 1927 and this probably accounts for the cryptic entry three days later and just noted, "No Baldwins out". It lay in the Port shed until January 1940 when it was given trials on the quay lines prior to loading on an L.M.S. well-wagon on the first stage of shipment to Western Australia . . . where they seem to have been more successful in operating it![60]

TREGARTH was the best of the poor trio; it ran until 24th April, 1929, two days after the aforementioned Sunday run – which may have been a trial trip after repairs. Obviously exasperation had set in as it proved impossible to cure the leaking fire tubes from which all suffered and it was pushed into a siding near the Coed-y-Parc marshalling sidings and left for nature to clothe it in a copse of bushes. Name and Works plates disappeared, but someone painted 'No. 3' where the name had been; it was scheduled 'for the torch' along with No. 1 and towed down to the Port to its fate – obviously the scrap man did not get the lot as a side tank was found in the Coed-y-Parc boscage years later!

Battersby was clearly patient with these engines and prepared to master their boiler and firebox deficiencies, but he could do little about derailments on the curve at the top of Dinas old incline; neither was he a lover of the American outline and went to the trouble of changing the chimneys (FELIN-HEN in 1925) to give them a more 'Hunslet appearance'; they also received the official livery and lining out. The open cabs were given backsheets (slightly variable in style) but he summed them up as "Troublesome and less reliable than the Hunslets, heavy on coal and limited to 45 wagons". They seemed to have escaped photography during their intermittent days of duty but one of the Liverpool schoolboys, evacuated to Bangor during World War II, took pictures of FELIN-HEN's steam trials at the Port prior to the engine leaving for The Fairymead Sugar Milling Co., Bundaberg, Queensland. Other opinions which filtered through from drivers who recalled them in the 1940s were "made a terrible fuss on main line trains . . . horrible rough riding and on the track . . . a very sharp blast which shot the fire up the chimney . . . they opened out the gauge on every curve".

Even if problems with boilers and fireboxes had been overcome, their official minimum curve radius was 165 ft (2½ chains); not surprisingly the Dinas curve of 85 ft (just over 1¼ chains) objected to them although TREGARTH seemed able to manage it. (For comparison, the Glyn Valley Tramway (3 chains), Snailbeach District Railway (3½ chains) and Welsh Highland Railway (3¾ chains) used Baldwin 4–6–0 tanks with the same fixed wheelbase.)

QUARRY LOCOMOTIVES PURCHASED SECOND-HAND – in date order of purchase.

Name	Date Purchased (delivery followed)	Cost £	From	Maker
SGT. MURPHY	1921	?	A.H. Richards, Chepstow. ex Admiralty, Beachley Dock, Chepstow, Mons.	Kerr, Stuart & Co. Ltd., Stoke-on-Trent, Staffs.
LILLA	12th May, 1928	150	Cilgwyn Quarry, Nantlle.	Hunslet Engine Co. Ltd., Leeds.
JUBILEE 1897	12th May, 1928	150	Cilgwyn Quarry, Nantlle.	Manning, Wardle & Co. Ltd., Leeds.
EIGIAU	June 1928	95	Aluminium Corporation, Dolgarrog.	Orenstein & Koppell A.G., Berlin.
SANFORD	July 1929	28	Maenofferen Quarry, Ffestiniog.	W.G. Bagnall Ltd., Stafford.
SKINNER	August 1929	90	Maenofferen Quarry, Ffestiniog.	W.G. Bagnall Ltd., Stafford.
BRONLLWYD (name applied 1937)	December 1934	95	Surrey County Council, Guildford. No. CP 39.	Hudswell Clarke & Co. Ltd., Leeds.
STANHOPE	December 1934	190	Durham County Water Board, Burnhope Resr., Wearhead. Contract 1931–1937.	Kerr, Stuart & Co. Ltd., Stoke-on-Trent, Staffs.
CEGIN	October 1936	140	Durham County Water Board, Burnhope Resr., Wearhead. Contract 1931–1937.	A. Barclay Sons & Co. Ltd., Kilmarnock.
OGWEN	October 1936	120	Durham County Water Board, Burnhope Resr., Wearhead. Contract 1931–1937.	Avonside Engine Co. Ltd., Bristol.
MARCHLYN	October 1936	120	Durham County Water Board, Burnhope Resr., Wearhead. Contract 1931–1937.	Avonside Engine Co. Ltd., Bristol.
GLYDER	January 1938	60	Durham County Water Board, Burnhope Resr., Wearhead. Contract 1931–1937.	A. Barclay Sons & Co. Ltd., Kilmarnock.

Works No. (Date)	Date re-gauged	Wheel Arrgmt.	Outside Cylinders	Boiler Pressure	Wheel diam. Wheelbase	Weight Working Order T. C.	Tractive Effort @ 75% B.P. lb.	Notes
3117 (1918)	1922	0–6–0T	8½ in. × 11 in.	160	22½ in. 4 ft 7½ in.	10 0	4238	1
554 (1891)	November 1934	0–4–0ST	8½ in. × 14 in.	120	26 in. 4 ft 6 in.	10 15	3501	2
1382 (1897)	January 1937	0–4–0ST	9 in. × 14 in.	140	26 in. 4 ft 4 in.	11 10	4580	3
5668 (1913)	(not known)	0–4–0WT	6 in. × 10 in.	175	22 in. 3 ft 6 in.	6 10	2160	4
1571 (June 1900)	(not known)[a]	0–4–0ST	6 in. × 9 in.	140	19 in. 3 ft 0 in.	5 0	1790	5
1766 (Jany 1907)	(not done)[a]	0–4–0ST	6 in. × 9 in.	140	19 in. 3 ft 0 in.	5 0	1790	6
1643 (1930)	March 1935	0–6–0WT	6½ in. × 12 in.	180 (later 160)	23 in. 4 ft 2 in.	6 17	2975	7
2395 (1917)	March 1935	0–4–2ST	7 in. × 12 in.	160 (later 140)	24 in. 3 ft 0 in.[b]	8 10	2940	8
1991 (1931)	March 1937	0–4–0WT	7 in. × 11 in.	180	23 in. 3 ft 11½ in.	7 10	3164	9
2066 (1933)	November 1936	0–4–0T	7 in. × 12 in.	180	24 in. 3 ft 9 in.	7 10	3307	10
2067 (1933)	December 1936	0–4–0T	7 in. × 12 in.	180	24 in. 3 ft 9 in.	7 10	3307	11
1994 (1931)	January 1939	0–4–0WT	7 in. × 11 in.	180	23 in. 3 ft 11½ in.	7 10	3164	12

(a)   Delivered as 1 ft 11½ in. gauge.
(b)   Total wheelbase 7 ft 6 in.

Notes on Second-hand Locomotives

Note	Name & date new livery applied (if at all)	New Firebox/ New Boiler (or) and location notes	Laid up[a]	Sold (or)
1	SGT. MURPHY (War Dept. design HAIG Class.[b])	Heavy alterations after fatal overturning 1932. (Boiler lowered) 16th Feb. 1932–7th Dec. 1932. Firebox May 1938. New tanks 1945.	pre 1945 1947–? (at Red Lion Level) "firebox gone". And again from 9 Oct. 1958 (at Coed-y-Parc) "officially scrapped by Jan. 1955".[c]	25th July, 1964
2	LILLA (delivered 21st May, 1923) August 1939	Firebox August 1939 (from A. Barclay Sons & Co. Ltd.)	Dec. 1946–May 1948 and from 19th Mar. 1957 (in store, serviceable after successful boiler test on 1st Feb. 1955.)	December 1963
3	JUBILEE 1897 (delivered 21st May, 1923) Painted but not lined Dec. 1946		At Coed-y-Parc pre September 1945. Oct. 1940–June 1943 and Dec. 1946–Nov. 1950. Withdrawn 1st January, 1955.	To Narrow Gauge Railway Museum, Tywyn, Dec. 1963
4	EIGIAU (delivered 18th July, 1928)	New chimney and cut down cab etc.	1949 (at Red Lion) "officially scrapped by Jan. 1955".[c]	February 1963
5	SANFORD (delivered 15th July, 1929)	Given new firebox on delivery @ £200. Firebox October 1930. Failed boiler test 31st December, 1935.	"officially scrapped by Jan. 1955".[c] Semi-derelict at Baldwin Shed September 1945.	Parts used for brake van 1956
6	SKINNER (delivered 15th Aug. 1929)	Firebars only August 1942. Part-dismantled by 1954.	? "officially scrapped by Jan. 1955".[c]	Sold as scrap 1967
7	BRONLLWYD (delivered 31 Dec 1934) July 1937	Steel tubes fitted May 1943. Boiler to PAMELA (q.v.) 14th August, 1951. Cast-iron front drag-beam fitted. Centre pair wheels flangeless.	1949 "defective boiler". "officially scrapped by Jan. 1955".[c]	January 1966 (less boiler)

Notes on Second-hand Locomotives

Note	Name & date new livery applied (if at all)	New Firebox/ New Boiler (or) and location notes	Laid up[a]	Sold (or)
8	STANHOPE (delivered 15th Dec. 1934) January 1937	Boiler lowered 6½ in. on arrival, and re-tubed. (First of maker's TATTOO Class: built for Holloway Bros, R.N. Dockyard contract, Rosyth, to D.C.W.B. 1930)	1948 "officially scrapped by Jan. 1955".[c]	November 1966 (Some parts pre-viously to Talyllyn Railway)
9	CEGIN (delivered 23rd Oct. 1936) March 1937	Overhauled 1947 Overhauled 1951 "In for heavy over-haul" (3rd April, 1962)	6th Jan. 1943–8th Mar. 1944 and 2nd Feb. 1948–27th July 1951 and 14th Aug. 1951–10th Sept. 1954 and 17th Dec. 1954–March 1955.	25th July, 1965[d]
10	OGWEN (delivered 23rd Oct. 1936) Nov. 1936	Last locomotive to work on upper levels (15th January, 1965)	June 1937–Apr. 1938 and alternate months to June 1939 and June 1939–February 1955 (in Port Engine Shed)	25th July, 1965[d]
11	MARCHLYN (delivered 19th Oct. 1936)	"An excellent loco-motive for the job" (June 1950)		25th July, 1965[d]
12	GLYDER (delivered 19th Jan. 1938) Jan. 1939 (D.C.W.B. livery 'touched up') Feb. 1957	Firebox August 1938 Last steam loco-motive overhauled at Coed-y-Parc	From acquisition to 1952 stored at Port Engine Shed with Saloon.	25th July, 1965[d]

(a) There are times in laying-up periods when certain locomotives were brought out and put into use for longer or shorter periods.

(b) 'THE NARROW GAUGE' No. 77 p.16 shows original ex-Work's condition of Class.

(c) "But not actually broken up".

(d) Date MANCHESTER PROGRESS left Manchester for Norfolk, Virginia. Loco-motives sold for £400 each.

Employment of Second-Hand Locomotives (where known)

(Note: it was often the practice to put engines into Port use when first entering service)

SERGEANT MURPHY	Intended to redress the overall shortage of motive power. Worked between water-balances and Mills on Red Lion Level, mid-1930s.
LILLA	Intended for main line haulage. Worked Red Lion Level mid-1930s–1950s.
JUBILEE 1897	Intended as for LILLA; had started at Port by early 1929, 'boiler weak'. To Quarry July 1930 (replaced by EIGIAU at Port) thence on Red Lion Level.
EIGIAU	Intended for use on insecure galleries. To Port July 1930; returned to Quarry February 1933. To Port January 1938 to replace CEGIN; returned to Quarry February 1938.
SANFORD	Intended as EIGIAU. To Port March 1931; returned to Quarry May 1931. By mid-1940s 'engine has dropped on its bearings and cannot be moved'.
SKINNER	Intended as EIGIAU. By mid-1940s 'on short length of rail in Blacksmith's Shop and has not been used for many years'.
BRONLLWYD	Intended for working rubbish trains in removal of old dumps to build new Ponc Sling – Coed-y-Parc; from March 1935 on this duty along with SANFORD until line found inefficient and SANFORD moved away. Later, BRONLLWYD to Ponc Ffridd and then, Red Lion Level.
STANHOPE	Intended as for BRONLLWYD. To Port January 1935 when Ponc Sling scheme only partially successful (see BRONLLWYD); returned to Quarry December 1936 (replaced by OGWEN at Port). Coed-y-Parc overhaul 1940. In 1940s on Ponc Twlldyndwr and Ponc Twrch, working rubbish trains. Out of use at Coed-y-Parc 1947. Parts sold: some donated to Talyllyn Railway.
CEGIN	Intended for Griffith's Scheme/Marchlyn contract. To Port June 1937; returned to Quarry January 1938. Back to Port February 1938 and works months-about there with OGWEN April 1938 to mid 1939, then doing the same with WINIFRED. When not at Port, on Red Lion Level marshalling wagons from inclines similarly on other Levels in mid-1950s. Noted working at Port December 1942, 1944, 1945, 1948, 1954 until put into storage at Port January 1955.

HUDSWELL / HUDSON CLASS "G"
0-6-0 W.T. LOCO. 60°/m GAUGE
W.D. N° 110 Works N° 1219-1915.
Drawn from the HUDSWELL CLARKE original by W.A.D.Strickland

Drawing: W.A.D. Strickland

BRONLLWYD originated to this War Department design.

OGWEN	Intended as for CEGIN. To Port December 1936; returned to Quarry June 1937 (replaced by CEGIN at Port). April 1938 to mid 1939 worked months-about with CEGIN at Port. Overhauled February 1955 then to Red Lion Level. Last steam engine in Quarry – ceased on Ffridd Level January 1965.
MARCHLYN	Intended as for CEGIN. To Port December 1936; returned to Quarry and working alongside STANHOPE mid-1940s mainly on Twlldyndwr. 'Stand-by at Quarry' January 1955.
GLYDER	Out of store May 1952; worked Port initially. To Ponc Garret November 1953. Stored at Port January 1955, 'stand-by'. Returned to Quarry; still active there May 1962.

PAMELA (II)

Such was the shortage of motive power that it was decided on a marriage of convenience – the old boiler on BRONLLWYD was taken off on 18th May, 1951 and, being suitable, it was placed on the frame of the PAMELA in January 1952, the cab (such as it was) of the former being adapted as well: a new saddle tank and smokebox were fabricated at Coed-y-Parc and the 'new' engine took up a trial period of duty at the Port on 18th March, 1952 replacing WINIFRED there. It remained at the Port (sometimes replaced by the returned WINIFRED or GLYDER) until December 1953, save for a return to the Works in July 1952 to check that all was well. Coed-y-Parc was proud of this conversion. From early 1954 it worked in the Quarry until the firebox was condemned, April 1958.

Employment of Locomotives in the Quarry

Steam engines might be moved from Port to Quarry but not used therein with complete freedom, due to the instability of rubbish tips; lighter engines were reserved for these even though the remainder of the level might call for a second heavier engine. (A single level at Penrhyn might be a great deal bigger than a complete slate quarry elsewhere!) From the first the de Wintons were allocated to the tips: the whole of the unstable 'Left Side' of the Quarry (East) was out-of-bounds to the 'Large Quarry' class; also, the line giving access to the pits below the hydraulic hoists having limited clearances, only the domeless Hunslets could be used there – and even they had their chimneys removed during delivery. Sinc Bach Level was an exception hereabouts as there was an alternative access.

RED LION LEVEL LOCOMOTIVE SHED

September 1945	*June 1950*	*May 1951*
HUGH NAPIER	MARGARET	MARGARET
ALAN GEORGE	ALAN GEORGE	ALAN GEORGE
LILLA	LILLA	JUBILEE 1897
EIGIAU	EIGIAU	EIGIAU
SYBIL MARY	SYBIL MARY	
BRONLLWYD		
SGT. MURPHY		

LAST ENGINE LOCATIONS – APRIL 1962

Main Line	*Quarry*	*Port*
LINDA*	MARCHLYN†	Rail Tractor
	GLYDER†	
	NESTA†	
	WINIFRED†	
	OGWEN*	

*In workshops August 1960.
†Also working in August 1960.

The end of steam was foreshadowed by J.H. Battersby writing on 10th January, 1955:

> The state of the steam locos is not very healthy. We have had several boilers which I have had to condemn lately and now things have come to a head and a decision will have to be made. I have been putting the boiler question for some years now, without result. The boilers are old, mostly the same age as the locos. We used to renew two fireboxes each year but since the start of the war 1939 have only put two in NESTA (1940) and WINIFRED (1953). The main line engines are not bad . . . CHARLES' old boiler but in fair condition . . . I have just had to scrap the boiler on HUGH NAPIER whilst SYBIL MARY, GERTRUDE and EDWARD SHOLTO are due for new fireboxes . . .

PETROL-ENGINED 4-WHEEL RAIL TRACTORS
(all built Coed-y-Parc)

Between 1929 and 1940, 25 cars with 4 or 6-cylinder engines, and 1 lorry (16th January, 1933) were purchased, the cars for an average £3 16s. 0d. each and the lorry for £21. They were converted into light tractors for use at Port or on insubstantial levels in the Quarry. No. 5, reputed to have been sold to Pen-yr-Orsedd Quarry, appears to be the

Fordson tractor used by Maenofferen Quarry in the Blaenau Ffestiniog yards until 1966.

No. 19 was an Estate Fordson tractor converted to rail by use of a Muir-Hill chassis, only to revert to road use again (1933/4).

The cars save one were purchased from local garages; all but one were of 'Morris' origin, the exception being a 'Rover' (probably No. 16) which cost £15 18s. 2d. in September 1937. Five of these units survived to 1954, three to 1960 (numbers not known) and No. 3 was extant in May 1965.

No.	Date	Cylinders	Notes
1	1931/2	6	For use at Port; rebuilt May 1946 with Lister diesel engine.
2	1931/2	6	For use at Port.
*3	1934	4	Last to survive (1965).
4	1934	4	
5	1934	4	May have been converted from Fordson tractor off Estate and sold to Maenofferen Quarry, Blaenau Ffestiniog.
†6	1935	4	
7	1936	•	
*8	1936	•	
9	1937	•	
10	1937	•	
11	1937	•	
*12	1937	•	
13	1938	•	
14	1939	•	
*15	1939	•	
*16	1939	•	
17	1939	•	
18	1940	•	Converted to Estate tractor -- rail wheels never fitted.
19	(see text)	•	

*Still in service 1949.
†Frame used in building diesel tractor No. 17 (q.v.)
• All probably 6 cylinders

Some of the early conversions from 'bull-nose' bonnet cars put the engine in a channel-steel frame chassis fitted with heavy end beams. Drive was taken from the gearbox on to the rear wheelset which was of standard wagon variety; the leading set was placed conveniently to take the weight of the engine. Later Morris 'flat-nosed' bonnets (e.g. No. 12) with temperature gauge on the filler cap were, like the 'bull-nose', retained on the conversions; parts of the car seating were used for a driving cab behind the gearbox, the driver sitting with his legs down between outside framework or chassis. From the mid-thirties heavy plate frames with curved beams carried the larger 6-cylinder engines; simple roofs were sometimes fitted but here and there removed if the tractor worked through low tunnels. The first conversions were originally springless (coil springs fitted later) and had to have weights added when in operation they were found to slip. Later conversions had coil springs from the start, running in customary horn-guides. Gearbox arrangements remained as for road usage, and the single reverse gear was an inconvenience; the Port tractors were turned on the wagon tables there but in the Quarry reverse travel was usually unvoidable. They retained the bulb motor horns from the cars and the full leather-covered seats.

These light petrol units did not replace steam – they were mainly to be found on weak galleries or replacing hand-worked methods.

	Wheel Diameter	Wheelbase	Length (over Chassis only)	Width
First Conversions	1 ft 3 in.	3 ft 0 in.	9 ft 1 in.	3 ft 1 in.
Later Conversions	1 ft 3 in.	app. 3 ft 0 in.	8 ft 9 in.	3 ft 1 in.

DIESEL-ENGINED RAIL TRACTORS   (all 4-wheel diesel-mechanical: chain drive)

All except Nos. 1 & 17 built by Ruston & Hornsby Ltd., Lincoln, most of these being Type 20 DL or the earlier 16/20 horse power.

No.	Maker's Number	Size or Class	Date	Source*	Disposal	Notes
1	—		1946	Coed-y-Parc. Fitted Lister diesel engine of 15th September, 1945 (£126 10s. 0d) Into service 16th June, 1946.	Scrap December 1967	ex-later conversion petrol tractor fully enclosed cab, one of Ministry of Works units used Sheds I & P 1941–46.
2	198292	33/40HP	1940	*November 1946 – used at Bethesda	Scrap 1967	
3	218033	33/40HP	1943	*April 1947 ex Hatfield	Scrap 1966	
4	218011	20DL	1943	* ditto	Scrap 1964	
5	222072	20DL	1943	* ditto	Scrap 1966	

No.	Maker's Number	Size or Class	Date	Source*	Disposal	Notes
6	223674	20DL	1943	* ditto	Scrap 1966	
7	223680	20DL	1943	* ditto	Scrap 1966	
8	187084	16/20HP	1937	*January 1948 ex Swansea	Scrap 1964	
9	183763	16/20HP	1937	* ditto	Scrap 1964	
10†	181818	20HP	12/1936	ex War Dept. ex Corsham	Scrap October 1957	
11	189994	16/20HP	1938	ditto	Scrap	Under repair at Coed-y-Parc when closed: left in pieces.
12	181812	20HP	1936	*January 1948 ex Swansea	Scrap 1966	
13	211596	20DL	1941	*April 1949 ex Bungey	Scrap 1967	
14	211605	20DL	1941	* ditto	Scrap 1964	
15	202976	20DL	1940	* ditto	Scrap 1966	
16	211640	20DL	1941	* ditto	Scrap 1964	
17	—	—	1949	Coed-y-Parc. Built on frame of No. 16 petrol tractor.	Scrap 1968	Used Lister engine of 3rd February, 1949 (£155 7s. 4d.)
18	223685	20DL	1944	* 1951	Scrap 1966	
19	223701	20DL	1944	* 1951	Scrap 1966	
20	222753	?	1944	* 1951	Scrap 1966	
21	226297	20DL	1944	* 1951	Scrap 1966	
22	226302	20DL	1944	* 1950	Sold 1964	Preserved 1985
23	229651	20DL	1944	* 1950	Sold March 1967	
24	382820	40DL	1955	New: too heavy for Quarry – used on main line.	Sold Autumn 1966	to Sir Robert McAlpine: left site.

*ex Ministry of Supply: most originally had open cabs with roof on pillars: many roofs later removed. A few had enclosed cabs throughout life.

†Ran over top of incline 2nd October, 1957: passenger being propelled in wagon, killed – tractor remains survive.

[Acquisition dates of Nos. 22–3 succeed Nos. 18–21 due later delivery of Nos. 22–3.]

All tractors had water-cooled engine and 3 speed gearbox.

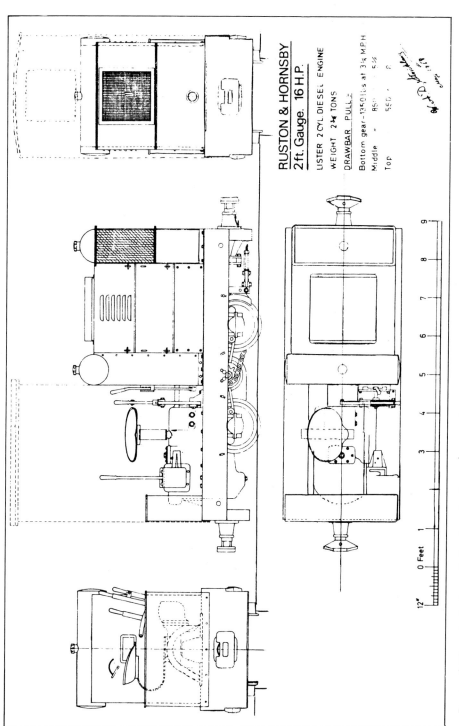

RUSTON & HORNSBY
2 ft. Gauge. 16 H.P.

LISTER 2 CYL DIESEL ENGINE

WEIGHT 2¼ TONS

DRAWBAR PULL

Bottom gear—1350 lbs at 3½ M P H
Middle   "   850   "   5¼
Top   "   550   "   8

Drawing: W.A.D. Strickland

Ruston & Hornsby Ltd. small diesel-engined tractor as used on insecure galleries of the Quarry.

Class	Length Overall	Width Overall	Height to Bonnet	Weight[a]	Wheel Diameter	Wheelbase
16/20HP	9 ft 0½ in.	3 ft 3 in.	4 ft 11 in.	2¾–3¼ tons	1 ft 3 in.	2 ft 7½ in.
20DL	(new no. for 16/20HP Series)			2¾–3½ tons	1 ft 4.5/16 in.	
33/40HP	11 ft 3½ in.	3 ft 3½ in.	5 ft 5 in.	4½–5 tons	?	3 ft 4¾ in.
40DL	(new no. for 33/40HP Series)			4½–6½ tons		
20HP				2¾ tons		

20DL built in large numbers for Ministry of Supply in World War II.
(20DL or 40DL is code for HP; D=Diesel; L=narrow gauge.)

(a) Depending on ballast weights.
Ref: 'RUSTON & HORNSBY LOCOMOTIVES' (E.S. Tonks) The Industrial Locomotive Society 1974.

Locomotive Liveries

Before 1890 de Winton engines were painted brown or carmine and the Hunslets similarly. An all-round black border was given to this and divided from the brown or carmine by a narrow blue lining (sometimes

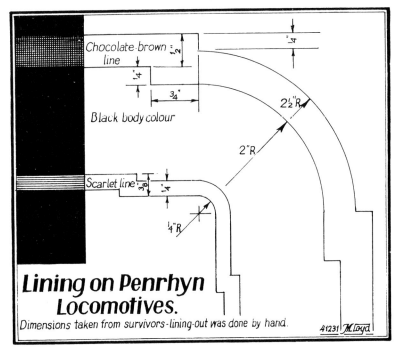

Lining on Penrhyn Locomotives.

Dimensions taken from survivors-lining-out was done by hand.

scarlet ?): this lining was given elaborate corners, the whole giving a most striking finish. Simplification was inevitable!

From 1890 painting of the main line Hunslet engines differed slightly from the remainder of the steam fleet; the main line stud was glossy black, with rear cab sheets lined at first with four panels and later, with three, the outer panels then being rectangles and the centre one a square. Cylinders were also lined in red; the remainder of the lining was as for Quarry engines (q.v.).

The Quarry engines had a more muted lining than used on the main line; both shared the use of an overall black with tanks and lower cab side sheets lined rectangularly with angular and radiused corners in a ½ in. chocolate brown, having a ¼ in. scarlet line inside this but separated from the chocolate brown lining by 1–1½ in. Frames were black, lined similarly: cylinders were not lined out. The main line engines had lining of bolder dimensions – see CHARLES currently in the Penrhyn Castle Museum, on which every opportunity for the fullest decoration has been taken (engines were never noted in traffic with white-tyred wheels etc)!

After 1936 the chocolate brown lining was replaced by sky blue.

Occasionally a non-main line engine had its cylinders lined in blue (not red, as on the main line). Buffer beams were once black lined in scarlet, but sometimes these colours were reversed, on the main line engines especially. Cab interiors were white and often showed the driver's name (discreetly!): brass and copper work was usually polished, including the dome-cover. The prominent bucket hung from a smokebox hook and chain on the main line engines (used to carry sand) was originally black, later white and latterly plain galvanized. There was only *one* bucket, carried by the duty locomotive; it was dented so the offending portion was usually hung towards the smokebox door.

Tractor Liveries

Petrol units were all-black, those having 'bull-noses' being highly polished there. Diesel units were usually green but Nos. 18–23 were maroon, lined in white and black.

CONVEYANCE OF PASSENGERS; PASSENGER VEHICLES AND WORKMEN'S TRAINS

16th January, 1880–9th February, 1951.

Spooner had already laid before Lord Penrhyn the possibilities of carrying public, estate and quarry passengers, but Lord Penrhyn was not convinced overall. A set of Rules (in Welsh) and the necessary

vehicles for a Workmen's Train had been agreed and ordered respectively between Quarrymen's Union and Management on 1st September,
1879 with a view to making the Quarry more efficient and conveying
employees to and from the districts where they lived. On 17th August,
1879 the service was foreshadowed by placing an order with de Winton
& Co. for eight vehicles @ £37 2s. 0d. each – they were ready by 20th
October but Lord Penrhyn instructed they were not to be delivered
until 5th November; and it was the men rather than Lord Penrhyn who
created the service. The train began running on 16th January, 1880.

The Rules laid down where the train was to stop; each place had a
slab-built waiting shed with a slate roof:

1) at Llandegai, where the old road was crossed by the Railway
2) at Pandy, at the west end of the Tregarth loop (later called Tyn-y-
   Lon)
3) at Felin-Hen, on the south side of the road bridge

though the Rules wrote of Llandegai Farm Road, Pandy Farm and
Pentir Crossing.

No time was lost – the carriages had been charged at de Winton's
price of £37 2s. 0d each at the time the Rules were agreed, and when
they were amended and published in May 1880, 8 vehicles and 2
buildings were ready.

The train was operated and funded by The Workmen's Train
Society, and a few records have survived. If a member died his initial
contribution was refunded and the next applicant offered his place. The
Society actually owned the carriages, but hired the steam locomotive,
crew and guard to work the train. (This ownership proved to be a
problem to the acquisition of certain redundant vehicles by the Talyllyn
Railway Preservation Society: in 1952 'H' and 'P' were donated, re-
gauged and sprung; 'C', 'D', 'E' and 'G' were purchased in 1953–4
without running gear. It proved difficult to find sufficient members of
the then-non-functioning Society to permit the transaction.) The Society also paid for a man to oil and examine the coaches, and have any
repair work carried out at Coed-y-Parc workshops. Just before the train
ceased to run an accident caused by a defective wheel caused argument
as to cost and responsibility; management was prepared to be lenient
when Society funds were low, (for instance when repairs proved rather
extensive, E.A. Young the Quarry Manager dipped into his own pocket
to find £3). Finances of the Train were for many years in the hands of
the Williams family (Quarry Overlookers) but as a shareholding the
scheme was wound up on 14th August, 1940 when the survivors were
paid out. The coaches thereafter were left at the Quarry and the few
men who used them during 1940–51 paid 1/- per week each; this
covered the train crew and the gatekeeper, but as the users became
fewer the train ran at a loss – subsequently the Quarry provided the
train free of cost to the men. Some reminiscences written in 1945

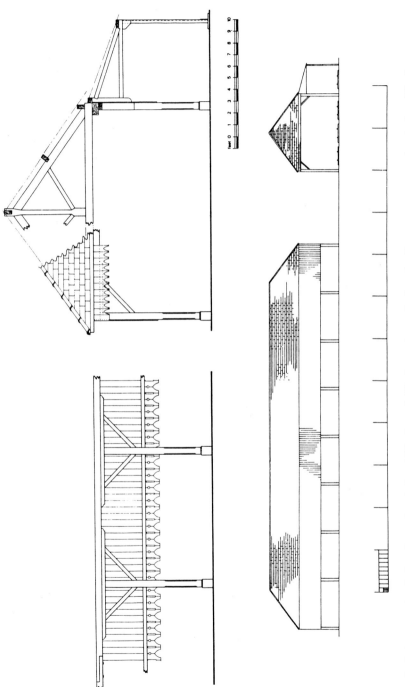

Built in 1880 the timber-framed and slated Workmen's Train carriages shed at the Port, was an attractive design. The lean-to was probably added as the number of vehicles increased, in 1903.

Drawing: C.G. Down

recalled the contrast with early days, when many Anglesey men worked at the Quarry by the week and it was necessary for open wagons to be attached to the coaches to accommodate them.[61] This would occur on Mondays and Saturdays only. 'In 1928–30 when the full number of coaches (13) were on the train, it was rather a heavy load coming up in the morning with a greasy rail as the locos had no sandboxes, only the familiar bucket hung on the smokebox door. I fitted sandboxes on the three engines about that time, which greatly improved things.'

Williams wrote in 1951: 'I cannot go further than January 1894; there were then 10 coaches 'A' to 'J' and they were carrying a full capacity . . . approx. 240 men . . . all were members of the Train and had paid an initial 33/2d. fee; in addition they were paying yearly about 7/3d.' (9 payments of 7d. and 4 of 6d. each year). He continued that it cost 6/7d. p.a. in 1895, but due to the strike in 1896 the accounts showed only for 10 months; the cost was 5/6d. per head. The strike ended in October 1897 and the three months when the train operated cost 2/- p.a. each; this became 7/7d. (1898) 7/1d. (1899) but the books were missing for the period of 'The Big Strike' (last seen in the hands of lawyers due to legal problems of train operation) 1900–1903.[62] From then to 1908 Williams recalls extra carriages made up a total of 16 but only 10 were regularly needed; cost in 1908 was 6/6d. p.a. per man; he adds that the World War I period books were missing, that another coach was added after it; cost 13/- per annum as a result of wartime inflation. By 1924 12 coaches were in constant traffic, this time the costing was altered to 1/- per month for Members; the amount for non-Members is not known.[63] In 1927 coach 'Q' was added; there were now 17 of them but only 13 operated.[64] By 1939 12 coaches were sufficient for the train; the Quarry closed due to wartime demands for labour elsewhere. When the Society was wound up the Members received 33/- each. In 1941 Quarry work re-started as due to bombs and fire, new slate for damaged roofs was urgently needed. There being no petrol (save rationed fuel) and road vehicle tyres being in limited supply, the train was re-started in 1941 with only 6 coaches. Soon road competition began to make inroads, and during the latter half of the 1940s it bit deeply; only 4 coaches were required by 1950 and the train was stopped on 9th February, 1951, buses being substituted.

During The Great Strike the train continued to run on a reduced basis apparently without the Society's permission or insurance cover, this state of affairs being possible whilst management/employee relations were at deadlock and legal responsibilities were of secondary interest. There was a greater need for the train than before as many who continued to work moved away from the Quarry area and even into Anglesey to live – for their own protection – and they needed the use of the train. Some never returned to Bethesda. Attempts were made to wreck it and on 31st July, 1901 six youths threw stones at the train from Tregarth road overbridge; five of them lived at Waen-Pandy. They were identified by women travelling on the train (the only reference found to the 'fair sex' using it) and as punishment Lord Penrhyn closed the station most convenient for these youths (Pandy) and opened one at Tregarth by the said bridge. During and after the strike it was found the main line engine could not handle the 13 coaches – 12 being the absolute limit in dry weather – so if needed extras were attached to the first Up slate empties train which ran 'mixed' until about 1910. At this time extra stops were added: at The White Bridge and Tregarth (where the 'punishment' stop was made permanent), but by 1906 Tyn-y-Lon (ex Pandy) had been unofficially re-instated: to the end there were five official stops and the two additional ones were retained.

[The writer used the train frequently at a time when there was no other means save walking – one had to be at the Port very early indeed to catch the morning Up train which left almost empty but quickly filled as it moved up the line; though obviously there were recognised stops, the driver never actually brought the train to a stand anywhere! The riding qualities of the coaches were very indifferent, and when a group of men joined the train together they all had regular places in one vehicle. The purpose of this was not simply social, for visitors were given an extra coach (brought from store at the Port) which was inevitably a lively rider with 'square wheels': the visitor was soon aware that he would be better to join the men, and effect a change of vehicle whilst in motion!]

The coaches carried identification letters and compartment numbers (cut from iron sheet) on each side: 'A'–'H' were delivered by 5th November, 1879; 'I' and 'J' by May 1880; 'K' 1st October, 1902; 'L' 26th November, 1902; 'M' 24th October, 1903; 'N' 3rd October, 1904; 'O' 30th December, 1905; 'P' 22nd June, 1908. 'A'–'J' were supplied by de Winton, 'K'–'Q' by Coed-y-Parc (and easily distinguishable as they had slatted seats whilst the de Winton ones had planked seats); lettering and numbering were done so as to allocate each seat. Williams recalls the full 16 in use, and the instance of 'Q' being built in 1927.

The wooden vehicles were four-wheeled, roofless, with three compartments having no doors and holding 24 skinny persons – on any railway open to inspection by the Board of Trade they certainly would not have been permitted! They had 'standard' slate wagon wheelsets (15½ in. diameter, with 7-curved spokes) and a prominent handbrake lever on one side which acted on one wheelset with large wooden blocks. Coach 'M' at Penrhyn Castle is (figures in brackets are dimensions taken from other vehicles): length over body 11 ft 8 in. (14 ft); width over floor 5 ft 1 in.; height of body only 3 ft 1½ in.; wheelbase 5 ft 6 in. (4 ft 8½ in.); total height of body above rail 4 ft 4 in. (4 ft 2 in.); colour latterly was a dark cherry red.

The Train ran at different times during summer and winter, and these were further modified to suit daylight or weather as necessary. Between 1896 and 1901 it left Port at 6 a.m.; returned from Quarry at

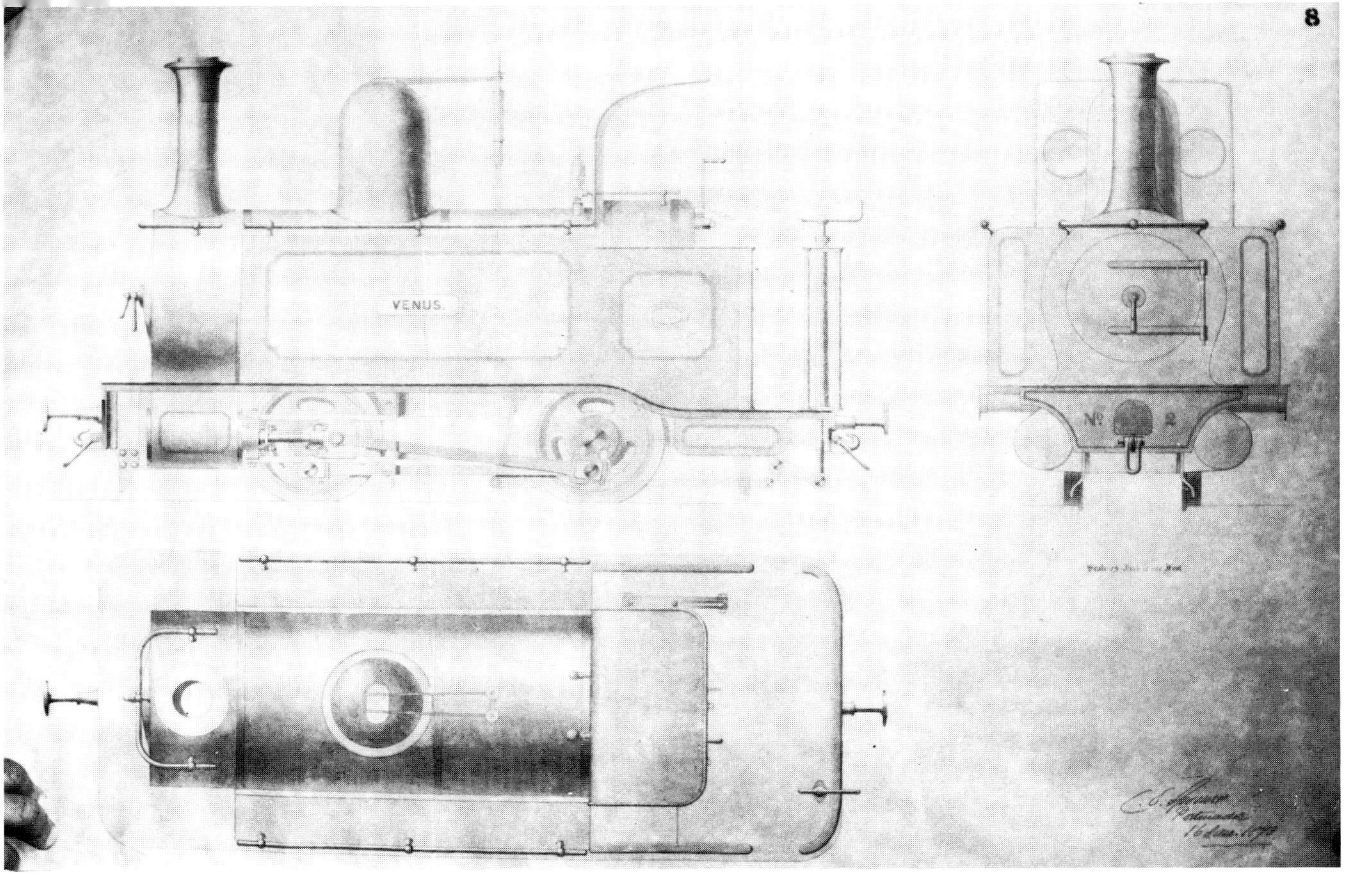

Plate XCI Proposed designs by C.E. Spooner are shown by this and the next six plates; herewith shunting engine VENUS. *Univ. College of North Wales*

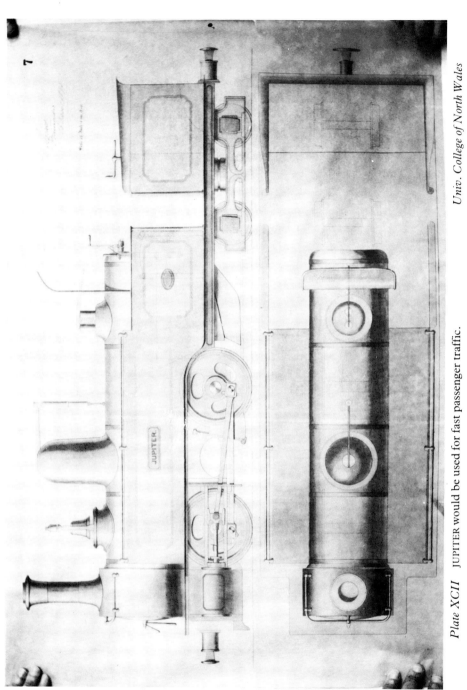

Plate XCII   JUPITER would be used for fast passenger traffic.

Plate XCIII   JAMES SPOONER was intended for mixed traffic.   *Univ. College of North Wales*

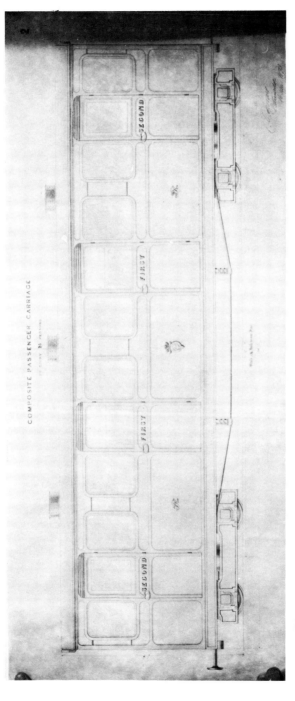

COMPOSITE PASSENGER CARRIAGE

Plate XCIV   This 1st & 2nd Class Composite was given F.R. No. 20 and Garter!   *Univ. College of North Wales*

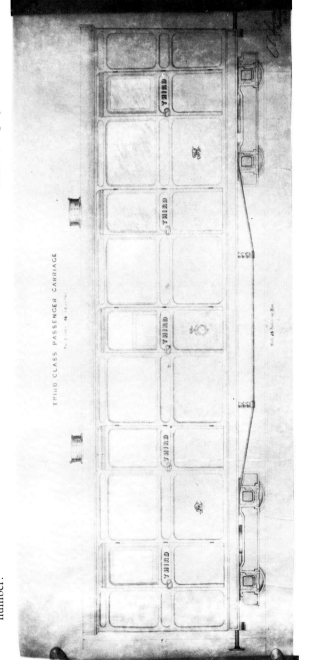

Plate XCV An all-3rd Class five-compartment coach with F.R. garters and monograms, but carrying no number.

Univ. College of North Wales

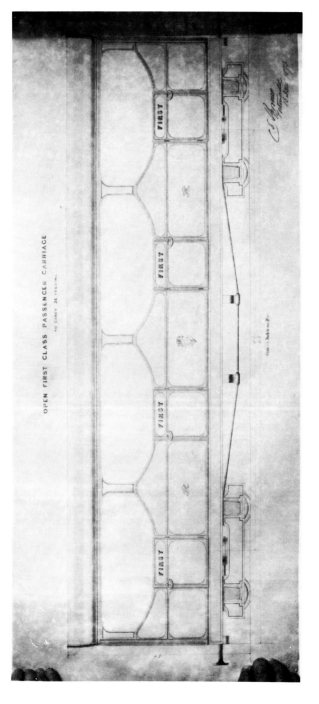

Plate XCVI A 1st Class partially-open-sided Observation Carriage carrying F.R. No. 22.

Univ. College of North Wales

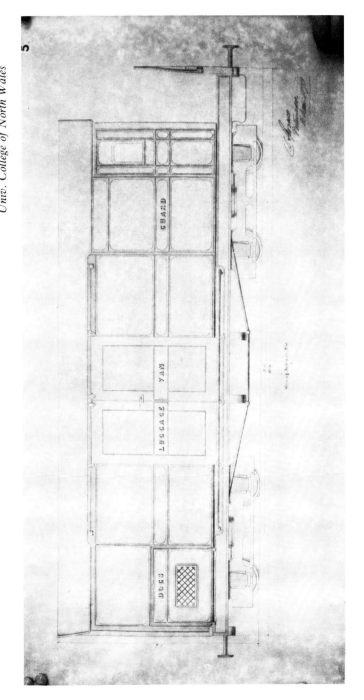

Plate XCVII A Luggage Van with Dog Compartment; the only carriage drawing which omits F.R. undertones.
Univ. College of North Wales

Plate XCVIII SYBIL MARY, last of the slate ships to ply from Port Penrhyn. Built by Scott & Sons, Bowling in 1921 and sold 1954.

National Museum of Wales

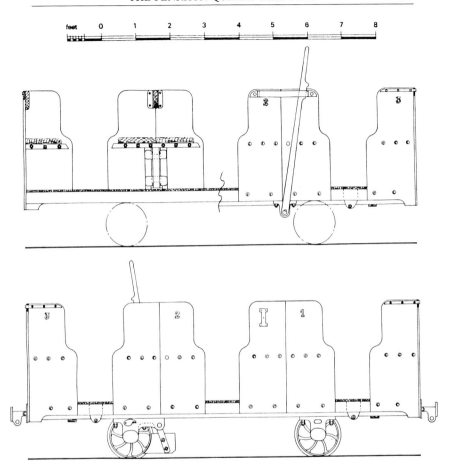

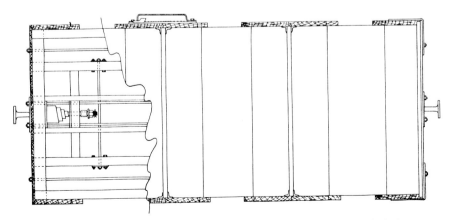

Workmen's Train carriage 'I', supplied by May 1880.　　*Drawing: C.G. Down*

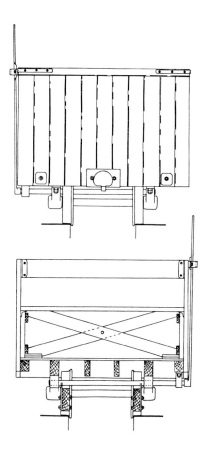

6.20 p.m. (pre-1886) and 6 p.m. (post-1886); these were summer times. From July 1901 the Up train left at 6.30 a.m. and the Down at 5.45 p.m. and in February 1904 the traffic had grown to require two Up trains (the second 'Mixed') to run. Only one train ran Down however; times were as for July 1901. The 'Mixed' did not run on Saturdays when slate wagon trains did not operate and only general goods were carried. The Saloon – in use as a Pay Carriage – was coupled on, firstly monthly, then fortnightly (and by World War I, once a week). The train carried on in this pattern until 1939 and after the irregularities of wartime, the last Down slate train (leaving about 5.30–5.45 p.m.) had the workmen's vehicles attached to it.

There was a strike of the Crosville bus services in May 1957 when the train was re-instated briefly, using four coaches.

Overlooker's Coach

A much older passenger vehicle is now in the Penrhyn Castle Museum, probably beginning life as an Overlooker's Coach dating from Railroad days. It has three 'compartments' seating two in each, with open sides and no roof, and suited for use on the Quarry inclines for its latter-day purpose was to carry V.I.Ps and officials around the workings. In construction it somewhat resembles the workmen's carriages, save that seating faces one way, and its varnished finish recalls the pews of any neighbouring Chapel.

A handbrake is fitted and operated by the passenger in the corner rear seat. It runs on 'standard' curved spoke wheelsets and is built on a wagon chassis suitable for horse haulage; the coupling arrangements and cast-iron footboard are more recent. Throughout its life the coach had been kept in a small covered shed. A log entry (13th May, 1840) may refer to it: 'New Coach at Quarry, with Yonge Family from Manchester' (it will be recalled the Yonges owned half the parish before the Pennant era: but it must not be assumed that the Yonges were *of* Manchester). As the log never makes reference to road vehicles, perhaps this is the earliest rail coach. Dimensions are: body 8 ft 1½ in. long; 3 ft 2½ in. wide; total height from rail 4 ft 5 in. with wheelbase 2ft 10 in.

Private Saloons

Also at the Museum is the private Saloon Carriage in which his Lordship made monthly visits to the Quarry; this is a beautiful small four-wheel Saloon, provided for a visit by the Prince and Princess of Wales on 12th July, 1894. It is a bijou replica of Wolverton (L.N.W.R.) practice of the times, and was probably assembled at Coed-y-Parc (according to an account in 'THE LIVERPOOL DAILY POST'); it was rebuilt there in 1926, though the latter work must have applied internally as the outward appearance and running gear remained unchanged.

An account in the 'NORTH WALES CHRONICLE' of the 1894 Royal Visit says: "At 3.30 in the afternoon (they) returned by way of Penrhyn Park to Port Penrhyn where they made a tour of the jetties and breakwater in a saloon carriage built by the carpenters at the quarry – they then embarked on a steam launch . . . and boarded the MIRA."

There are strong reasons for thinking that Crewe or Wolverton delivered the body as a complete unit; E.A. Young the Quarry Manager had links with the L.N.W.R. The body is carried on sawn-down standard gauge railway sleepers to which running gear of typical quarry-availability has been added, and though *this* vehicle is credited as having been that of which Young had made a gift to Lord Penrhyn, there is no contemporary confirmation. There are five equal windows on each side and a door. Seats are arranged along each side and at the doors' end and the interior is finished in blue leather cloth in the sumptuous manner of Edwardian times; there are loose cushions, floor mats, high seat backs and curtains.[65] At the non-door end is a wooden handwheel which operates the brake. The sides are waisted, the livery of 'Crewe' fashion, being cream upper panelling with blue/black on the lower; lining out is in gold-edged vermilion and there is a small coronet on the doors. The body is all timber including the framing, (but the running gear is a cast-iron assembly with laminated springing, and tie rodding all bolted up to the frame), and is 11 ft 10 in. long and stands 8 ft 4 in. above the rails; the maximum width is 5 ft 6 in. and wheelbase 5 ft 6 in. also; in the Museum the coach stands on 'Dowlais Steel' rails. The records are unsure whether the official capacity is 14 or 15 persons but with this form of seating it is not critical! The coach was also used when the wages, calculated fortnightly but paid weekly, were brought up from a Bangor bank in the train from Port Penrhyn: "by then the Penrhyn family had no need of it".

A predecessor of this Saloon has not survived (although a photograph of it dates as recently as 1935–36) but it had a quilted upholstery interior. Its general layout was similar though smaller, being perhaps about 9 ft long × 5 ft wide and 7 ft 6 in. above rails and having the appearance of being built on wagon running-gear components. There was vertical panelling at ends and boarding up to waist at the sides; above the waist the sides had four windows on the west side. On the east side there was probably one door positioned as for the existing saloon – there was no doorstep. Each end contained two glazed 'portholes' at eye-level about 6 in. diameter, positioned so that when inside, corner-seated passengers could observe the train or line in either direction. Though exact dimensions are not known, the roof was scarcely high enough to allow a grown man to stand inside! One pair of wheels was braked. Like the Overlooker's Coach, it was finished in varnished timber and may well have been the conveyance of the Agent as between Port and Quarry. Local tradition has it that Queen Victoria declined to travel in it . . . and with equal firmness declined to sleep in the slate bed specially made for her at the Castle!

It is believed that about 1877 the Quarry Manager made a gift to Lord Penrhyn of a passenger coach. It also played a double role by bringing up the wages' money, prepared in the Port Office. The 'CARNARVON & DENBIGH HERALD' refers to a fire in a Port shed (April 1935) which burnt a coach; perhaps in this way this Saloon was destroyed.

Man-Riding Cars in the Quarry

In very recent times, a set of man-riding cars was provided for taking men up and down the inclines in the Quarry, run in pairs, each vehicle having a pair of angled back-to-back seats with footboards set lengthwise upon it so as to maintain the level of the riders on the incline; the appearance of the 'train' resembled a flight of steps mounted on a flat moving platform. End handrails curved from sole up to central backrest divided each set of seats, which were slatted. These vehicles would have been quite useless on level ground; their place of work was the inclines system between Red Lion and Ponc Holywell (611 ft to 1,090 ft).

WAGONS

Writing in 1826–7, Von Oyenhausen and Von Dechem summarized their comments on the rolling stock with enviable exactitude:

> The wheels of the wagons which run on this railway have double flanges, which is very unsuitable; the wheels are 12½ in. high, with a rim 2¼ in. wide; the nave is 3½ in. long. The axles of the wagons themselves turn, and the wheels also turn on the axles.[66]
>
> Wagons for the transport of finished slates have only a wooden or iron railing standing up from the strong bottom of the wagon; they hold one ton, or 20 cwt. of slates. In the quarry, tipping wagons with wooden frames are employed for carrying away the refuse. The wheels lie inside of a wooden frame upon which a small pedestal is erected; on this one half of the body rests and is hung so that it may be turned. The other end of the body is held by a sloping pair of supports held fast by a cross-bar. As soon as this bar is withdrawn, the support falls down; the wagon body becomes free on the pedestal and is then easily tipped over.

Contrastingly, a commentary on wagons in recent times is full of pitfalls, for although there was an annual stocktaking, no inventory of wagons has survived.

Prior to January 1877 wagons were marked only with their tare weight, but in that year those working between the Quarry sheds and the Port were given numbers. Within the Quarry, the quarry and mill sleds and the three-sided rubbish wagons usually carried a mark or stencilled name to show to which Quarry District they were assigned. There may have been c.2,250 vehicles in this category.

All stock ran on double flanged wheels until 1878, when de Winton supplied slate wagons singly flanged: thereafter all wagons for the new Railway also had such 1 ft 3 in. diameter wheels (more recent wheel sets were 1 ft 4 in. diameter); while certain single flanged stock also ran in the Quarry, most remained double flanged.

The wagon central buffer-coupler came into being in December 1877, but steam operation on the main line had already begun without such a refinement.

A daily log of 1950 includes the following stock: slate wagons Nos. 1–400; 'Fullersite' wagons Nos. 1–80; coal wagons Nos. 1–60; main line sleds Nos. 1–40; but this was not a complete coverage.

Records now reveal the dates and batches of wagons added, but when surviving stock was taken to store in the Quarry in the 1960s such records proved unreliable as survivors do not fit into categories. Stock was allowed to run down and renewed or repaired in forms which were convenient rather than in similar style to the original: wagons carried numbers higher than those of the 1950 log.

Slate Wagons

(Not numbered before 1887 and numbered 1 onwards thereafter.)

Penrhyn may claim to be the birthplace of this most Welsh of narrow gauge wagons. From earliest days the installation of weighing machines demanded that the overall lengths must correspond, though differences of an inch or so in basic dimensions were usual. There were several periods of development from the pioneer 'crate' bodies riding on a heavier chassis with the 'crate' inside the wheelbase, to the adoption of similar but heavier bodies in wood or metal having the wheels totally beneath the body. There are a number of paintings and engravings of the Quarry area made in the early part of the nineteenth century; many of these show one or two varieties of open wagon in use, but somewhat naturally the attention paid by the painter to detail is not always helpful. All paintings show a four-wheel vehicle, some with heavy wooden frames almost hiding the wheels behind them and carrying a heavy wooden body tapered upwards and outwards like a chauldron wagon with two upright frame members on each side; others show the same principle but suggest a sheet-iron body with large spoked wheels outside it. Other renderings stress right-angular bodies and most show a number of horses at work (so perhaps not painted before 1828) – not to mention track in wooden rails (?) or exaggerated bar forms.[67] By 1817 there were about 220 'crate' slate wagons but in 1833 the wooden framed body appeared, carried on a wooden chassis and loading 1¼ tons . . . up to 1837 all new building involved wagons of this pattern and the conversion of the three preceding forms into something similar. (The 'REPERTORY OF ARTS AND MANUFACTURES' Vol. III engraving (1803) shows this early form of wagon, but the chassis has been distorted.) Two hundred iron-framed bodies on heavier wooden chassis began to appear in May 1859; all of these had been built by 1862. Totals were 380 for c.1837 and 420 for 1860, the latter including a batch of iron type made in 1859, plus survivors from earlier days.

Up to this time the wooden solebars of wagons had been extended to form simple 'buffers' projecting beyond the body to suit the chain and ring couplings of the period, and all had double-flanged wheels. The 1874 wind of change (heralded by modernisation of the Railroad) was followed on 24th November, 1877 when de Winton was given an order for 200 slate wagons of their own completely new design, a pattern already used by competitors hereabouts. It was intended to fit every vehicle with a wooden brake block operated by hand lever, but when it was found they caught fire, iron shoes were specified on 7th July, 1879; on 4th March, 1880 the brake lever (with its securing rack) design was revised. Wooden floors were fitted. Delivery was to be made at eight per month but after the first batch on 5th October, 1879 the makers found they could not supply more than four per month.

Single-flanged wheels and central buffer-couplers have already been noted; and at last the rolling stock of the line was on a par with the best of rivals in the trade.

By November 1877 the old slate fleet had been reduced to 340 wagons, and now any new wagons were given numbers previously allocated to the old. All old stock – much rebuilt – was now withdrawn, and no 1801–37 wagons survived. With the addition of certain of the 200 wagons of iron bodied/wood-framed 1859–62 batch, about 400 slate wagons were available.

de Winton & Co. received two further 1879 orders each for twelve wagons having longer bodies on 6 ft 3 in. wheelbases; these followed the last of the 1877 batch. The instructions were included among another for rubbish wagon bodies thus:

13th September, 1879 20 iron rubbish bodies (only)
13th September, 1879 12 'long' slate wagons (probably braked)
15th November, 1879 12 'long' slate wagons (probably not braked)

The very last slate wagons were delivered October 1886–July 1895 spread over several orders to The Midland Railway Carriage & Wagon Co. Ltd., bodies only being supplied, Coed-y-Parc completing them. On these the central coupler was altered from de Winton type to a sprung pattern to prevent wagons 'snatching', the cause of slate break-ages. Brakes had now become a mixed blessing . . . about half the former de Winton wagons so fitted had had them removed, and none of the Midland bodies batch had them. (Photographic evidence confirms removal of certain brakes very early in the existence of some wagons.) On the Caernarvon-built wagons the brake rod was left in situ as a strengthener. Wagons fitted with the conspicuous central buffer remained unique to the end; it was only certain of these slate wagons which had them and the rest – as was common to all other stock on the line – had a curved buffing plate, in primitive form being simply of timber faced with an iron rubbing strap. Despite all this modernisation some older wagons survived into the 1950s; these were certainly of 'nine-life category' for even when the first Midland order was placed, only 96 'old' wagons survived in a grand total of 296, and all through the ensuing years the traffic tonnage was falling.

To prevent breakages in transit, after 1908 wooden pads were placed inside the bodies to protect the load when being lowered down Felin-Fawr Incline; capacity was slightly reduced; due to 1925 changes in layout at the Port wagons might become turned, so pads were fitted to both ends of some stock. During the winter of 1912/3 a major overhaul of stock was given, and a wagon of quite different outline would result, sometimes of dissimilar dimensions. When the Railway closed only 5% of the original 400 wagons was unaccounted for, a remarkable testimony to good husbandry. The complete de Winton wagons had cost £30 3s. 0d. each; the Midland bodies averaged £10 15s. 0d. each and even bringing in the cost of repairs over 80 years, each wagon must have expended little more than 60 new pence per annum . . .!

A summary of slate wagons appears on pages 142 and 143.

First Phase

The open-sided form of slate wagon may have been derived from the similar crates used in the pottery trade, and the Llandegai Tramway used demountable bodies of like design whereby flint 'cakes' could be taken up to the Mill, finished products brought down again and the loaded bodies shipped to Toxteth. To keep these bodies as low as possible to save lifting, they would be carried on wheeled frames with the wheels taken above and through the frame: an acceptable frame would accommodate one crate, so a small wagon of narrow gauge sufficed. It would be natural to base the first slate wagons on this principle and perhaps adapt the pottery crates. A local tradition maintains that the bodies were derived from the panniers used by pack animals which were used in collecting heather from surrounding hillsides, brought into Bangor for 3d. per crate and used for cattle feed (the 'crate' was contemporarily a conventional transport container). [See drawing page 141: speculative design and original draughtsmanship by Eric Foulkes.]

Wagon building took place at the Port between 1801–15, firstly on a batch of 75; ultimately 105 were made. Thomas Knowles (surely a Liverpool man?) of Allt-Ucha, Pentir, was responsible; the frames were of oak with wrought-iron fittings. The double-flanged wheels "weigh 14 lbs." were 1 ft 2 in. diameter on 1½ in. axles which ran in plain cast bearings outside the wheels and bolted up through the outside frame; cross members supported the body: the tare weight would be about 3½ cwt. and load 16 cwt. In an 'overlap' period 1815–17 the bodies were gradually replaced by raising the height of the sides about 3 in. Loading was now 17½ cwt. and at the end of this time there were 220 slate wagons. In and from 1823 the bodies were again changed and increased in capacity by building them out to the full width of the frame; this was too much for the old chassis and increased loads (about 1 ton) cracked the frames. By now all such rebuilding was carried out at Coed-y-Parc.

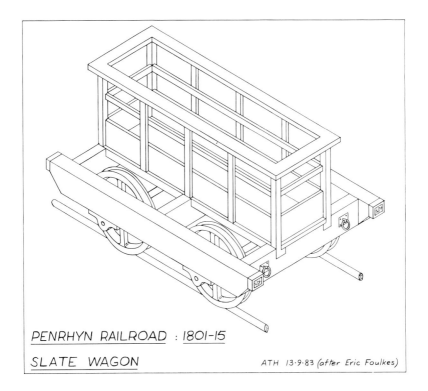

PENRHYN RAILROAD : 1801-15

SLATE WAGON   ATH 13·9·83 (after Eric Foulkes)

Second Phase

In 1833 to 1837 a larger all-wooden wagon was evolved at the Workshops of 1¼ ton capacity and the general dimensions adopted were to remain for the rest of time. By 1837 about 380 wagons were available.

Third Phase

This was an important step; iron-framed bodies replaced wooden ones on a wooden chassis – all made at Coed-y-Parc. Building occupied from May 1859 to June 1862 and during 1860 the fleet reached its highest number, 420 wagons. The substantial chassis frame had four longitudinal members and resembled closely the wagons of more recent times; the obvious difference was in the wheels which, to give the load a degree of 'cushioning' (no wagons were sprung) wooden-centred Mansell wheels were fitted[68] – but having a double-flanged cast iron tyre fastened on. For some reason these were disappointing; however by this period Hadfields Ltd. of Sheffield was offering single-flanged wheelsets with a guarantee; these were available ex-stock at all times and there

SLATE WAGONS

Phase	Type	Dates	Body	Frame	Wheels	Wheelbase	Capacity	Body approximate external dimensions			Builder	Notes
								Length	Width	Height		
First	1)	1801–15	Wooden	Wooden	1 ft 2½ in. diam. d/flanged	2 ft 0 in.	c.16½ cwt.	4 ft 4 in.	1 ft 6 in.	1 ft 6 in.	Thos. Knowles of Pentir (at Port)	A
First	1a)	1815–17	Wooden	Wooden	ditto	ditto	c.17½ cwt.	ditto	ditto	1 ft 9½ in.	Coed-y-Parc	B
First	1b)	1823–27	Wooden	Wooden	ditto	ditto	1 ton (later reduced)	ditto	?	?	Coed-y-Parc	C
Second	2)	1833–37	Wooden	Wooden (oak)	?	ditto	1¼ ton	approximately as Fourth Phase			Coed-y-Parc	D
Third	3)	1859–62	Iron	Wooden (oak)	1) Mansell (wood centre, iron tyre;) 1 ft 3½ in. diam. 2) later; cast iron same size, 7 curved spokes.	2 ft 10 in.?	1¼ ton	approximately as Fourth Phase			Coed-y-Parc	E
Fourth	3)	1879	Iron	Iron	1 ft 3½ in. diam. 7 curved spokes.	2 ft 10 in.	c.2½ ton	6 ft 3 in.	3 ft 3 in.	1 ft 7 in.	de Winton & Co.	F
Fifth	4)	1878–81	Iron	Iron	1 ft 3½ in. diam. s/flanged	3 ft 0 in.	2 ton 6 cwt.	5 ft 6 in.	2 ft 9¾ in. ★	2 ft 1 in.†	de Winton & Co.	G
Fifth	5)	1886–95	Iron	Iron	ditto	2 ft 9½ in. or 2 ft 10 in.	2 ton 5 cwt.	5 ft 6½ in.	2 ft 10¾ in.★★	1 ft 10¼ in.†	Midland R.C. & W.Co. and Coed-y-Parc	H

Dimensions taken from surviving wagons confirm that figures can only be a rough guide. Many wagons heavily rebuilt and beyond categorisation.

NOTES ON WAGON TABLE (opposite)

A   Initial building of 75 wagons; c.105 ultimately built. Oak frame. Wrought iron fittings to strengthen frame. Wheels inside framework but projecting above it. Body on top frame and between wheels – very narrow in consequence. Body possibly demountable and design possibly prompted by crates used in pottery trade.

B   Existing bodies replaced with substitutes of higher side; about 115 higher bodied wagons resulting.

C   Used existing frame but bodies rebuilt over full width. Frame unable to accept heavier load; rebuilds had short life.

D   Hardwood frames used for first time?

E   Wooden centred wheels replaced at early stage. About 200 wagons involved.

F   Fitted buffers/double brakes – see text.

G   Wheelsets supplied by Hadfields of Sheffield. First batch to carry vehicle numbers and central drawgear.

H   Wheelsets by Hadfields of Sheffield or Charles Hanswell & Co.

*Some 2 ft 11 in.
   ″ 3 ft 1½ in.
†Measured top body to underside of frame (remainder top to topside of frame).
**Some 2 ft 11½ in.

were few railways of this nature which did not utilise this service. This batch of wagons was given them in place of the existing Mansell pattern, being the first at Penrhyn to receive them, thus simplifying the task of Coed-y-Parc; they had seven curved spokes, were made in cast iron and ultimately all 200 wagons in this lot were so fitted. Hadfields long remained a reliable supplier.

Fourth Phase

This was obviously based on the Fifth Phase series when steps were taken to increase the individual loading of wagons but not perpetuated. Dimensions in the table (p.142) were taken from a survivor but variations in repairs have made it impossible to conceive the exact form as built. No. 104 of this series complete with brake was in service October 1953 and had buffing plates, not buffers; No. 161 (16 cwt. tare) retained buffers and brakes. 'THE LOCOMOTIVE MAGAZINE' for 1917 quotes these wagons' dimensions as forming the "standard wagon" to carry about 27 cu. ft of load.

Fifth Phase

By November 1877 (with the wagon fleet down to 340 units) de Winton's new design with central sprung drawgear with handbrake lever on one side but operating on all wheels was accepted and 200 wagons, delivery of which was to be spread over 4 years, were ordered. As each reached the weigh-table at Coed-y-Parc it took the number of an old wagon to be replaced. Hadfield wheelsets appeared and such was their success that in March 1881 it was decided to fit them under *all*

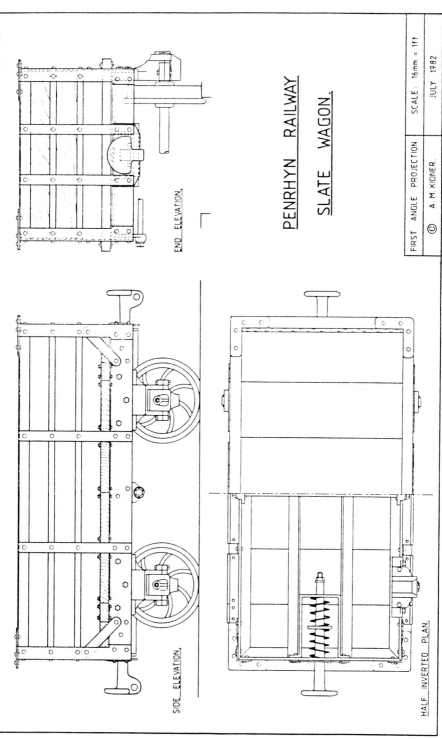

END ELEVATION.

SIDE ELEVATION.

HALF INVERTED PLAN.

PENRHYN RAILWAY.

SLATE WAGON.

| FIRST ANGLE PROJECTION | SCALE: 16mm = 1ft |
| © A. M. KIDNER. | JULY 1982 |

Fifth Phase Slate Wagon built by de Winton & Co. as running latterly with a number of modifications made at Coed-y-Parc.
Drawing: Alan M. Kidner

stock used on the main line i.e. to include certain coal wagons and slab wagons. [Though these Hadfield sets were widely respected for their security of wheel to axles, nonetheless on lines such as the Festiniog and Penrhyn the constant friction between brake shoe and tyre would in exceptional cases heat the wheel to the extent that it became loosened on the axle and caused a derailment. On the Penrhyn however, down-going trains had the added brake power of the locomotive at the head and a braking vehicle behind, features which the Festiniog gravity slate trains did not enjoy!]

Penrhyn trains were assembled so that the brake handle was on the west side; there was a temporary phase during the change-over in coupling methods when stock was fitted with two rings to take chain hooks.

The last batch of bodies from M.R.C.&W.Co. Ltd. of Birmingham was completed at Coed-y-Parc using such stocks as were available and had wheelsets from Hadfield or Charles Hanswell & Co. Only the sprung couplers distinguished them from the Caernarvon 'lot'; they had no brakes.

Finally, tare weights of wagons; it was in the interest of everyone that the loading of each wagon was known by weighing; the practice of marking each slate wagon with tare weight may have begun quite late in the period of the Railroad; J.J. Evans (Quarry Engineer) writes 26th November, 1877: ". . . we had commenced since January to weigh and mark them . . . I found those which were weighed today had a great difference all against Lord Penrhyn and for the Men . . ."

There remained always the suspicion between employer and employee that the weights were calculated in favour of one party or the other, each knowing how dependent they were on accuracy. An empty de Winton wagon of 2 ton 6 cwt. capacity weighed approximately 12 cwt.

Coal Wagons (Numbered 1–60)

Coal was delivered by sea, usually loaded at Point of Ayr Colliery, Flintshire, and when the steam age first reached the workings this new commodity had to be handled from Port to places up-line; the wharf nearest the Port bridge was fitted out to unload and store it on the quayside and if required, move it around the Port premises where it could bunker one of the Quarry's steamships.[69] It might travel south-wards for (1) locomotive coal for use on the main line or Quarry galleries, (2) use at Coed-y-Parc workshops and the five blacksmith's shops scattered within the Quarry, (3) domestic use, (4) to heat Quarry buildings, (5) fuel for the steam pumping engine boilers. Domestic coal – quite apart from heating the Quarry offices, Overlookers' cabins etc. – was delivered free of charge to certain employees on the Estate, and in this instance the Railway was a carrier for Estate purposes; also employees living in the Bethesda district used this supply.

At the Port the unloaded coal was stacked behind a low wall on the wharf edge. Slate-carrying coal-burning ships included the Anglesey Shipping Co. fleet, an associated concern. For internal use at the Port this company had its own wagons, but in 1904 A.S.Co. assets passed into Quarry ownership and the wagons were worked up the line if convenient. The first two steamships acquired – as opposed to sailing ships – were principally coal carriers and of shallow draught to enable them to berth at the coal wharf at low tide.

Coal wagons were four-wheeled, with single-flanged wheels; some had bodies of sheet iron (later sheet steel) but the early types had wooden ones with iron strapping; each variety – and there were several variations – had a single door, either at end or side. There was a changeover in 1886 from the short curved end-buffer pad to a curved pad which extended the full width of the wagon end coinciding with the death of the Coed-y-Parc wagon-builder.

The first batch[70] was begun in January 1856; later they carried the numbers 1–6: supplied to begin this business, the traffic was confined to Saturdays when slate carrying was suspended and on that day all sundries were moved along the line. The contents of these Saturday trains reflected the nature of the Railway as on no other day; whilst Mondays–Fridays were given over to the slate business, Saturday emphasised that the line was an Estate Railway; various commodities which traditionally arrived by coaster would be lying on the wharf ready for the weekend Up run. Coal, potatoes, grain, lime, timber, in fact all the ingredients of domestic life for the quarry community. (Even pigs would be sent down the line on their way to market; perhaps one of the strangest loads carried by the Railroad was a 'Large Suckling' which left Dolawen Farm en route for the Herculaneum Pottery, Toxteth, where it was roasted for an 'Official Opening' of a furnace (21st December, 1806). It cost £1 0s. 1d.) The batch was built in Coed-y-Parc but not put into use until October 1857 when trade commenced; the first lot had plain open wooden 'box' bodies without any door (!), but this was rectified by giving them a side opening hinged at the top. A distinguishing feature was a heavy horizontal rubbing strake on either side of the body; these held open the various occupation crossing gates as the horsedrawn rake passed by (it was apparently the practice to leave these closed across the line and they were probably weighted to move back into that position). Oak frame members were 7 in. × 3 in. One was later fitted with a removable roof to carry lime from the Port kilns and could usually be found standing idle by the Port weighing machine; this batch was distinguishable with its heavy outside wooden framing and top rail, all in square section.

A new venture was begun in the mid-1880s when a business was set up to sell coal to non-employees; in consequence the then Manager, E.A. Young, found there was a shortage of suitable wagons, so on 1st July, 1886 he ordered twelve further wagons from Coed-y-Parc. They were distinguishable by their deep wooden frames, and strapping of iron, their upper sides having iron angle; later they took numbers between 7 and 38 but certain other types had numbers in between. Nos. 8 and 10 have survived. In due course this batch was also given rubbing strakes even though their bodies were smaller than the first batch.

Coed-y-Parc was lethargic in supplying these wagons and displeased Young considerably, especially as it became clear even when they were in service the business would still be short of them; he had no choice but to order a further twenty similar to those in work but having steel in place of wooden frames. Once again the bodies were to be smaller than before.

A fourth variety resembled the traditional coal wagon as used on other Welsh narrow gauge systems i.e. an all-iron bodied vehicle carried on a wooden frame (which in the Penrhyn type was even more traditional for the frame side members were extended to form dumb 'buffers'; later these were removed in favour of the curved buffing plate before-mentioned). A dated photograph shows nine of these wagons at the Port in 1894 and it is possible they came from an outside source. Two body sizes were noted in recent times: they had top hinged end doors and some had corner straps.

Some coal wagons defy recognition; standing disused in 1945 and marked 'No. 1' was a large iron body wooden framed open wagon marked in chalk 'Loco Coal'. It had been long in this service and had post-1886 buffing plates and possibly had a full length but lower-portion-only side door on one side: its origin more nearly fits a purchase from M.R.C.&W.Co. Ltd. in early 1891 against their design for side tip wagons (an order dated 16th December 1890). They were bought by the Estate (not the Quarry) for use at The Ogwen Tile Works. This fleet was operative by August 1891 for a wagon-load of 4 tons of slate dust 'covered by a tarpaulin' was sold at 5/- ton by the Liverpool agency.[71] In 1893 the wagons (no details of size or number are available) were sold to the Quarry; No. 1 may be from the batch – it would carry 4 tons, and retain its original number; possibly such wagons would only be suited for after-use in coal traffic.

The two before-mentioned wooden-bodied coal wagons built 1892/3 passed from A.S.Co. in 1904: both wagons were identical with three plank side/ends having (except in 1953) a central drop door (No. 1) and a full drop door (No. 2) on one side only. There were anxious moments when these wide vehicles first passed up the Railway, being larger than anything heretofore, but all was well. Evidence in the frame construction of No. 1 suggests it may have embodied parts of the original brake van of 1876.

Confusingly by September 1964 either some renumbering had been done or a third wagon had appeared – the latter is unlikely! In store at Red Lion Level was No. 1, a full-drop side door specimen, whilst that having the centre door was marked No. 3; evidence of the renumbering scheme following closure of the main line . . . and to prove as pointless as re-arranging the deckchairs on board the sinking TITANIC.

Details of certain survivors at the Quarry in March 1967 may prove valuable; No. 10 of Young's first order had the deep wooden frame and beams, 3-plank sides and full end buffing plate. There was a top hinged iron end door, held by a catch each side of the end. Its number was painted on left top plank, '11½' on top right end. Another type had a 3-plank body but an iron frame, with iron end door having two catches, at one end, the other end being a plain iron sheet. The top plank (left) read 'C^1 T^{10}', in the centre 'No. 2' and on right '12½'. All lettering was white but body paint had almost gone. Originally the number had been 2A (see 1A in Museum, aforementioned) but the 'A' had not been repainted. All wagons of this pattern retained rubbing strakes to the end – they were of course useless by then.

Regarding the reference made to latter-day re-numbering, it may be confusing to add that there were coal wagons Nos. 1A, 5A, 8A, 13A, 15A . . . and more besides as there was a last minute decision to give 'A' numbers to wagons having fixed bodies and 'B' numbers to those with side drop doors. The former took coal to Overlookers' cabins and were run off the track on Spoon Points and then manhandled to tip sideways and rest on wooden chocks set in the ground, which supported the rubbing strake. The 'B' wagons went to loco sheds, blacksmiths' shops etc. Each wagon was properly destination-labelled at the Port.

Also noted were iron-bodied/wooden framed wagons with lift-up iron end door, doubly-catched, viz. No. 20 tare 15 cwt.: No. 22 tare 17 cwt.

At the beginning of the present century the foregoing were sufficient, but wear and tear was such that at the eleventh hour of the existence of the Railway another design was evolved in May 1956 and in fact, the last of this new type was not delivered from Coed-y-Parc until after the Railway had closed! The pattern is quite distinct from predecessors having steel frame and sheet steel sides to which were fitted suspension straps and eyes to allow lifting by the 'Blondins' in the Quarry; there was an end door, top hinged. One or two of this series survive, including No. 5.

The operation of these wagons was unique in certain respects. For instance, those used to supply the engine sheds on the galleries had to be taken into the shed for unloading. Each shed had a small annexe on one side (usually at the rear end), part of which contained a coal bunker; the loaded wagon (with its drop side correctly positioned!) was pushed inside when the engine was away and the top hinged side door propped open to allow the coal to fall into the side bunker. It was largely a hit-and-miss affair and any that fell to the floor was piled up with a shovel into the bunker and on to the footplate floor. Presumably body rigidity demanded the top hinge, but a door which fell to provide a transfer platform between wagon and bunker would have been preferable.

As to rubbing strakes, they were not confined to coal wagons, as certain early slate wagons also carried them; the horse-hauled rakes were led by a horse(s) in charge of a lad who would push open the single gates as they were reached – there were portions of wagons which would snatch the gate if it was unable to rub clear of them e.g. the catches which held the end doors closed. The strake on the slate wagons took on an extra role for when a hobbler was used to load/unload, (a hobbler was a form of gangplank) it could be rested on top of the strake.

Painting was red oxide for wooden bodied wagons, with black ironwork: iron wagons were black.

	Builder	Overall Length	Overall Width	Wheelbase	Note
First type 1856–7	Coed-y-Parc	7 ft 1 in.	3 ft 9 in.	2 ft 5 in.	
Second type 1886	Coed-y-Parc	6 ft 1 in.	3 ft 1 in.	2 ft 9 in.	Tare 11½ cwt. Load 2½ ton
Third type 1886	Coed-y-Parc	5 ft 11¾ in.	3 ft 0 in.	2 ft 7½ in.	
Fourth type pre 1894	?	5 ft 3 in.	3 ft 0 in.	?	Iron bodies, timber frame, e.g. No. 13
	&	6 ft 6 in.	4 ft 0 in.	?	(no No. visible)
ex Anglesey Shipping Co. (pre 1894)	?	10 ft 0 in.	5 ft 5 in.	4 ft 0 in.	All wooden Tare 18½ cwt. Load c.6 ton
Fifth type 1956	Coed-y-Parc or	6 ft 0 in. 6 ft 3 in.	3 ft 0 in. 3 ft 2 in.	2 ft 7 in. 2 ft 10 in.	All steel bodies 2 ft 6½ in. deep (incl. solebar)

During World War I minesweepers filled the Port (their R.N.V.R. skippers hit the sea walls frequently!) and some coal wagons were then fitted with hooks for tipping into naval bunkers.

Tar Wagons

Resembling the gunpowder vans which ran on the Festiniog Railway (but which were owned by the gunpowder contractor) there were two 'wrap over' type covered vehicles of strange purpose and having firedoors in the centre of each side. They ran on iron chassis and might be taken for travelling crematoria! There was a long rectangular but narrow opening running along the roof top, complete with hinged lid and chimney each end. They were in fact tar boilers running on standard wheelsets at 2 ft 10 in. wheelbase and were used at the Port installation to heat up pitch into which the slate dust was thrown, producing the bitumenlike substance for road repairs etc. and known as Penrhyn Grout. They were made by the Phoenix Engineering Co., of Chard, Somerset, and were in use betwen 1929 and 1943 when, rather surprisingly, the grout production suddenly ceased. They were rail-mounted, as the warehouse where the pitch was offloaded from ships did not have road access.

Rubbish Wagons

These were confined to the Quarry and were employed (1) between working face and the tips to carry away waste which could not be processed, (2) to carry away waste offcuts from the cutting sheds and mills to the tips. In an industry where up to 90% of the stone extracted became useless, there was a high demand for suitable wagons – all were carried on double-flanged wheels and were basically a three-sided box on four wheels, the open end having no door and had their working location within the Quarry either stencilled or rough-painted on the sides. Early types were carried on wooden chassis ('Wood Rubbish Wagon'), and the later ones on steel channel; they were simple, efficient and suffered extremely hard usage – some channel framed had lifting eyes for attachment to the 'Blondins' ('Iron Hanging Wagon'). On close examination the bodies would be found to be non-rectangular, the open end being 'mouthed' to assist discharge of rubbish over the tip end. There were 871 in the fleet (January 1928) increased to 1,057 two years later!

Average dimensions would be: body 5 ft 1½ in. long; 1 ft 5 in. high on 2 ft 1 in. wheelbase; the open end 3 ft 5 in. wide, and the closed 3 ft 1 in. wide. Some bodies (only) were supplied by de Winton & Co. in 1879; most others came from Coed-y-Parc.

Painting originally was medium grey with a white symbol denoting the district of allocation to which they were expected to be returned!

Sleds (Flat Wagons)

These were of three types: Mill, Quarry and Main Line: the two former had double-flanged wheels and the Mill type being moved around by hand singly, had no couplings. They were simple four-wheeled 'flats' for carrying slabs. Mill (of wood) and Quarry types were of wood or iron, with 1 ft 10 in.–2 ft 1½ in. wheelbase; some Quarry sleds had 'Blondin' eyes ('Hanging Sleds').

The Main Line type ('Large Sleds') were altogether larger, being 8 ft 6 in. long by 3 ft 1 in. wide and carried on 2 ft 8 in.–2 ft 10 in. wheelbase, although some were 10 ft long carried on a 3 ft 6 in. wheelbase. They had sheet iron floors and securing rings on the solebars to affix chains to secure the slabs they carried on low supporting ribs to keep them clear of the floor; if these moved or were too wide they would occasionally jam in the narrow cutting below Tyn-y-Clwt! No. 11 survives – tare 7¼ cwt. (A few had short buffers and other traces of the pre-1877 coupling methods, together with traces of the two hook rings at each end.)

Painting: the wooden parts were left plain, with incised numbers and tare weights; the metal ones once were in medium grey but more commonly in iron oxide.

Bolster Wagons (Timber Trucks)

These were made up in sets of three wagons, and were to carry long loads; there were two large sets and one small: the sizes were 6 ft 3 in. (or 5 ft 6 in.) long by 3 ft wide on a 2 ft 10 in. (or 2 ft 7 in.) wheelbase, and they were carried on singly-flanged wheels and used on the main line. The end wagons would carry a bolster to which the load could be chained, the middle wagon being a flat. The 'set' at Penrhyn Castle Museum is not one . . . having a bolster wagon from each of two sets (the other 'pair' also survive). Painting was as for sleds.

Gravel Wagons

These served the gravel pit near Felin-Hen; there were about 25 of them, supplied for a traffic which began in 1908. They were converted at Coed-y-Parc from rubbish wagons, and their wheelsets exchanged for those with single-flanges. No. 21 had a steel frame, but the rest were wooden. From 1926 they were recruited for the Saturday coal traffic run as their 5 ton capacity suited them well for the Coed-y-Parc smithy coal supply. A top hinged door at the wider end of the body was added, and they were immediately distinguishable by having their sheet sides and ends raised using material from another redundant body. Short iron straps were simply welded on the sides to hold the new materials in the same plane! Body dimensions were similar to the rubbish wagons, but with 2 ft 10 in. high body sides.

'Fullersite' Wagons

To cater for the new post-World War I business in graded, finely-ground slate powder trade named 'Fullersite' (used with bitumen for road surfacing etc.), developed in 1923–24, suitable plant was erected on Red Lion Level at the Quarry and at the north-eastern end of the Port; 'Fullersite' and bitumen were made into a mastic 'asphalte'. Ninety wagons suitable for the main line were ultimately in use for this traffic alone, the first two score having an all-timber 2 or 3 plank body construction with a hinged drop down door on one side; outside wooden or cast-iron framing was prominent on many variations. Following the first twenty, materials were more mixed, some having loose sheet iron and a few wooden ends; of the remainder, dimensions were varied; some had loose sides which could be lifted out as the stout vertical stanchions were extended down and dropped into sockets on the solebars. In the last wagons there were 2 plank dropside doors with iron strapping, and sheet iron fixed ends (e.g. No. 85).

An interesting exception was a smaller wagon only 6 ft long which was possibly based on a design drawing by Edwyn John Jeffrey Dixon, the manager of the nearby Bryn Hafod-y-Wern Slate Quarry (then worked by The Royal Slate Co.), who seems to have been something of a 'Heath Robinson' in his day and full of ingenious but often fallible ideas! A surviving drawing of the early 1850s shows a similar wagon to this exception; the wagon itself was probably the one listed in a sale lot "23 old wagons and a turntable" purchased at Hafod-y-Wern Auction 17th October, 1898. This wagon probably formed the basic inspiration for the 'Fullersite' stock but which was built initially to enlarged body length of 8 ft. Some bodies had full width buffing plates and others half-length . . . in this case nothing to do with the 1886 changeover. Wagon numbers and tare were chiselled deeply into the wooden solebars and no vehicles seemed to have been painted; they always worked under a layer of grey powdered dust even though the load they carried was always bagged or sacked. Ironwork was painted black.

This traffic never grew as it might – as with earlier bricks and tiles from waste, the method was too costly. A trade in bagged 'Fullersite' remained on a limited scale. Some was used in the then-new plastics industry.

Tare weight was 13½–16 cwt.; No. 77 survives in the Castle Museum, No. 85 in a private collection.

	Body Length	Body Width	Body Height Sides	Height Overall	Wheelbase
First batch (hinged door one side)	8 ft 0 in.	3 ft 1 in.	1 ft 6 in.	3 ft 4 in.	2 ft 6 in. to 2 ft 10 in.
Later vehicles (lift-out etc. sides/ends)	8 ft 6 in. (see note below)	2 ft 10 in. to 3 ft 3 in.	1 ft 8 in.	2 ft 8 in. to 3 ft 6 in.	3 ft 3 in.

(These are average dimensions only: some later vehicles were only 6 ft 6 in. (No. 46) and others 8 ft long.)

No. 96 had 3 plank sides, a wooden drop door and prominent sheeting eyes for securing a tarpaulin cover; with only ninety wagons in total, not all could have been numbered serially! Sample numbering bears this out e.g. first batch: 61, 63, 70 and later vehicles: 7, 17, 38, 46.

Steam Navvy or 'Auto-Tipper' Tubs

Seventy-two large hopper-bodied end-tipping iron/steel wagons were supplied by an unknown maker, carried on 1 ft 4 in. diameter double-flanged wheels for use to serve the four 'American Devil' steam powered excavators by Ruston-Bucyrus engaged mainly in clearing up rubbish on working floors in the Quarry (they are first mentioned in an accident report of 16th April, 1928). The 'diggers' were self-propelled on caterpillar tracks and were not rail-mounted: the wagons had tapered bodies in sheet iron, 5 ft 10 in. long with a 4 ft 10 in. top width reduced to 3 ft 10 in. at the bottom, and with maximum height of 2 ft 6 in. they were hinged to tip endways and carried on a channel steel frame 5 ft long by 3 ft 1 in. wide having 'open' steel buffing stops (two per end) and on a 2 ft 6 in. wheelbase. Painting was black bitumen and they carried no markings. A quantity was also supplied to Dinorwic Quarry at the same time.

Special Wagons

Hand cranes, rigger's sleds etc. were adaptations mounted on sled wagons. There were five 5 cwt. hand cranes (of which two were on Red Lion) used for installing 'Blondin' masts, telephone poles etc. and occasionally to re-rail after accidents; they swivelled in a kingpost and a 'tray' to the rear was loaded with slab (or) counterweight.

Rigger's sleds (single-flanged in case of need down the Railway) carried tools, ropes, hooks and slings for maintenance work anywhere on the site.

Certain inclines operated as water-balances were counter-balanced by a dozen or so tank wagons supplied by Ratcliffe & Sons, Hawarden Ironworks in 1883; an additional purpose was to supply locomotive needs on Levels above Ffridd where there was no natural water supply.

Coed-y-Parc had the use of three all-steel side-tipping skip bodies mounted on channel steel frames; there was a solitary side-tipper by Robert Hudson Ltd., Gildersome Foundry, Morley, Leeds, supplied in 1908 which passed its life shyly on an unused Level!

Sleds were usually 'acquired' by other trades e.g. painters or slaters would employ two as bogies to which they might lash their ladders.

General-purpose Wagons

A supposition regarding a general-purpose open wagon arises from traces of coupling hook fastenings behind the end beams of certain wooden-framed 'Fullersite' wagons built or rebuilt pre-1877. Such might suggest that until the opening of the L.N.W.R. Bethesda branch in July 1884 there was a number of wagons to carry general merchandise and especially for Bethesda. Materials to build the first batch of 'Fullersite' wagons may have come from such disused goods wagons.

Brake Vans

A practice to employ a guard in a special van on the rear of the Down trains was already established by 28th December, 1875 when the guard broke his arm in an accident. By 1880 a guard was no longer employed as the new 1877 slate wagons allowed "pinning down" 'on the last three wagons instead'. However, as to a brake van, "one was in use up to around 1914 . . . a Mr. Mackay used to take the wages up to the Quarry in it every Friday . . .", so writes an informant.

In 1946–48 the frames and wheels of a Muirhill rail tractor (not identified) had a water tank mounted on them, and a 'woodshed' stuck on to one end; the latter may have been intended for the brakesman's shelter but in practice he rode on an adjacent wagon and reached the handbrake through an end door; the ride was so rough that even the inducement of such shelter was eschewed. The length was 10 ft 2 in. on a 4 ft wheelbase which, with a loaded water tank containing no interior baffles, may have had much to do with the awful riding! The tank was filled for the downhill run, and came back empty when no brakes were strictly necessary; it ended its days as a mobile water tank on Red Lion Level.

The third van was an effort to improve on the second; the water tank was removed but still without the addition of baffles, it was put on the lengthened frame of the then-discarded steam engine SANFORD which, stored out of use on 25th June, 1956, by August had become a brake van. The wheelbase had been elongated to give it stability, and the original cab was retained but cut down in height. This time there was no end 'door' and the cab was fully sheeted; it was impossible for the brakesman to do anything but stand and ride in that sentry box and once again the water was responsible for a very wild ride – J.G. Vincent said: "In 1957 I had a very rough ride in this, but I kept fairly dry in the brake van." Its life was short. The tank was then removed and the last brake van then made its appearance, using the same chassis.

At first a shallow open 'tray' having two lids and filled with odd scrap iron was tried, then a block of concrete was laid permanently over the frames, the wheelbase modified to 5 ft 6 in. long and one of the open cab sides blanked off to give added weather protection. After less than five years of active life, this van survived to the end.

A Note on Brake Power

It must be said that brake vans were unnecessary; the fitting of so many slate wagons with handbrakes and then their wholesale removal confirmed that locomotive men were quite capable of restricting the Down speed of loaded trains. The design of the slate wagon brake was such that, when a loaded train was moving down the line it would be virtually impossible for the guard to apply the brakes except by lying flat on top of the load, reaching down, and pulling up the brake handle . . . an uncomfortable business when it is remembered that to assist counting the load, certain slates would be left standing up proud of the remainder . . .! At an early stage the customary division between the theoretical minds which provided the brakes, and the practical operatives who had to use them was soon demonstrated; before the Down train left Coed-y-Parc sufficient brakes were either dropped in their hangers or tightened down and as this was quite sufficient, the guard was left with little to do. On Up trains it was only necessary for the guard, riding bravely in the open on the last fitted wagon, to reach down and control the brake, but on his own wagon, to ensure control of the train.

As for the rest of the brakes on an Up train, they ran with their brake handles lifted off, for which purpose the Operating Department (not the Design staff) supplied themselves with a length of string to tie up the handles so they would not fall back. *Verb. sap.*

Train Formations in 1956/57/59

Timetable: Three Up and Down trains daily Monday–Friday.

October 1956	9.30 a.m. ex Port	BLANCHE	14 empty slate, 1 'Fullersite', 1 brake van (ex Loco) = 16 vehicles
July 1957	11.20 a.m. ex Quarry	BLANCHE	7 loaded slate, 12 'Fullersite' = 19 vehicles
May 1959	10.45 a.m. ex Port	LINDA	5 empty slate, 5 empty 'Fullersite', 4 loaded coal (middle of train) = 14 vehicles
October 1959	? ex Port	BLANCHE	21 empty slate (last braked, with brakes- man in attendance), 4 loaded coal = 25 vehicles

It was the practice to have slate wagons (braked or otherwise) at each end of the train, with other vehicles grouped together intermediately.

REFERENCES

1 A HISTORY OF THE NORTH WALES SLATE INDUSTRY (Dr. Jean Lindsay) Chapter 2 covers the Penrhyn situation 1731–1782.
2 THE PENNANTS & JAMAICA 1665–1808 (Dr. Jean Lindsay) Trans. C.H.S. No. 43 (1982) gives a detailed background to the inheritance.
3 Escott, Devon. The Yonges were more strictly of the nearby Colyton, living in a mansion built 1688 (replaced 1810) but had a family house in the diffused settlement of Escott (2 miles N.W. of Ottery St. Mary). They were not noted for their active life-style; of Sir William Yonge his friend Horace Walpole had said – on hearing of his death in 1755 – 'extinct so long, at last is dead'. The moribund condition of the Penrhyn Estate at this time may be thus accounted-for! Sir George was a promoter of the Grand Western Canal in 1793 which could have been a factor to engage the attention of Richard Pennant.
4 QUARRY MANAGER'S JOURNAL: March 1944 p.316.
5 A SURVEY OF THE ANCIENT & PRESENT STATE OF CAERNARVON (Williams 1806) (N.L.Wales MS.821C (Ty Coch MS.7)) contains pertinent background information to this period.
6 The idea was also claimed by Rev. Dawson, uncle to the Earl of Portarlington.
7 Penrhyn Castle Papers (1939) 811–15 (U.C.N.W.)
8 Trans. C.H.S. Vol. 13 p.22 has details of Turnpike Roads.
9 Wyatt had had experience of road building in Staffordshire but nothing as challenging as here. He became Clerk & Treasurer to the Capel Curig Turnpike Trust formed by Act of 1801 to improve the Llandegai–Pentre-Voelas road.
10 Lindsay; gives further detail pp. 89 etc.
11 Contemporary advertising read that the Pottery was 'Late, The Copper Works' on 'The East side of Salthouse Dock' and in 1797 offers his products to 'Merchants, Captains and Owners'; by June 1798 he was offering 'A constant supply of Bangor Slates, for home consumption & exportation'.
12 Dodd, p.207.
13 At Worthington's family home, Worthington Hall, Standish, near Wigan, tramways already existed on the Estate.
14 Other early wooden tramroads in this district of Flintshire include the Latchcroft and Sandycroft systems, both connecting with the river.
15 Llanberis copper mine had an underground tramway by 1796.
16 Samuel Holland: see THE FESTINIOG RAILWAY Vol. 1 (Boyd) Chap. 1. He was cousin to Elizabeth Gaskell, the novelist.
17 Penrhyn Castle Papers 2032 (U.C.N.W.)
18 Penrhyn Castle was built with special muniment rooms lined with slab; some material from this source has still to be recovered and catalogued.
19 One argument in favour of the plateway was that the plain wheel, having no flange, would be lighter. However, this was not always so; The Herefordshire Railway wheels were heavier than equivalent flanged wheels for though the tread was narrow (¾ inch) they had substantial centres with thick hubs and ribbing.
20 THE CANALS OF THE WEST MIDLANDS (Charles Hadfield) contains extended information on Dadfords. (Likewise THE CANALS OF SOUTH WALES AND THE BORDERS p.17 etc.)
21 A HISTORY OF BRITISH RAILWAYS DOWN TO THE YEAR 1830 (Dendy Marshall) pp.108–9.
22 A PRACTICAL TREATISE ON RAIL-ROADS AND CARRIAGES (1825) pp.24–5.
23 THE WYATTS: An Architectural Dynasty (J.M. Robinson) p.137 on.
24 Penrhyn Castle Collection (Book 4 p.463) (U.C.N.W.)
25 Younger brother of William Provis, an assistant to his brother on the road and the attendant Menai and Conway suspension bridges; William was Resident Engineer for the Menai Bridge from 1819.
26 Due to the efforts of the Holyhead Road Commission 1815 Telford was employed to survey the entire London–Holyhead road and William Provis was his senior surveyor (see also THOMAS TELFORD (L.T.C. Rolt) Chap. 8.).
27 Also 8 & 9 Vic. Cap. XXXIII of 30th June, 1845.
28 Bethesda: Trans. C.H.S. Vol. 41 (1980) 'Community & Social Structure in Bethesda 1840–1870'.
29 THE FESTINIOG RAILWAY (Boyd) Vol. II p.578 on.
30 THE FESTINIOG RAILWAY (Boyd) Vol. II p.343 – isometric drawing – and pp.361–63.
31 There was a further fall to the west of this on 6th September, 1879 and a fall created beneath both sites on 3rd June, 1881 was contrived to make the area safe.
32 W.J. PARRY: QUARRYMAN'S CHAMPION (Trans. C.H.S. Vol. 24 (1963) esp. pp.235 on).
33 He was also Engineer to the Anglesea Central Railway 1866, but had no other railway connections.

34 Reference to that portion where the new railway would be on the old Railroad site; a suggestion that both might exist together and legislation would demand parallel courses.
35 Penrhyn Castle Papers 856–63 (U.C.N.W.).
36 Somewhat confusingly, the 'Right' side was the western and 'Left' side the eastern portion of the workings i.e. they were viewed as from Lord Penrhyn's lodge below the quarry, Ogwen Bank.
37 By 1913 this cart road was the course of 18″ gauge tramway 500 yds long between the Penrhyn Iron Mine at Rhos-Uchaf Farm, and the Bangor–Bethesda road "where it (the iron ore) is shot into carts and taken about 200 yds to the Penlan Siding on the L.N.W.R. . . ." most of the ore going to Brymbo for smelting though some was shipped from Deganwy. At the head of this tramway was a balanced incline, 150 yds long. The owners were then The Silurian Iron Ore Co. Ltd., of 45 Wind Street, Swansea, and the site was worked 1912–1921, employing 40 men in 1916. In the past proposals for a Pen-Lan Siding by the L.N.W.R. would have given the standard gauge access to the mine – another proposal to link it with the Penrhyn Rly. was turned down for fear of interference with slate traffic.
38 British Rail records suggest the junction here was at first by a turnout; Telford's plan of 1815 shows what may be a later alteration, by turntable.
39 There is some evidence that the tunnel was not built until 1852 or 1853, in which case the main road must have been crossed by a level crossing.
40 J.H. Battersby: (letter, 24th January, 1961).
41 EARLY WOODEN RAILWAYS (Lewis) p.54.
42 An unintentional 1 in 33 was created near the Port.
43 Originally held by heather roots twisted into 'rope', this form of fence is said to have originated in France.
44 Ref: Public Record Office, M.T. 27/49.
45 Based on SURVEY OF NORTH WALES (Davies 1810) and other contemporary writers.
46 "The part below the oval" (of the rail) ". . . cast to the end of each rail 3 inches long to let into the sills, which have a double notch to receive them."
47 Chairs were first used at Lawson Main Colliery in 1797 but were of completely different design.
48 This rail first introduced by Charles Vignoles in 1836 but found no favour on the main lines of this country for the next century; it was basically designed by R.L. Stevens of New Jersey, as was the attendant rail spike (and the fishplate).
49 A few 'T' and flat-bottomed rails have been found drilled to take a four-bolt fishplate, but this was not universal.
50 A name quoted in the documents accompanying the first delivery and inferring the use of 'turnrails' said to have been invented by Richard Fothergill of Tredegar Ironworks whilst 'doodling' in the sawdust of the church floor during a sermon.
51 When the strike ended the whole Quarry management, Francis among them, resigned. (In consequence of the strike, the new Felin-Fawr Incline, ready 22nd August, 1874, did not pass its first train until 23rd November.)
52 STEPHEN LEWIN & THE POOLE FOUNDRY (Wear and Lees) Industrial Railway Society 1978 pp.43–45, has the well-known photograph of the engine in Lewin's yard.
53 NARROW GAUGE RAILWAYS IN NORTH CAERNARVONSHIRE (Boyd) Vol. 1 West pp.240–3.
54 THE FESTINIOG RAILWAY (Boyd) Vol. II has later history.
55 Bangor 25273 (U.C.N.W.).
56 The strata here tended to undercut the supported 'step' in the gallery and the Ministry's inspector would not permit even the small Hunslets to work there.
57 All dimensions taken from manufacturer's official fact-sheet.
58 HISTORY OF THE BALDWIN LOCOMOTIVE WORKS (1831–1923) Philadelphia 1924. Chap. VIII gives background information – see also LOCOMOTIVE NEWS & RAILWAY CONTRACTOR 8/1919 p.112 and 9/1919 p.11 and 10/1919 p.76 (weight diagram).
59 GLIMPSES OF THE NARROW GAUGE (Boyd) May 1952 p.117 shows these engines as built.
60 Illustration of locomotive operating at The Fairymead Sugar Mill, Queensland – as 0–6–2. THE NARROW GAUGE No. 71, p.3.
61 Reminiscences of Messrs. John M. Williams of Tregarth and J.H. Battersby, 1945.
62 Dr. Jean Lindsay writes in A HISTORY OF THE NORTH WALES SLATE INDUSTRY, p.270: "Some men such as fitters, joiners, and some of the daymen, continued to work in the quarry; and a 'dastardly attempt' to wreck the workmen's train was made by those locked out. The engine driver 'noticed that the line was blocked with large stones in a manner which would have inevitably wrecked the train and possibly have caused fatal injuries to the workmen had not the obstacle been providentially seen'." This event occurred in late 1900, on the sharp curve at Dinas.
63 Another source gives the 1930s charge as 4d. for boys and 6d. for men per month.
64 It is sometimes stated there was an eighteenth vehicle, the missing one being a de Winton built for Quarry officials in 1896, later converted to a coal wagon. (INDUSTRIAL RAILWAY RECORD, No. 98, p.169).

65 In May 1951 extended interior details were: buttoned blue leather seats and upholstery up to the waist; mahogany panelling above waist; luggage racks at door end; dark blue curtains sliding on rings over a wooden rail; lincrusta cream ceiling, in panels; rubber matting between doors.

66 In C.E. Spooner's Estimate of 1868 the necessity of changing to tyred wheels, fixed axles on wheels and single flanges is costed for.

67 Penrhyn Castle currently displays such a painting; THE ILLUSTRATED LONDON NEWS frequently featured Quarry engravings. A number of engravings is available in the National Library of Wales.

68 Richard Mansell's Patent wheels first appeared in 1848; they had teak centres and were used on the main lines of this country until the 1920s.

69 A typical and early entry in the Letter Book is one to Snape, Coal Agent, Runcorn, re: "50 tons not exceeding 3/6d. ton freight, immediately." Ships included the TALACRE and ROBERT.

70 One of this batch is No. 1A and survives in the Penrhyn Castle Museum. It is wrongly attributed to the A.S.Co. and does not conform to other dimensions being 6 ft 3 in. long, 3 ft 3 in. wide and having a 2 ft 9 in. wheelbase.

71 This enterprise to manufacture bricks and tiles from waste was a failure; machinery, wagons, and the whole Works was sold to the Quarry in March 1893 for £500. Its products were the genesis for the later 'Fullersite' plant.

MAIN INDEX

Abandonment
  Penrhyn Railroad 35, 41.
  Penrhyn Railway 42.
  Quarry Rail System 42-43.
Algeo, Robert 33, 37, 41, 60, 62.
Anglesey Shipping Co. 68-69, 146-147.

Barber, H. 38, 60-61.
Beatson, John & Co. (etc.) 35, 92-95.
Bethesda
  Griffith Scheme 42, 112.
  L.N.W.R. Branch & other proposals
    33, 37-41, 57-59.

Canal (1799)
  Proposal & Survey 10, 12.
Carriages
  Man-Riding 137.
  Private, etc., & Saloon 134-136.
  Workmen's 129, 131-132.
Cegin River 6, 9, 41, 47, 60.
Chester & Holyhead Rly. 26-27, 29, 47,
    60.
Cilgwyn Quarry 4.
Closures (list of)
  Penrhyn Railway 43.
Coal traffic 28, 145-146, 148-149.
Coed-Hywel 37, 59.
Coed-y-Parc 21-23, 26, 41-42, 44-45,
    54-55, 72-74, 86-87.
Construction
  Penrhyn Railroad 15.
  Penrhyn Railway 35, 37, 41.
Croesor Quarry 21.
Crown Land (etc.) 20, 64.

Dadford, Thomas (Snr)
  Surveys & Reports 10, 13-16.
Darlington Iron & Steel Co., Ltd. 88.
Dawkins, George Hay 5.
Dinorwic Railway 24, 28, 83-4.
Drainage tunnel 45.

Edgeworth, Richard L. 13.

Felin-Fawr 22, 45, 54-55.
Felin-Hen 37, 59.
Festiniog Railway 5, 28, 92, 112, 149.
Flint-grinding 8-10, 23, 25.
Francis, John 34, 93.
Francis, William 22.

French wars 5-7, 20, 25.
'Fullersite' 151-152.

Gallery system 21.
Gibson, Benjamin 87-88, 91.
Gravel pit 59, 87.
Greenfield, James 10, 21.
Griffith Scheme (of 1938) 42.
Guest, Keen & Nettlefold Ltd. 88.

Henderson & Glass 91.
Herculaneum Pottery 8-9.
Holland, Samuel 9.
Horse Tax 7-8.
Hughes, Thomas 80, 90.
Humble, Michael 9.
Hurry, Nicolas 9.

Inclines
  all principal subjects – see also 'Quarry'
    20, 22, 26, 34-35, 42, 45-50, 52-54,
    56, 58, 84, 86, 153.
Inheritance
  The Penrhyn Estate 2.
Iremonger, P.A. 21.
Isca Foundry 89.

Jamaica 3-5.

Leases 4, 9, 64.
Leslie & Hall 91.
Lewin, S. & Co. 94-95.
Lime kilns 23, 28.
Llandegai Ty
  Purpose & Construction 8-9.
  Eclipse of 10, 14.
Locomotives, Steam
  general 92-93.
  de Winton & Co. 34-35, 37, 41, 92-99.
  Early types 34-35, 92-95.
  Employment 92, 119, 121-122.
  Livery 127-128.
  Locations 92, 110, 112.
  The Baldwin Loco. Works 112-114.
  The Hunslet Engine Co. Ltd. 108.
  The Hunslet Main Line 95, 99, 101-103.
  The Hunslet 'Large Quarry' 106-108.
  The Hunslet 'Port' 103-104.
  The Hunslet 'Small Quarry' 104-106.
  Second-hand for Quarry 108, 110, 112,
    115-119, 121.

INDEX TO DRAWINGS AND MAPS

NOTES

NOTES

Location Map of
The Railways of Caernarvon[s]

SYMBOLS

These are standard throughout all volumes. Where a symb[ol]
a suitable note is made on that map. In the interest of clar[ity]
used in some areas, e.g. Nantlle Valley, Gilfach Ddu (Dinorwi[c])

RAILWAYS:

	NARROW GAUGE	STANDARD GAUGE
Railways Built	▬▬▬	▬▬▬
· Projected	··········	▬ ▬ ▬
· Abandoned	▬ ▬ ▬	✕ ✕ ✕

SPECIAL SYMBOLS:
Padarn Ry 4ft gauge
Nantlle Ry. 3ft "
Snowdon Mt RY Abt system
Rigi system proposed
2ft gauge quarry lines

Course doubtful or }
Existence questionable}
Tunnel   S.G.
  "   N.G.

OTHER SYMBOLS:

Waiting shed or Station   S
Goods shed   G S
Loco shed   L S
Weigh Bridge   WB
Locomotive shelter
Level Crossing   LC
Gated Crossing
Stop Board
Altitude Board
Signal Box
Ground Frame
Signal post   •SP
Semaphore signals
Branch subsidiary signals
Point disc (F.R.type)
Canals
Aerial Ropeway
Pier

Incline with Drum House indicated

Wharf or platform edge with higher
          level feathered
Crane
Water crane
Water tank   WT
Locked Scotch
Turntable, loco
    "   wagon
Turning plate
Catch point or trap   CP
Gradient post
Mile post   •MP
Mining level   L
    "   shaft   •.S
Stop board   • SB

ABBREVIATIONS

Slate wharf (see also wharf edge)	SW	Goods platform	GP
Railway	Ry.	Carriage shed	CS
Tramway	Ty.	Quarry	Qy.

County Boundaries (pre 1974)
         A   B   uncl.
Roads
Volume limits, see also key

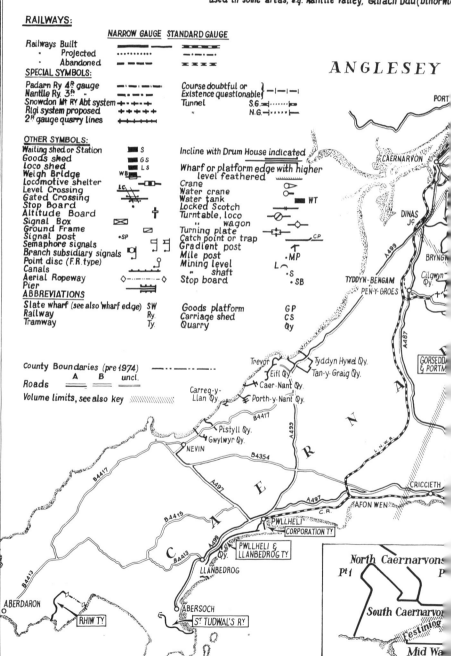

ANGLESEY

PORT[...]

CAERNARVON

DINAS Jc.

BRYNGW[...]

Cilgwyn
Qy.

TYDDYN-BENGAM
PEN-Y-GROES

A499

A487

A4

GORSEDD[A]
& PORTM[...]

Trevor
Eifl Qy.
Tyddyn Hywel Qy.
Tan-y-Graig Qy.
Caer-Nant Qy.
Carreg-y-
Llan Qy.
Porth-y-Nant Qy.

B4417
A493

Pistyll Qy.
Gwylwyr Qy.
NEVIN

B4354

R

E

A

C

CRICCIETH

AFON WEN
A497
C.R.

B4415

A497

B4413
A499
PWLLHELI
CORPORATION TY

PWLLHELI &
LLANBEDROG TY
Qy.
LLANBEDROG

B4417

B4413

ABERDARON
RHIW TY

ABERSOCH
ST TUDWAL'S RY

L.N.W.R.

North Caernarvon[s]
Pt 1   P[...]

South Caernarvon[...]

Festiniog

Mid Wa[...]